Women's Psyche, Women's Spirit

Women's Psyche, Women's Spirit

THE REALITY
OF RELATIONSHIPS

Mary Lou Randour

Columbia University Press New York

Columbia University Press
New York   Guildford, Surrey
Copyright © 1987 Columbia University Press
All rights reserved

Printed in the United States of America

Library of Congress Cataloging-in-Publication Data

Randour, Mary Lou.
  Women's psyche, women's spirit.

  Bibliography: p.
  Includes index.
  1. Women—Psychology.   2. Interpersonal relations.
3. Spirituality.   4. Self-perception.   5. Self-actualiza-
tion (Psychology)   I. Title.
HQ1206.R36   1987   158'.2   86-17180
ISBN 0-231-06250-8
ISBN 0-231-06251-6 (pbk.)

c 10 9 8 7 6 5 4 3 2
p 10 9 8 7 6 5 4 3 2 1

To: Ellen Sydney Fox, whose spirit endures
and Pearle E. Mathewson, my mother

Contents

Part II: Portraits of Six Women

Acknowledgments

Acknowledging all of those who have helped me, in so many different ways, is both difficult and pleasing. I will never be satisfied with my ability to convey how much I value their contribution to the creation of this work. But I am pleased to try, and gratified to have the opportunity to recognize them publicly.

My husband, and friend, Sam Black, always assumed I could succeed, never doubting my competencies or my capacity to persevere. His unwavering confidence provided me with a quiet backdrop of assurance from which to work. Equally important, whenever I called upon him, he patiently spent time discussing ideas for my writing with me. When I felt most mired in the particulars of my data, his seemingly inherent ability to grasp the "big picture" advanced my thinking.

Julie Bondanza, long-time friend and respected colleague, also critically influenced my thinking throughout this endeavor. She read, and usefully commented on, many versions of my manuscript. Most significantly, her observations, along with Sam's, allowed me to step back and understand what the book was about, and to write the concluding chapter to Part I.

Luckily for me, Betsy Cohn, another friend, also is a professional writer/consultant and competent teacher. I went to her for advice with the earliest versions of my manuscript. She started me off in the right direction by focusing my attention on the need to find my own voice in my writing.

There are still others: Mary Hunt supported me with her friendship, intelligence, and humor; she continues to do so. Shirley Cloyes, whom I had just met, kindly read an early draft, helping me significantly to reorganize and improve it. I also was a stranger to Carol Ochs, but she graciously agreed to talk to me about my ideas for the book when I made that request of her. And Harry Oliver, a wise and good man, spoke to me about the metaphysics of relatedness, and expanded my horizons.

I am grateful to Susan Koscielniak, executive editor at Columbia University Press, who found value in what I was doing. Her professionalism and receptivity gave me a most pleasant introduction to the world of book publishing. The thoroughness and interest of Joan McQuary, managing editor at Columbia University Press, made the editing and checking process, surprisingly, most enjoyable.

I hope my gratitude to the ninety-four women of this study is apparent. I will always appreciate their willingness to participate in this endeavor, and I will never forget that this work was possible because of them.

Women's Psyche, Women's Spirit

Prologue: The Meaning of Relationships

All of us, I believe, seek meaning. Being human, we are aware of our history, our mortality, and the possibilities for a future that we may not live to participate in, but which we can imagine. We can find meaning in any moment of life—be it brief or enduring. Writing a book may provide meaning by its ability to reach people that will otherwise never be met, or watching the graceful arched soaring of a bird against a spring sky may do so, or meaning may be derived from knowing that you have done as much as you can to help a friend.

I came to realize with greater clarity as I pursued this project that it is precisely in the fact that we are makers of meaning, that we ask "questions of ultimacy,"[1] that defines us as humans. For ours is the "burden of understanding," the burden of making meaning out of ourselves, out of our relationships with one another, and out of our relationship with the world. Langer tells us: "For good or evil, [we have] this power of envisagement, which puts a burden [on us] that purely alert, realistic creatures do not have—the burden of understanding. [We] live not only in a place, but in Space; not only in a time, but in History. So [we] must conceive a world and a law of the world, a pattern of life, and a way of meeting death. All these things [we know] and [we have] to make some adaptation to this reality."[2]

Not only do I believe, with Langer, that the search for meaning is what sets humans apart from other forms of life, I also believe, and hope to illustrate with the spiritual stories of the women of this study, that the essential part of our humanness is that we seek meaning in relationships.

Kohut, commenting on the importance of relationships to our psychological life, observed that we may no more become independent of relationships than we can become biologically independent of oxygen.[3] As we live and breathe, we psychologically depend upon, in Kohut's terminology, our self-selfobject relationships. Other theorists—such as those from the Interpersonal School of Psychiatry and from the British Object Relations School—join Kohut in redirecting our attention away from a purely intrapsychic, instinctual, psychological world, to a world of human relationships.[4] More recently, neo-Piagetian theorists like Kegan and Noam, recognizing both our desire for independence and our yearning for inclusion, have emphasized human development within the context of self-other relationships.[5]

The most vigorous claim made about the significance of relationships in the construction of self, and in the actuality of our lives, comes from those who study and write about the psychology of women. For example, Baker Miller, Gilligan, Dinnerstein, Lewis, and Chodorow, who have attended to the lives of women, radically changed, or at least challenged, existing psychological theory.[6] Baker Miller and Gilligan, in particular, tell us that women live within an interpersonal matrix in which relationships often are of primary concern. Instead of seeing separation as a psychological given, they find psychological growth, for women at any rate, occurring as a result of their attachments to others.

A reading of the women's spiritual stories, with their resounding theme of a relational spirituality, lends credence to the view that women find meaning and construct self in a world of interpersonal relationships. The narrative language used by these women has been heard before by those who have stopped to listen to women tell of their experiences, whether the context was one of an ethical dilemma, or of being in a therapeutic relationship. In this instance, they were describing a spiritual experience, and as they spoke they told of becoming and being in relationship.

But how, I wondered, can we understand the psychology of women who do not seem to live as much within an interpersonal matrix? While the theme of relational spirituality was prominent in many women's stories, it was not an exclusive expression. A sizable minority of women told stories in which they were the lone character. These women did not specifically refer to another person in their spiritual story. The significant moment they told us about was a moment when they appeared to be alone.

However, by adopting a more comprehensive definition of relationship, we then can see that the women who seemingly described a moment of self transformation when they were alone, also were in relationship. The understanding that we all are in relationship from our conception to our death does not originate with me. What I propose here is that we appropriate the other conceptions of relationship—intrapsychic, imaginary, self-reflexive—and add those to the crucial understanding we have gained from those writers who have described the interpersonal matrix of many women's lives. I do not want to distract any attention from the psychological significance that relationships have for many women, or of the value this way of being has for all of human living. I would like, however, to place alongside this vision of women's interpersonal relational world a view that includes other types of relationships, not just the interpersonal.

Much of our lives, of course, we spend in significant interpersonal relationships with an actual other. We are held by our mothers, sung to by our fathers. We learn to give our love to friends, mates, and children, as we also learn to live at work with our colleagues. The women who told of a relational spirituality spoke of these kinds of relationships.

But we also carry these and other relationships within us, even when no one seems to be present. From the beginning, we internalize aspects of significant others in our lives. We identify with our parents, emulate our peers, aspire to become like our heroines in substantial or superficial ways. Some of the others with whom we are in relationship have a real physical presence in our lives; others are mythical figures. Little girls can imagine a relationship with Wonder Woman even though they never will, or can, actually meet her. And the development of a little girl's self is formed in this imaginary relationship with the mythical Wonder Woman, as much as it is in the physical world where she jumps rope with her friends.

As we "take in" these others, we carry them with us intrapsychically. These internalized, intrapsychic representations of others, at the highest level of adaptation, give form to our ego identity.[7] The nature of being human is to be in relationship with all of these internalized others, as well as with actual others.

Finally, we also have relationships with ourselves. At times, we step back and from some perspective look at some aspect of ourselves. We think about our thinking, review our performance, evaluate how we responded in a certain situation. At times, we talk to ourselves. At those moments, we are a self-in-relation-with-self. Even then, of course, we are not alone since our selves are formed by the relationships—real and imaginary—we have had with other beings. As Ochs has described it, "When we speak of an individual . . . we are actually referring to a conglomerate."[8]

If we look at relationships from this perspective, we then find that all of us are in relationship, it is only the *nature* of the relationship that varies. A majority of the women in this study expressed a relational spirituality, that is, they spoke of a self-transformation that occurred within an interpersonal matrix. Not only these women, however, but the other women as well were in relationship. These latter women were in relationship with mythical others, internalized others, and with parts of themselves. Instead of a relational spirituality, these women expressed a relationship-in-imagination.

One more point needs to be made by me about the nature of our relationships. Kegan has observed "that the activity of being a person is the activity of meaning making,"[9] and I would like to stress that the activity of being a meaning making person occurs in the activity of relationships. We are never complete. As selves in a world of relationships we both constitute and are constituted by this world of others. The configuration of our relationships—intrapsychic and interpersonal, mythic and real—are continually evolving. Borrowing from Mary Daly's trenchant remark that God is a verb, we, too, are verbs. We are as much a process as an entity.

I came to realize how we are constituted by our relationships as I became engaged with the process of this book. I found myself in relationship with the ninety-four women who wrote of their spiritual experiences. As I imagined who they are and reflected on the meaning of their experiences, I changed. Many I carry in my memory. I also changed as I came into relationship with the thinking of others, both through their writing and by talking to some in person. As I added their visions to my own, I reconstructed what I saw. And as I write this now, I am in relationship with you, the reader, whom I can only imagine. The possibility of your reading this book provided me with the inspiration to write it. I also can only imagine how this conglomerate I call myself might influence you, as we come into relationship as you read this book.

Part I
Women Speaking
of Relationships

One: Women's Lives and Reality

In the following pages, you will find the stories of ninety-four women, as selected and told by them, each relating what was for her a memorable spiritual experience. As you read these women's stories, and my commentary on them, I hope you will learn more about these particular women, about women's spirituality in general, and about what a study of women's spirituality can teach us about women's psychological development and expression.

I write about these women's spiritual experiences as a psychologist with an unflagging interest in what makes us human, and with a curiosity about many of the rich paradoxes implied by much of human behavior. Supporting my interest in knowing more about the human adventure and dilemma is my conviction that we become empowered and whole as we discover and accept all that makes us who we are—our strengths, weaknesses, limitations, and our freedom. I know that the processes of awareness, acceptance, and integration guide us down the path of self-development.

A Woman's Path

I also know from my own personal and professional experiences, and from the observations of others, that the path to a woman's self-development and self-definition is littered with obstacles. These obstacles, placed in her path by a society that sometimes subtly, but rather consistently, devalues female and whatever becomes associated with female, are so pervasive they appear to be inherent. For example, ask any number of people of different ages and backgrounds to check off which adjectives describe women and which describe men on an adjective check list of personality attributes and you will find a remarkable consensus. We typically associate women with passivity, dependency, timidity, vulnerability, helplessness, emotionality, while men are associated with those attributes seen as their opposite—activity, independence, adventurousness, reliance, and rationality.[1] But the differentiation of personality attributes along gender lines does not end there; once differentiated the traits associated with female are seen as inferior and either dismissed, demeaned, or despised. Phrases that label men as having feminine characteristics—sissy, she-boy, pansy, smock kisser—are pejorative, whereas the assignment of male traits to a woman is meant to be a compliment, e.g., "you think like a man." (Admittedly enlightened segments of our society now see this particular reference to be the insult to women it has always been, but the underlying attitude still prevails. In a more subtle fashion our cultural norms still imply that men possess more highly valued traits.)

Growing up female in a society that devalues females certainly does not produce the most conducive environment for human development. Undoubtedly women today, and throughout history and across nations, have paid unnecessary prices—psychological, physical, and economic—because of the fact of their femaleness. These burdens may be reflected in women's greater tendency to express distress, as well as in their greater willingness to participate in psychotherapy, although whether this is a sign of psychological need or psychological strength—or a combination of both—is debatable.

Although I feel justifiable anger at the unnecessary suffering that has been inflicted on women, I also know that women are not defined by their victimization. Despite a historical weight of oppression, women have not only survived, but thrived. By some transformative process, many women seem to have been able to translate their societally defined inferior and demeaned status into an increased capacity to meet and enjoy life. I have witnessed women willing to risk the pain and uncertainty of looking into their inner lives, motivated by a desire to live a full existence and a belief that there was more to life than they were now experiencing. As a psychologist, I probably will always associate courage with the willingness to face one's self as directly, honestly, and completely as possible.

I think we now recognize that women's less than advantageous position in society has resulted in the development of a women's culture with many exemplary characteristics. It has even become fashionable to express envy of women for their ability to express so much of themselves and to lament the burden of restricted expression that so many men seem to feel. The question I have is whether that has occurred *because* of women's position in society or *in spite* of it. It seems that the pain of suffering has forged in many women a deeper, stronger capacity to appreciate life. By overcoming the obstacles in their path, many women have developed a greater capacity to respond fully and creatively to life than they would have without the test.

I am not the only one who has pondered the irony of how women's strengths seem to have arisen out of such unfavorable circumstances.[2] Baker Miller has observed that all psychological characteristics are two-sided and that the characteristics of vulnerability, helplessness, and dependency, which societal arrangements have fostered in women, are not just weaknesses but also sources of strength. She understands the harm that has resulted to the individual when, in the past, these characteristics were exhibited in situations of subordination and powerlessness. But she also reminds us that "the dialogue is always with the future . . . women's psychological characteristics are closer to certain psychological essentials and, therefore, both sources of strength and the bases of a more advanced form of living."[3]

Understanding Women and Ourselves

Like others, I, too, want to understand what it is like for a female to grow up in a world in which her sex has been assigned an inferior status, and how this has affected her, for better and for worse. I want to understand a woman's inner psychological world, to come to know her inner psychic life. To do this, I chose to look at women's "spiritual experiences" because I understand spiritual experiences to be reflections of a woman's religious imagination and of how she symbolizies self. When I use the terms religion and religious imagination, I do not assume the existence or actuality of a transcendent being—whom some have called God—or even of a transcendent truth. I do assume, with Langer, that what distinguishes us humans from the other animals, with whom we share this earth, is our need to symbolically tranform and understand our experiences.[4] Some seek such transformation within the context of an institutional church and traditional religious beliefs, others through their participation, for example, in art and literature. The possibilities for our transformational settings are only limited by our own vision. Whatever means we chose, our choices testify to our need to symbolize, to imagine, to make meaning.

I believe, then, that women's spiritual expressions will offer insights into how women see the world and themselves in it. In our spiritual expressions I see a reflection of our psychology, and in our psychological expressions I see the influence of our spiritual understandings and religious beliefs. Because of this interaction, I think that we can arrive at a deeper realization of women's psychological development by looking at the spiritual stories of the ninety-four women who responded to my request to describe a memorable spiritual experience.

I also understand that I am making this inquiry into the psychological-spiritual world of women in a historic period in which we are witnessing a paradigmatic shift being made, not only in psychology, but in other disciplines as well.

Until recently the study of men has been equated with the study of humans. Not too many years ago it wouldn't have occurred to me to write this book, and if it had, I wouldn't have imagined many would be interested in reading it. Whether, for example, in history, psychology, or sociology, women were either ignored as subjects of study, or, using a deficit model, they

were studied in comparison with men. Comparing women's behavior, attitudes, and achievements to men, often the yardstick
used to make the comparison was built on male experiences. Not
surprisingly, as a result of using this method of measurement,
women often "came up short." Now, however, a number of
writers—mostly women—are focusing our attention on women's
lives and, no longer comparing women to men, are seeking to
understand how women experience the world.

Most of these authors assume, as I do, that women's
and men's experiences do not fall neatly into two dichotomous
groups separated along gender lines. But I believe, as they do, that
the experiences of women "reveal in a more emphatic fashion
certain aspects of the human situation which are present but less
obvious in the experiences of men."[5] So, as we study women we
are learning more about the "human situation" that we previously
ignored. And as we look at women's lives without our previous
assumptions of male-as-the-norm, we discover that many aspects
of women's lives can be seen as sources of strength and as models
for more advanced forms of human living.

Jessie Bernard,[6] a self-described sociologist-at-large,
was convinced that we had a lot to learn about our society and
ourselves by studying women's lives. Gilligan,[7] writing as a psychologist, shares this view. Doubting that the current male-derived theoretical formulations of moral development can adequately explain most women's behavior, Gilligan also opted to
study the world of women's lives. By doing so she was able to
appreciate women's experiences for what they were, in and of
themselves, not as deviant or deficient expressions of male-based
norms. She adds an essential dimension to the existing male-based
theory with her complementary model of moral development. In
the dimensions of women's experiences, moral development occurs in an interpersonal world as well as in the more masculine
world of abstract justice. Because of this different context, a
female-defined sense of justice does not emphasize abstract principles at the highest levels of moral development, but rather relational responsibilities. With the placement of moral development
within interpersonal relationships we find that a tension between

self and other inheres in every moral choice. The dilemma becomes: when does the decision for self contribute to a larger good and when does a decision to acquiesce to the other's right or need contribute to the larger good?

We not only learn more about the human situation from Bernard, Gilligan, Baker Miller, and others, but, just as significantly, we see revealed how certain societal assumptions about what makes us human, and about our relationship to the world, have limited our thinking. We have assumed as givens of existence what turn out to have actually been societal artifacts. Expressions of dependency at any age and for any sex are not necessarily inappropriate or unhealthy; and placing concern for others before a sense of abstract justice is not necessarily an expression of inferior moral development. We have incorrectly assumed that male experiences and responses to the world are natural, and we dismiss the possibilities of ordering our world from a perspective based on female experiences. We find these androcentric assumptions embedded within all of the different areas that govern and reflect our feelings and our thought. They are contained within psychological and sociological theories, in the way we analyze history, and in what we see as possible economically.

We doubly benefit by a focus on women's lives, then. First, we have a more complete realization of the human situation. Second, we understand that certain societal assumptions are carried in our myths, written in our law, and entrenched in our academic theories, and that, explicitly and implicitly, they guide our thinking and behavior. Until recently these assumptions have been unstated and their male-centered bias has been unrecognized. But now we see an emphasis on uncovering the societal assumptions, on discussing their mertis, and of including women's experiences in the assumption building process.

A Feminist Theological Perspective of Our Reality

Nowhere is it more emphasized that we need to draw upon women's experiences in the construction of our societal theories and concepts, and to expose our androcentric assumptions, than it is in feminist theological writing. I turn now to a discussion of feminist scholarship in religion because I think we can benefit from becoming acquainted with some of the issues raised by these feminist theologians, as we try to better understand the psychology of women. Women writing in religion may use different language than women writing in psychology, but they often describe a similar phenomenon, although from a different perspective. Because of these common conceptual concerns, we often can infer psychological correlates to many of the theological categories raised by women in religion. I think we can benefit by explicitly integrating their insights about women's lives into those suggested by women working in psychology. As a step in that integrative direction, I will use a framework of theological categories, as suggested by feminist scholars, as well as a paralleling psychological perspective, to orient us as we read the women's spiritual stories in the following chapters. Next, as introduction, I present an abbreviated description of my interpretation of the basis of feminist scholarship in religion, and then describe the three theological categories that I will use as framework, and suggest some possible psychological correlates.

Feminist theological scholarship takes many forms and offers different theoretical, methodological, and political viewpoints. But within the variety of feminist religious writing, there is common agreement, as expressed by biblical scholar Elisabeth Schüssler Fiorenza, that its theoretical and practical aim is "to undermine the legitimization of patriarchal structures (and) also to empower women in their struggle against such oppressive structures."[8] These scholars concur that patriarchal structures oppress women, children, animals, the earth, and most men, and that patriarchal ideologies are so deeply entrenched in our society, culture, and history that "these ideologies . . . make social structures look 'natural,' inevitable and divinely given."[9] They describe a patriarchal stamp that, imprinted on our reality, makes us believe that we cannot manage without hierarchical arrangements; that nature and animals exist to be used by us humans; that war is inevitable; that the body is separate from the spirit and often its enemy; and that death is opposed to life. Feminist religious writers strip away that innocence, exposing many of the patriarchal ideologies for what they are: a system that exploits the many for the few and endangers the planet. Clearly rejecting patriarchal values as destructive to all, they do not, however, seek to substitute the rule of women for the rule of men. Ruether summarized the goals of most when she said, "the commitment of women today continues to be what it has always been: a commitment to the survival of children and of the earth."[10]

The feminist critique of religion—mostly addressed to the Judeo-Christian traditions—and the alternative theologies they offer, may be one of the most fundamental challenges faced by any religion for centuries. At least one feminist theoretician believes that the challenges made have already been won, and that we are witnessing the beginning of a "changing of the gods."[11] The basis for the feminist argument in religion is similar to the feminist argument in other disciplines. Feminist religious writers contend that all extant theologies are incomplete because, just like our psychological theories, they are based primarily on the experiences of men. We will not have a complete understanding of the divine reality and our relationship to it, and to each other, feminists argue, until our theologies have considered and used the experiences of women.

Although the feminist religious scholars make a similar argument as feminists elsewhere, the stakes seem exponentially higher. The arguments around the reformulation of psychological theory revolve around empirical observations, clinical experiences, and scientific judgments. Theological arguments, however, imply or directly refer to an ultimate higher authority, and, once a particular theological argument is accepted as divinely inspired, further discussion and argument is stunted. Psychological arguments, which are presumably derived from scientific-rational reasoning, are made between one individual or group to another. Theological discourse, operating at a mythic and symbolic level, often pits human invention against claimed divine inspiration of an absolute authority. So, when feminists challenge the nature of God, they also challenge what some see as the most fundamental and ultimate authority for the way we live our lives.

Feminist theological thought is rich and abundant. I would like to focus here, however, on three essential arguments: on a critique and reformulation of how we conceive of sin; on the sex and nature of God; and on the paradigms we use to discuss our spirituality.

A New Conception of Sin

It was Valerie Saiving, writing over twenty years ago, who opened the discussion on the androcentric incompleteness of sin. She questioned the traditional view that explains sin as growing out of self-assertion, self-centeredness and pride. In this traditional view, associated with Christian religions, we become estranged from God as we forget we are but one small part of the whole, not the whole. We sin, in other words, when we fail to remember that we are in relationships with all those others who together form the whole. Saiving, however, challenges the implicit claim of universality made by those who describe sin as pridefulness, or the "imperialistic drive to power." Arguing that sin as pride and self-assertion is more common to the experiences of men than of women, she offers another understanding of sin which would encompass the experiences of women. Sin, she explains, also arises out of denying self, of abnegating responsibility, of forgetting oneself in the everyday minutia of life.[12]

Saiving's argument is summarized by Plaskow, who observes that this "flight of responsibility before God . . . involves orientation toward what is not God."[13] Extending this line of thought, Plaskow contends that the experiences of women are never free from cultural role definitions, and that cultural pressures move women toward a denial of self and an unwillingness to initiate unless she does so for others. The cultural expectations for a woman's role and her psychology are to maintain, help, and nurture. We expect a woman to sustain relationships, even if this means that her own individuality will never be realized. The Christian stress on self-sacrifice and obedience, then, as a counterweight to human (male) tendencies of pride and self-assertion, redundantly emphasizes this cultural message. Culture and theology combine so that a woman's sin, Plaskow and Saiving contend, is less likely to be associated with an excess of self, but rather from her failure to disembed from her relationships when it becomes appropriate to assert and define self.

Using impressions gained from clinical observations, I think we can find the beginning of a basis for using Saiving's and Plaskow's perspectives to inform our understanding of women's psychological development. We know that psychiatric symptoms often fall along gender lines; women are more likely to be diagnosed as hysterical, depressed, or agoraphobic, and men seem to be more prone to obsessional neurosis, addictions, sexual deviations, and psychopathy. Helen Block Lewis' thinking on shame and guilt has added to our knowledge of these differential diagnoses by sex.[14] I will use that part of her presentation that applies here, by recounting her observation that the phenomenon of shame is experienced and expressed more often by women, while feelings of guilt seem more common to men. Both shame and guilt, she explains, are different modes of affecting reparation. We experience guilt for those real or imagined transgressions against others for which we feel responsible. Acting as psychic censor, guilt repairs the relationship with others that has suffered from our real or fantasized hostility. In contrast to the externalized process of guilt, Block Lewis describes shame as "an 'implosion' or momentary destruction of self"[15] that occurs with the real or imagined loss of affectional ties. This happens because our satisfaction with our self often comes from the "mutual delight" of an internalized affectionate interaction, i.e., we carry within us our mother's delight in us. Shame occurs because of our perceived failure to earn the delight of this loved other, but, instead of directing anger at the other, shame turns our hostility against ourselves. In states of shame, the internalized other is still loved, only the self is hated. It seems then that this self-hatred is offered as penance to our loved object for our imagined failure. Shame may temporarily destroy the self, but it seeks to repair the relationship. Block Lewis hypothesizes that shame is more common to women because, being raised by the same sex and making an early identification with the same sex, women then find it more difficult to establish a separate sense of identity.

I think Block Lewis' views are helpful, but I also think that we can expand on her explanation of shame in women if we use the theological propositions advanced by Saiving and Plaskow, adding material of our own. They tell us that in Western Christian society, women grow up within a culture that has defined sin as "the imperialistic drive to power." At the same time, women have been directed by that same culture to define themselves, and to gain their satisfaction, through their relationships with others. As Plaskow has suggested, these cultural demands make redundant the emphasis on self-sacrifice meant to counter human (male) aggressiveness. But, if we add knowledge derived from the psychological research literature we can contribute further support for Plaskow's contentions. The greater tendency of males to express physical aggression is one of the few consistent sex differences that stands up after scores of studies on the topic.[16] For whatever reason, or combination of reasons—biological, cultural, psychological—boys and men are more likely to be physically aggressive and more often try to achieve dominance over their peers than girls and women. Expressed in theological nomenclature, men are more likely than women to express "an imperialistic drive to power."

I think that, in part, the phenomenon of shame in women also may result from unnecessary cultural and theological demands for self-sacrifice and dimunition being directed against the very group least likely to need that direction. If men are more likely to experience their own aggressiveness, they also are more likely to understand and apply the theological conception of sin as too much self-assertion. They may even welcome such a restraint. But women, because they are less likely to feel the same aggressiveness, and because of the cultural role demands made on them, make a different interpretation. The theological restraint on women's aggressive drives finds no target, no exaggerated feelings of aggressiveness. As a consequence, women internalize the image of "an imperialistic drive to power," and, having no object, turn it against themselves. The phenomenon of women's shame, or the "momentary destruction of the self," is fed by this unnecessary check on women's self-assertion. Perhaps sin as "the imperialistic drive to power" gives a necessary control to male aggression, and the damage that aggression can do to our societal relationships and social order. But when it is directed at women, who typically express less aggression, it does not lead to a balance between self and other, but to the self-destruction that shame brings.

The Sex and Nature of God

As a society we have begrudgingly begun to clean up our sexist language, replacing the "generic" he with whatever pronoun, she or he, is appropriate. Letter carriers now deliver our mail, not postmen, and chairmen have been replaced by chairs, chairpersons, and chairwomen—take your pick. Women, once linguistically subsumed under men, are now emerging in our speech as visible agents. Although some recalcitrant traditionalists continue to make snide comments about the importance of this linguistic revolution, as a society we are slowly accepting the need to acknowledge women's presence in our language. Textbooks are being changed, government bureaus and forms are being revised, and television commentators have started using inclusive language. By changing our language, we as a society are making an essential shift in our attitude toward women. As we include women's presence in our language, we acknowledge and encourage the agency of women in our lives.

Feminists working in religion also are acutely aware of what it means to include women in our language and therefore in our thoughts. Again, feminists challenging certain religious assumptions may face even greater resistance than those working similarly in other fields. They not only require that we use sex inclusive language in religious scripture, writing, and practice, but that we reconsider the sex of God. They understand that our God-language fundamentally establishes our relationship with the divine.[17] In a later chapter, "Views of God," we will see how the

concept of God is inextricably linked with the psychological process of self- and object-representation. For now we need to know
that how we speak of God affects, in the most basic way, not only
how we think about God, but also how we think about ourselves.
Language gives form to our concepts, which, in turn, becomes
our psychology.

For example, if I think of a mythical relationship with
God the Father I imagine one type of God. For me, he is parent,
authoritative, judgmental, and powerful. By comparison, I am
dependent and look toward him for guidance. And, as a female, I
understand that the ultimate authority and power is male, and I
equate authority with maleness, especially when societal arrangements support this conclusion.

If I think of God the Mother, however, an entirely
different image emerges, and, with it, a different relationship. The
connection I now feel to God, as Mother, is much more primitive
and as elemental as the umbilical cord that initially ties all of us to
our mothers. A Mother God has authority, judgment, and power,
too, but it is not of an abstract nature; instead it seems to flow
from some primordial beginning. And, finally, one more example
of how the naming of God shapes our relationship to the divine. If
I call God neither Father, nor Mother, but Friend, another relationship emerges. God is still God and therefore with an ultimate
and supreme essence. But when I imagine God as Friend, I enter
into a more mature relationship. Although still not equal with
God, for I am human and God is God, there seems to be a different
expectation for me. I can rely on God, but I also am expected to
rely on myself. God provides wisdom, support, and counsel, but I
share responsibility with God for who I am. Spatially, I picture
God across from me rather than above me.

These are some of the ways in which I respond to
different conceptions, or images, of God. You, the reader, may
share some of my reactions, or you may differ in your responses.
But I think you will agree that how we name God—as Father,
Mother, Friend—becomes the basis for our relationship to God.
And how we name God can bring us into closer relationship wth a
"greater power," or it can create an alienating distance.

The example of God as Friend refers us to a related

issue raised by feminist theologians and the women's spirituality movement, although this topic has not been stated as explicitly or treated as comprehensively. Although not a consensus of opinion, I think we can find within feminist religious thinking and practice a representation of a God, or divine spirit, that is more immanent than transcendent, and of a God, who as friend and partner, shares power with us rather than threatens to use it against us.[18] The form of this God-other relationship does not have an a priori hierarchical arrangement.

I think the question I have about how we are psychologically influenced by a conception of God with ultimate authority and judgment that exists external to us is shared by many women scholars and activists in religion. I formed these questions as I worked with women struggling with their sense of self-definition. Many of these women grew up equating self-assertion and self-definition with egocentricity and selfishness; they were given both spoken and unspoken messages to conform and to be directed by outside forces. As adults they could not trust their own inner sense of who they were and what they wanted, yet they also deeply yearned to find that self. Their conflict was whether to listen to their own innate, creative desires, or to an authority external to themselves. Their training had been to do the latter. An essential part of the therapeutic process was to establish a context and a relationship in which the woman could feel free to explore and express all of who she was without first looking for approval or consent from others. Slowly she would learn that one could, at the same time, consider the other and express and define self. (While my point here is about external authority, the reason for women's hesitancy to assert self also stems from the point raised in the previous section. In addition to being oriented toward an external male authority, they also are being influenced by the cultural and religious ideas about the role of women in society and the nature of sin.) Again, we will see explicated in the later chapter, "Views of Self," the psychological processes that translate societal values into self-images.

Much of the psychological work of these women was to shift from an external to an internal authority. So, it comes as little surprise to find an immanent, less fearsomely authoritative God, or spirit, depicted in the women's spirituality movement. Either intuitively or consciously, I think women working in religion understand that our conception of God influences the psychology of self, and that the characterization of God as external and authoritative exacerbated many women's well learned response to look outside of themselves for direction.

Being-in-Relationship

The psychological and spiritual experience of being-in-relationship is the third issue I would like us to consider as we read the women's spiritual stories. I think that it is this category of being-in-relationship that has a distinctly female influence and that most uniquely characterizes the female experience.

As we learn about women's lives from a variety of settings and from different perspectives, we see strengthened the observation that women live in a world of interpersonal relationships. Bernard saw this in her discussion of women's world; Gilligan described women's moral development as set in an interpersonal matrix of attachment and connection to others. Based on her clinical observations, Jean Baker Miller reformulated the concept of self for women as a "self-in-relation." Arguing that psychological theories place too much emphasis on independence as a developmental goal, she understands maturation as a process of developing a capacity for relationships.[19]

Certainly the psychological and psychiatric literature is richly endowed with clinical theories and techniques that are built on how our, mostly early, relationships with others influence our development and existence.[20] But it has been predominantly those writers who have chosen to examine and describe the experiences of women who have helped us to see that an interpersonal relational mode of existence is not theoretical speculation, but a practical lived reality of many women's lives.

The interpersonal relationality of a woman's world

also receives attention from women writing in religion. One major contribution to this effort comes from Carol Ochs who uncovers and brings into light the sacred and spiritual significance found in the everyday lives of women. Ochs offers a definition of a "new spirituality" that has as its central task the "process of coming into relationship with reality."[21] Rejecting traditional male-based developmental models of spirituality which stress the separation of self from its supporting environment—e.g., the "desert experience"—she uses the female developmental model with its focus on relationship. We all begin relationships with our experience of being mothered and it is to mothering that Ochs turns her attention. She discusses how mothering is a context for spirituality, or for "coming into relationship with reality."

Ochs, of course, was not the first to lift up the spiritual significance of relationship to our awareness. Buber's "all actual life is encounter,"[22] provides part of the basis for her proposition that mothering is a context and a process in which we experience the spiritual and come into relationship with being. Implicitly accepting the idea that there is the divine presence within each of us, Ochs, as others have done, builds on Buber's presentation that we "become an I through a You."[23] We form one another through the encounter, a moment when we enter into another's world, momentarily dissolving boundaries that separate us from the rest of life. Experiencing oneness with the other, we are transformed by that experience. We then carry part of that other within us; they have helped shape our being. And, understanding that there is something of the divine within each of us, we also understand that it is in the fullness of the encounter when we meet and touch the divine presence. Ochs, then, urges us to expand our conceptions of the spiritual process to include not just dramatic, independent events that occur in physical isolation from others, but also those everyday experiences, more common to women, that lead us into relationship.

Writing about women's friendships, not mothering, Mary Hunt describes new models of relationship. She explains that she intends to reclaim the word "lesbian" for what it has always meant, "women loving women without fixating on the presence or absence of genital activity." Expanding lesbian to include any woman who feels the love and closeness of another woman's friendship, she understands that it is in friendship with another that "something new may be born."[24] Like others who write about woman's world, she finds self-definition and growth occurring in relationship to another, in this case, to another woman friend.

In one sense, the concept of a self-in-relation (as Jean Baker Miller would say), or of "coming into relationship" (as described by Carol Ochs) or Mary Hunt's model for women's friendships, contains and depends upon the essential points raised in the two other theological categories. Before we can feel comfortable with the constantly shifting demands between self and other that we experience in our interpersonal relationships, as well as intraphysically in our internalized world of actual and mythic others, we need to become accomplished in a number of psychological tasks. First, we need to have a well defined sense of self, and a conviction in the appropriateness of our self-assertion. We must acquire a sense of our "self-ness," of being more than the sum total of our relationships, but also of having a cohesive sense of identity that is not just defined by, but also defines, our self-in-relationship. At the same time, we have to be aware of our dependency on others, and remember that we form, and are formed, by all of those who are important in our real and mythic lives, throughout our life. This balance is never finally achieved, of course. What we learn, at best, is some type of homeostatic control so that we never tip too far to one side—toward self or other—for too long a period of time, or for too great an extent. However, we can be severely impeded from learning this type of regulation if we continually hear one position emphasized. As I discussed in the section "A New Conception of Sin," cultural demands combine with theological conceptions of sin, placing too great a stress for women on self-denial. Societal and religious pressures become an impediment to learning how to balance self and other. And, again, we find the danger that women may neglect self-interest and miss their own integrity when they grow up and live in a world governed by cultural and theological assumptions that place authority outside of themselves—either because authority is invested in males or in a male, externalized God.

Whether we speak of a new conception of sin, or of the sex and nature of God, or of a self-in-relation, it seems to me one fundamental issue is being raised: how can we live in harmony with ourselves and with others—the others that inhabit the physical world we share, and all of those others we have internalized as parts of our self. What feminists in religion and psychology have been saying is that our desire to achieve some type of dynamic moral balance between self and other cannot happen unless we understand the incompleteness of the male-derived assumptions that govern our existence and include other assumptions, more compatible with the experiences of women.

These three theological categories—a new conception of sin, the sex and nature of god, and being-in-relationship—provide us with an orientation to understanding the women's spiritual stories. My hope and intent is that an examination of the women's spiritual stories, using this perspective, will not only teach us more about the psychology of women and the human situation, but also reveal a broader range of assumptions we can use to govern and interpret our existence.

Two: Introducing the Women and Their Stories

No one group of women can speak for all women. But I think that, as a group, the women whose stories will be told here represent a diversity of backgrounds, of ages, and viewpoints. I will let you, the reader, be the judge of their diversity by briefly describing how I found the ninety-four women of this study and by briefly detailing the characteristics of this group of women. After being introduced to the women, I hope you will agree with me that, although they cannot speak for all women, their stories can tell us something about the lives of many women.

Finding the Women

Ninety-four women responded to a questionnaire I designed, requesting them to "describe what was, for you, an important or memorable spiritual experience." In addition, I asked these women to "describe the situation and how you felt in the situation as completely as possible." Explaining that I was conducting research on women's spirituality, I also asked for their age, religion in which raised (if any), religious affiliation or identification at present (if any), and their race or ethnic group.

I had to ask hundreds of women to respond in order to collect the number of responses I finally obtained. The nature of the questionnaire distribution, however, makes it difficult to arrive at an exact count of how many questionnaires were distributed. I often gave questionnaires in bulk to women who distributed them at conferences and it was impossible to ascertain how many were actually disseminated. Other women distributed questionnaires in classes and to friends and colleagues, and some women Xeroxed questionnaires to hand out to colleagues and friends, which also confounds exact accounting.

My search for women who would respond began in May of 1983 and ended in August of 1984. I found the women wherever I could, relying on the help of family, friends, neighbors, colleagues, and the women's network. My mother distributed questionnaires to her friends in Florida: my sister to her colleagues in Thailand. I wrote to other relatives in Pennsylvania. I distributed questionnaires at professional conferences I attended, and to the women at various churches. I gave them to those women students in my classes who expressed a willingness to respond. Friends distributed them to the women in their classes at local universities. Questionnaire distribution spread as the family members of friends distributed them to neighbors. I placed the questionnaire in newsletters of women's religious groups. I also sent questionnaires to the National Black Sisters' Conference, and contacted ministers of local black churches. A number of lay and clergy women, active in religious networks—such as the Women's Alliance for Theology, Ethics and Ritual (WATER) in Silver Spring, Maryland, and the Lay Ministry Project—kindly assisted me with distributing questionnaires. Most of the women who resonded were strangers to me, until I met them by reading their stories.

Meeting the Women

Something can be learned first, I believe, from the women who will not be met. Most women who were asked to respond to the questionnaire chose not to. I can speculate, with some confidence, what those reasons for not responding were. Women's lives are busy and spending time to respond to a stranger's request understandably might have low priority. If a woman sees some benefit to herself in responding, such as becoming clearer about her own spirituality, then a response is more likely.

If no benefit is perceived, then response is less likely. Some women may have felt the request, to describe a spiritual experience, an intrusion in their personal life. One woman wondered, "what the question is to point up or prove?" And there must have been women who, with the best of intentions, forgot the questionnaire under an accumulation of papers.

But I do not have to rely solely on speculation to understand why many women chose not to respond. I spoke with women who did not respond, with some who did so reluctantly, and with women who, acting as my agents, talked to women who were asked but did not respond. Some non-responding women described the request as "too overwhelming." Describing a spiritual experience seemed, to them, to demand too much introspection. Mixed in with this sentiment was the expressed desire of some women to respond to a structured questionnaire rather than an open-ended question. This, of course, would have defeated the purpose of the open-ended format. I deliberately avoided placing limitations on a woman's description, as I was seeking self-definitions of spirituality, not how women's responses fit into an established structure. It was a deficiency of my approach that this rationale was not successfully conveyed to some.

Other women seemed to agonize over what I wanted, or expected. What did I mean by "spiritual?" they asked. One respondent wondered with two other women whether her participation in a friend's birthing experience would be considered a "spiritual experience." They decided together it could not, assuming it failed to meet some implicit standard for "spirituality."

When I was able to talk directly to the women who questioned what I meant by "spiritual," I explained that I wanted to know how they defined it for themselves. This answer did not usually satisfy them, and, I think, frustrated many. And there were women who thought that they had never had a spiritual experience, or who thought anything they might consider spiritual to be inconsequential. Some women who did repond apologized for what they considered to be the banality of their stories.

Other women did not respond because they thought I wanted a specific event, and they had a process over time to describe. This was another inadequacy of the questionnaire design, not of their judgment. One woman explains why she will not respond, "this (her faith) has been just a steady, simple, and I hope *growing* thing all through the years, never having experienced . . . any sudden, or revealing insights, or any specific instance of a time of 'conversion.'"

Most women chose not to respond. Some women responded with reluctance. But many of the women who chose to respond did so with gusto. Often lengthy typewritten and handwritten accounts were sent. Many described more than one spiritual experience. Many more gave their names and addresses. A few expressed an interest in talking to me; others wanted me to inform them of my findings.

The vast majority of the women who responded (75 percent) identified themselves with a traditional religious affiliation. Many traditions are represented—Baptist, Lutheran, Presbyterian, Episcopalian, Quaker, Jew, Roman Catholic, Methodist, Seventh Day Adventist, United Church of Christ, Greek Orthodox, Mormon, Congregational, Christian Science, and Disciples of Christ. A smaller group of women (13 percent) described either a syncretic religious affiliation—Catholic-Feminist, Roman Catholic-Buddhist-Hindu—or just called themselves Christian, Protestant, or "God's Free Agent," not specifying any denomination. Almost as many women wrote "none" when asked to name their present religious affiliation (10 percent). Some of these women talked of God in their response; others did not. All described some felt sense of a larger presence.

Two women described themselves as witches. And one, at nineteen years of age, declares herself an atheist. A Lebanese, she explains her experiences with near death episodes during the war in Lebanon. Instead of turning toward religion, she found that "witnessing all the horrors of death, war, poverty, and the like cause me to find NO acceptable reason for believing in a god." She ends by emphatically stating, "I (underlined three times), know or believe, if you will, that there is no omnipresent force, and see no reason to believe."

As a group, these women have a rich variety of religious backgrounds. Diversity can be found not only in their religious affiliations, but in the variety of their ages. The three youngest women who responded were nineteen years of age, the oldest was eighty-one. The largest group of women were in their twenties (27), with the next largest group of women in their forties (22). But there were also ample numbers of women in the other age groups, nineteen of the women were in their thirties, five were in their fifties, eight were in their sixties, and nine were in their seventies.

These ninety-four women also came from a variety of ethnic backgrounds. Nine of the women are black, two are Asian; some of the remaining eighty women who identified themselves as Caucasian also cited their ancestral nationality. Eleven called themselves Irish-Americans, and five noted their German ancestry. Two described themselves as Italian-Americans and one as Italian-Irish. The Baltic states are represented by one woman who identifies herself as Lithuanian and two others who describe a Latvian heritage. Finally, one woman described herself as Greek, and two others as Polish-American.

The women come from different parts of the United States; one lives overseas. They live in the northeastern states of Massachusetts, New York, and Pennsylvania and in the mid-Atlantic states of Maryland, Virginia, and the District of Columbia. They also live farther south in Florida and in the southwestern states of Texas and Oklahoma. Two women from Minnesota represent the Midwest. The woman who responded from the greatest distance was living in Thailand at the time.

The Women's Stories

In each of the following four chapters I have described one major theme of women's spirituality, as found in the stories of the ninety-four women. Those parts of their stories that illustrate a particular theme are quoted exactly as the woman told it, with the exception that some minor, but identifying, details have been changed or omitted to protect each woman's anonymity.

In the following chapter, "Views of Self," you will find

women's stories which seem to emphasize some concern or experience with self, or that focus on their sense of their individuality or personhood. Next, I recount the stories of women to whom being in relationship with another seemed to have been an integral and common characteristic; that chapter is entitled "The Interpersonal Event." Other women's stories also depict being in relationship, but for them the distinguishing feature of their association with another was that it occurred in the context of death and dying. Their stories are told in the chapter by that name. And, not surprisingly, experiencing and defining some kind of larger presence occupied the thoughts of many women. I discuss their stories in the last theme chapter, "Views of God." All four themes—"Views of Self," "The Interpersonal Event," "Death and Dying," and "Views of God,"—also have sub-themes. So, for example, in "Views of Self" you will read about emerging women and mystical women, and in the chapter entitled "Views of God," you will hear the stories of women who speak of a time of being "in sickness and in health," and others who talk of "seeing and feeling the hand of God."

As you read the women's stories in the following four chapters, I think you will be struck, as I was, with both the richness and diversity of their expression. They experienced their spirituality in a variety of settings—in churches, at home, in nature, in cars, and in the hospital. Sometimes they were alone, often they were with another or in a group. Some women described a discrete event that occurred in one setting, such as a near car accident on a bridge, a vision in a bedroom, or harvesting peanuts in the fields of Africa. Other women described more of a spiritual process. One woman reported a new sense of self after a feeling of struggle, another after a long period of hopelessness. Others described moving from alienation to community and from sickness to health.

There was a generous offering of expressions in the self-descriptions of these women's feelings and attitudes during their spiritual moments. Many women spoke of acceptance—acceptance of self, of accepting others, of being accepted by others and by God, and of accepting one's fate. Some cast acceptance in terms of forgiveness. In addition to acceptance, themes of one-ness, with others and with God, of a connectedness to other life, of a sense of being a part of a larger whole, are used to describe their feelings. Sometimes the women's descriptions of feeling-in-union took on a mystical tone. Then they spoke of timelessness, of entering spaceless voids, of "tasting Jesus."

The women told of feelings of acceptance and of being in union; they also described a sense of contentment and peace. Words such as goodness, love, comfort, warmth, and security illustrated the women's sense of satisfaction. Other women's stories drew a definite form of a felt presence, such as a guardian angel looking over them, of Christ by their side or leading them forward, of cones of energy, and of sensing the Goddess within. As the women experienced these different emotions, some report a heightened sense of presentness, of centeredness and balance. Contrasted to this were those who talked of crying, or opening up and release, of being knocked to the ground on their knees, of being struck in their solar plexus by a greater power, and of feeling sexually aroused.

The other major motif found in these women's stories was adumbrated by the discussion of women's self as a self-in-relation, and of women's ontological posture as a "being-in-rela-tionship." With this prior understanding, perhaps it should come as no surprise that so many of the women's stories pulsate with their connection to life and to otherness, and that it is through this relationship with otherness that so many apprehend the divine. Time and again, we hear their stories of being in relationship with another—with a parent, a friend, an adversary, a dying person, with nature, and even with a ferret! Sometimes they speak of their relationship with an actual other person, as the woman does who tells of how she derived inspiration and feelings of connectedness with all life from her dying friend. Other times a relationship is implied. For example, one woman writes a poem while alone, but the poem she writes is a highly emotional rendering of her rela-tionship wtih her mother, and of how, as a mother, she is in relationship to her daughter.

These two motifs—diversity of experiences and the

commonality of relationship—appear throughout these women's stories. Each woman's story helps paint a picture with a uniquely personal experience, so that a definite form emerges from both the diversity of the stories as a group and the uniqueness of each individual woman's experience.

In the following four chapters, I will discuss within each theme how the women's stories may illustrate the issues raised in the three previously discussed theological categories of "a new conception of sin;" "the sex and nature of God;" and of "being-in-relationship." Additionally, I will offer some speculation on what implications may be found in these spiritual expressions for women's psychology.

Three: Views of Self

In discussing the development of his client-centered framework, Carl Rogers noted that he began his work with the idea the "self" was outmoded, too ambiguous, and an unscientific psychological concept, useful only to equally outmoded introspectionists. Over time, as he listened to clients tell him of their problems and their hopes, he realized that, for them, self is not a vague notion, but "an important element in their experience."[1] Rogers found that his clients not only spoke about self, but that becoming their "real self" was his clients' ultimate goal.

More recently, however, psychologists, who use a social-cognitive or clinical-developmental perspective, have been systematically studying what Carl Rogers and his clients experientially understood. Their interest is in the development and organization of self, which Noam, Kohlberg, and Snarey have defined as the mediating structure and process encompassing the two psychological subsystems of cognition and emotions. In the discussion by these, and other theorists, self also is equated with ego. Whatever term is used, ego or self, both refer to a fundamental structural unity of personality organization or an organized activity or system of functioning.[2]

The development of self is seen by these theorists, who begin with Piagetian principles, as occurring in an invariant developmental sequence of stages. Structural stage theories can be distinguished from other developmental approaches, which have organized development by culturally defined ages, or functionally defined phases (e.g., achieving autonomy in early childhood or identity in adolescence). These theories, with their focus on structure, understand the development of self as occurring through a continual process of the organism differentiating from the environment, reconstructing its relationship with the environment, and then integrating the original structure that defined the relationship "into a bigger system of which that structure is now a part." Some theorists, like Kegan, who have postulated a holistic self-structure, conceive of six developmental stages—incorporative, impulsive, imperial, interpersonal, institutional, and inter-individual.[3] Other theorists have studied a subdomain of self and arrive at different descriptions and numbers of stages. Kohlberg and Gilligan have examined moral development; Fowler is concerned with faith development; and Selman's theory focuses on the development of reasoning about the social environment.[4] Regardless of the delineation of stages, and whether or not a subdomain or a holistic structure of ego is the topic of study, at each developmental stage a reformulation of the relationship between organism and environment, self and other, is made with greater differentiation and integration achieved with each advancing stage.

Differentiation from the environment is required in order to gain a perspective on an experience and on the relationship to another; integration then allows this enhanced perspective to be accommodated into a re-elaborated self-other relationship. For example, in Kegan's model, at the impulsive stage of development, which typically occurs at about age two to five years, the child is not differentiated from her impulses or perceptions. She does not "have" impulses at this stage, she "is" her impulses because she cannot observe, manipulate, or mediate them. At this stage, her impulses are a subject of her experience; they are not yet object, or other. By the next stage, the imperial, she has differentiated from her impulses and they are now an object of her awareness. She is capable of mediating or coordinating them. What is now subject is not her impulses, but her needs, interests, and wishes. At later stages of development, such as the interpersonal, institutional, and inter-individual, what is subject and object in the relationship becomes less oriented to biological principles of impulses and needs, and more toward social organizing principles. At each stage of development, however, what is subject and what is object changes; according to Kegan's schema, the self is defined by this subject-object, or self-other, relationship.[5] Also important to remember is that, especially when the other, or object, is defined from a social perspective, the other can be an actual person, a symbolic other, or an internalized other.

There are two critical features of structural stage theories of development that can contribute to understanding the experiences of the women in this chapter who speak of self. First, these theories emphasize the relational nature of the self. From their perspective, the development of self occurs in interaction with the environment, and their theoretical model directs our focus to the importance of the social environment in development. Through a process of differentiation and integration with the environment and others in it, a dynamic activity of balancing subject-object relationships constitute self. With the transformation of what was once subject into an object of experience, a reelaboration of the self-structure is made, and a new relationship with the environment is achieved. Of course, differentiation is not always achieved, or desired. At times, the decision is to assimilate the environmental information into an existing self-structure, preserving the status quo. A second essential feature of this perspective is that it conceives of the self not as an entity but as a process, a process which mediates between an organism and its environment. The goal of this mediation is self-consistency or equilibration, "the basis for self-environment integrations and attempts at synthesis of contradictory demands, influences, or social conditions."[6] In these women's stories to follow, then, we may see examples of a woman who has achieved greater differentiation and integration with the environment, or other, as well as examples in which a woman has opted for the status quo. Whether the outcome is greater self-complexity, or self-maintenance, throughout their stories we also can witness the human striving to seek consistency and equilibrium. The conatus of self is to extract meaning from the environment.

In the stories that follow, many of the women describe a time or a process that challenged or developed their idea of who they were as a person, as a self. The largest number of women in this category who speak of self describe the emergence of a stronger and a more complete sense of self as a spiritual experience. These emerging women speak of affirmation, wholeness, and of a more complete sense of self as a spiritual experience. These emerging women speak of affirmation, wholeness, and of a more individuated self. A smaller number of women who describe a spiritual event that happened when twenty and twenty-one years old, are the youngest in this larger group of women who speak of self. These younger women report struggling with an opposition or tension they feel between self and God, self and other; for some, the struggle remains unresolved. A third group of older women, one over forty years of age and the others over sixty years of age, show resoluteness in their conviction that their task is to submit to God's will. They do not talk about a need to find their "real self," instead they strive to turn themselves over to God's higher authority. Defying usual categories of thought, a fourth group of women speak in the language of the mystic. These mystical women talk of being "in God," of moving toward God; they incorporate and identify with God.

Emerging Women

The emerging women of this study, whose voices tell of the beauty and power of discovering who they are, describe a sense of spirituality as a larger and more definitive sense of self develops. These women's stories tell of an affirmation of their identity, as they discover, integrate, and accept previously unacknowledged or unknown parts of themselves. A time when she consolidates her identity is recalled by one woman, who tells us;

> Three years ago I visited my father's home for the first time. It was in a part of the Soviet Union which is inaccessible to tourists from the West. It was a long journey, done in secret. My feeling at being, for the first time, in my ancestors' ground was . . . amazing. I felt so right, so whole. This is where I should be. I felt as if I had always been there, [I] knew where everything was,

wanted to encompass everything. It was a feeling of "yes, this is it, this is me!"

Discovering and acknowledging previously unknown parts of herself is the process another woman experienced as spiritual. As she participates in a guided imagery exercise, she recalls,

> I imagined a garden with flowers, a big tree (oak) and green lush lawns . . . running water and butterflies, insects, birds. I had feelings of warmth, of sunlight and blue sky and white clouds. I loved this garden of my creating . . . nothing was separate from me; there was a community of essence.

Guided to bring a loved one into her garden, a "masculine presence" emerges for her.

> It was not a male person of my acquaintance, just a smiling, loving, presence. There was this intense sense of love and intimate understanding between me and it. It was the most warm, understanding and comforting sense of love I've ever experienced. The "presence" knew me so intimately that there was absolute mutual knowledge, nothing to be explained . . . It was indeed a garden of love. I can't describe the feelings very well except that there was a sense of unity—essential unity that went beyond differences in time and space. The love I felt from and for the "presence" was the intimate love I guess everyone dreams of . . . permanent . . . with compassion. About a year later I realized this masculine presence was the masculine me.

The woman quoted above experienced a spiritual process in which unnamed and unknown parts of self are differentiated and then integrated, leading to a larger and stronger self-vision. For other women, this process is characterized by struggle, birth, and then a feeling of self-acceptance and wholeness.

A woman reporting on a three-day retreat she attended, entitled "Women in Transition," describes how

> We would use images (i.e., water), Bible stories, and fairy tales to examine our lives . . . The first two stories we looked at were Genesis 17—Sarah being told she would have a son—and Sleep-

ing Beauty/Brier Rose. We looked at the images—barren-ness/100 years of sleep, pilgrims on a journey, a waiting time. We were given questions to use for further meditations . . . Slowly a sense of myself began to emerge, even that first night. In our initial introduction, we were asked to give *one word* that came to mind to describe ourselves and the first word that came to mine for me was "struggle." As the evening progressed and I had time to process some of the questions posed, the second word that came to mind for me was "birth"—and isn't birth a struggle?! I began to see that part of my struggle in recent years came from not having tied up loose ends from a transition made thirteen years ago . . . the weekend enabled me to do that . . . to finish one stage before moving on to another. I couldn't complete the birth until I had "let go" the struggle—but I couldn't even do that until I identified what the struggle was. And this weekend helped me to do that. I began to recognize my strengths and weaknesses—and even beyond that, to accept myself, *just as I am.*

Thoughts of struggle, transition, and birth stay with her, culminating in the certain knowledge of

now *being ready* to accept the responsibility of giving birth to myself—and not being *afraid* any more of giving birth . . . It has stayed with me—that same sense of serenity and peace, of new-ness of life, and most importantly of *wholeness* and healing.

An exhibition of feminist artist Judy Chicago's *Dinner Party* occasioned one woman to open her sense of self, for the first time, to a conscious and reverent valuing of her femaleness. Recalling that moment, she tells us:

It was with a real sense of anticipation that I got on a subway to make the journey out from the Bronx to Brooklyn. It was November, one of those first days when you know that the segue from autumn to winter had begun. The subway runs under-ground most of the way, and then comes out over one of the bridges before going under again . . . I got to the museum . . . and . . . I was able to go right in. I walked past the banners on the wall, and then into the darkened room where the illuminated triangle seemed to float and shimmer. My first impression was that it was much larger than I had expected. Then I began to read the names on the Heritage Floor, and to move around to the beginnings of the first table and the first place setting for the Primorial Goddess. At that point I knew what the angel's words to Moses had meant: "Take your shoes from off your feet for the place you stand on is holy ground." The place where I was at that moment was for me, holy ground. I was in the presence of hundreds of my foresisters, the Goddesses of the ancient past, women who had lived and suffered and died to bring me to this moment. I felt a profound respect and love for the artisans and artists who had created the Dinner Party. I was ashamed that I did not know more about the women whose lives the plates and table runners created for me in symbol and color and fabric. I was infused with a sense of being part of a much larger and longer process of life and struggle—a connection to a people, my people, women and a Woman Spirit which I had never before experienced so clearly and powerfully. . . . It was hard for me to leave . . . For days afterward I found myself thinking about the beautiful flowers and vaginal images of the plates. Gradually I came to realize that this was a part of myself, a holy part of my body which I had never properly valued.

Through the transformational power of art, this woman acknowledges a previously unknown part of her self. With this realization she has a more complete sense of self, and a larger vision of holiness that encompasses her, as female, within it.

Like the woman at the Judy Chicago exhibit, another woman also relates a more powerful sense of self to her female-ness. Instead of her sense of self as female arising from the trans-formative power of art, it derives from the cleansing power of pain and fury. The rage one woman identifies within herself because of the exclusion of women from the clergy of her church metamorphoses into renewed strength as she "name(s) what I had dimly *felt.*" She realizes that the rejection of female clergy meant that "*I* as a woman was considered inferior." After the naming of what once was only "dimly felt," the "pain and rage were em-braced and experienced as *healing.*" Later, "this culminated in a spiritual experience when I attended the ordination of women in Philadelphia . . . *claiming* my and our rightful place, not waiting for men to grant us permission, but claiming what is ours." She, and others, move from awareness to anger to an enlarged vision of themselves and of their place in their church.

A third woman, who describes herself as "a feminist Jungian," learns to value her female wisdom, whom she knows as Sophia, after a ten-year period of "animus ecstasy." She remembers this time;

> I [was] focused on . . . a form of more "personal," ecstatic (read: traditional mysticism) experience à la St. Theresa of Avila. It was what I call "animus ecstasy"—or essentially a spirituality borne of my need to come to terms with the masculine in myself (in dreams, God imagery, a male figure) and I did so by projection of it onto male clergy, professors, colleagues, and a male "God-head" whom I allowed (unconsciously) then . . . to "possess" me . . . sweep me off my feet . . . "lift me up" in the traditional mystical sense of feeling a "floating—disembodied" state. Somehow I was fortunate enough, after some ten years of rather mindless possession (read: as in a cult follower) by "spiritual" mentors/guides, to run into one such male who held me at a distance and refused to be flattered by my devotion . . . and he educated me to what was going on. He turned me inwards to see that the traits I admired and exalted in him were actually in *me*.
>
> Thus began an inward journey to "own" my own inner spiritual guide. In the process of six-seven years of dreams/guided imagery dialogue with my own masculine self, I integrated the male symbol into my growing "self" image so that males are no longer primary figures in my dreams. For example, thieves breaking into my house . . . In early adolescence my father was the one to defend me and my house from the intruders (with a gun). In later adolescence . . . it was always male lovers, colleagues/mentors who defended me. Now I rarely (if ever) even dream of intruders . . . and if I do . . . I . . . defend myself . . . and/or a new older woman figure who appears variously as an Indian or Mexican woman . . . or as a faceless "spiritual presence" befriends me. She *nurtures* me silently when she appears in the incarnational form . . . and she speaks to me in the first person when she is in her more "spiritual" form. Since I did a lot of biblical research on Sophia . . . I see her as Sophia . . . God's *wisdom within me* . . . who enters me and embodies me . . . makes me "real." . . . She first spoke to me in a dream/revelation

the night after I attended a large conference of Catholic and Protestant feminists ... so I connect her with the collective power—the incarnate (yet corporately transcendent) spirit of women gathered together to *grow* spiritually and find *themselves* in the process.

Not all women who spoke of self used psychological language to do so. Understanding her place in history became a self-forming and spiritual moment for one woman. Having recently returned from two active years of doing religious work in another country, she recalls,

I was walking by the chapel, not in the habit of stopping by as the pious would have it. I suddenly heard the grandmother clock in the hallway, something I had passed numerous times on my way from one end of the building to another. It was still in the chapel and the steady tick of the clock was as loud as a heart monitor. It simply ticked off the seconds, one after another, as the day went by. I felt myself part of a long procession of people who had heard that clock. I felt myself key as the one who was hearing it at that particular moment. I was both part of a progression of history and an integral, essential part of it now. If I did not fulfill myself my little tick would be lost and somehow the whole flow of things would stop. These thoughts were not those of an egomaniac, but, rather, came from the realistic sense that our world does have intentionality and our places in it are secured by history.

One woman sums it up for all of these emerging women when, commenting on her emotions at the time of her spiritual event, she describes feeling "strong as an individual." These women experience their spirituality as they develop and assert a more differentiated sense of self—sometimes by integrating a masculine presence, other times by affirming a female identity and wisdom, and by taking their place in history.

All of these emerging women speak of experiences in which they transformed their relationship with the environment, and others in it, thereby achieving a more complex sense of self. Each woman's story gives an example of her participation in the process of developing, differentiating, and expressing newly found aspects of her personality.

Related to their greater self-complexity and self-definition is how these women speak of God. Over half of these emerging women do not talk of God, although all describe some sense of felt spirit. Of the women who do speak of God, none talks in a language in any way familiar to traditional religious nomenclature. One speaks of her experience as "a gift from the Goddess in myself." Another tells us of the electrifying realization that, without doubt, "God is (also) Female—I felt it, I knew it." A third woman identified the God within as "She (Sophia) . . . the Goddess of Kairos experience and not Chronos . . . womb-like mysteries of creativity surround her . . . She is the counselor/Holy Spirit/the transforming creating Christ, who was incarnate in the man Jesus, and, who is present to us now in the 'resurrected Christ'/God's ever creating/mediating/wisdom." These emerging women either eschew God-talk or speak of God as female, or also female. Not one of them speaks of God the Father. Speaking of self-definition as a spiritual process, they not only reject the notion that pride and assertion offend God, their stories also suggest a presence and authority found within themselves, not external to them. Implicit in their stories that tell of a process when they consolidate and enhance their sense of self is a rejection of the traditional Christian conception of sin as pride and assertion.

Selves-in-Conflict

Contrasted to these women are a group of younger women, under twenty-one years of age, who seem to be struggling with their self-definition in the context of their relationships. These younger women do not speak explicitly about feeling an undue emphasis to sacrifice self to other or to God. They show no conscious awareness of the observations made by feminist theologians who criticize the traditional conception of sin, or of the alternative view of moral development offered by Carol Gilligan. However, whether one uses a theological framework suggested by feminist theologians to look at the tension between the excesses of self-assertion and those of self-denial, or a parallel perspective on the opposition between responsibility toward self and other, implicit in each young woman's spiritual story is her struggle to achieve some balance in her relationship between self and God, self and other.

Recounting her reaction as a teenager to her family's move away from the country to a more urban area, one woman describes herself as "bitter, hostile, and angry" at her parents. She expresses her anger by recalcitrantly refusing to help around the house and by withdrawing from family life. Suddenly she is turned around. Looking up at the stars one evening, she talks about being "overcome with a sense of the presence of God and the goodness of all things, a sense of love." After this experience, her attitude toward her family changes. She once again happily participates in family life, relinquishing self-interest for the realization of a higher order relationship. She lets go of her individual yearnings for a sense of being connected to a larger reality. Emphasizing her responsibility to others, in this case her family, she serves the larger good.

Like this young woman, another young woman reports an adolescent conflict with her family. She remembers,

> my parents were very strict, they wouldn't allow me to go to any unorganized parties or events (where there were no adult chaperones), not go on any dates. Dating, and a social life were such important elements within my peer group's attitudes, and I felt very angry at my parents (even though we were close, and could talk openly). I would sneak out a lot and date behind their backs. Before long I started turning to the Lord, asking him to guide me safely through these situations. Sure enough, I realized the Lord had helped me and my parents, for I went through late high school with no problems at all (except a little guilt) . . . they wanted to keep me safe, and they loved me dearly.

By the end of this adolescent development episode, she has apparently completely internalized her parents' values which now have become a part of her self-construction. She predicts that "if I ever raise children, I will do it in the same manner as my parents, for the adolescent pain is worth the life you receive after adolescence."

A young musician, less clear about her decision than the young woman who eventually identifies with her parents' values, wavers between a stated desire to make her music a selfless "gift or contribution to God" and the pride in her accomplishments she attempts to deny, but unconsciously reveals. She sets the scene,

> I was standing by the organist, my flute in my hand, and I had just finished playing a song before the congregation. It was at that moment that this experience took place. I had such a feeling come over me that it is difficult to explain. But I can tell you what I saw that made me feel that way. As I looked around, the church was covered with flowers, the candles were lit in rows down the aisles. I saw families together and they all seemed to be at peace, even the little children were quiet. I had such a peaceful feeling that I had never had before. I felt that I had made a gift or contribution to God in playing my music, and I could tell that everyone else received it in a positive way also.

But her story doesn't end here. She remembers,

> I have had "peak" experiences similar to this that I wouldn't consider spiritual experiences. They all seem to deal with my accomplishing something, such as the end of a gymnast performance, receiving a good grade . . . or cutting off from things I know aren't good for me but that I enjoy.

She seems to distinguish her "peak" experiences, based on satisfaction and pride of accomplishment, from spiritual experiences which she sees as freely given gifts of self. In her definition of spiritual experience, there can be no self gain. After making her distinction between a peak and spiritual experience dependent on whether or not one gains a sense of self-accomplishment or gives of oneself, she contradicts herself. "I think that the feelings of *accomplishment,* contentment, and peace are what add together to give me a significant spiritual experience." After dismissing accomplishment as inappropriate for that which is defined as spiritual, she now includes it. She seems to feel a need to make a definitive choice between self-accomplishment and self-sacrifice, or getting something for herself versus giving to others, yet she understandably reveals a reluctance to give up one for the other.

Another young woman's story, while different, has a similar message. Expressed in secular terms, her dilemma is how to reconcile self-aggrandizement with responsible action or, expressed in the language of religious myth, when is it better to give than to receive. She experiences herself "acting like a lazy, spoiled brat . . . I wasn't studying as diligently as I should have been, I was spending too much money, and I was eating poorly." After hearing an inspirational address at an ecumenical service, she shifts from self-indulgence to a posture of striving to realize her potential and acknowledges "all of the goodness life has to offer." In the surface message or her self-described spiritual experience, she moves from self-indulgence to responsible action, with the implicit goal of responsibility to others. Her desire to satisfy her self-interests still predominates her thinking, however, as she speaks of her decision to be happy and how she wants "to start making things go in my direction."

Some women of this study describe moments of conflict between self and other that occur in their actual relationships with other people, such as the young woman who at first withdrew from her family when they moved. Others, like the young woman who struggled with her desire to make a purely altruistic gift of her music to God in the face of her own undeniable satisfaction she gained from her music, trace a relationship conflict that occurs more in their imaginations. But both conflicts are real. Each woman wrestles with the pull she feels to meet her responsibility to another—whether her family, people in general, or God—and the urge to express and feel her own needs, satisfactions, and desires. Each tells of her attempt to achieve some balance in her relationship of self with other, and in the balancing of this relationship we see the process of self-construction. Unlike the emerging women who expressed no ambivalence about their self-assertion and self-definition, these younger women tentatively explore how they can assert and be proud of themselves and at the same time make the contributions to others that they all see as important to make. Like many others of their age, they do not seem quite ready to differentiate from the other in such a way that they feel free to make their own claims and, at the same time, remain in relationship with the other.

Resolute Women

While these younger women may seem unsure of how to accommodate their needs with the demands they feel from others, the stories of a group of older women tell of finding a balance in their relationship to others; in their cases the balance tips toward the other. These women, resolute in their understanding of their spiritual task, do not waver between seeking to satisfy self and seeking to satisfy others. Talking in the tones of the traditional religious voice, they strive for submission to a higher authority, not self-enhancement. Accepting the traditional Christian conception of sin for them means that self-assertion endangers their relationship to God and that acquiescence enhances it.

Speaking of feeling "spiritually alive" and how "all things are new," one woman redefines freedom. "I was born to be free—free from my *limited* will." This freedom from her own will comes with a price. She acknowledges, "The pain comes when I must bend mine (will) to God—the eternal question." The freedom from fear and the courage she feels because of her relationship to God outweighs any pain she may feel from acquiescing to a higher authority. Trusting in God and "letting go and letting God" forms the basis for her faith.

Although these women do not waver in their conviction that their task is to surrender to God's will, they do report on the difficulties they encounter in fully living up to their own expectations. One woman talks about the need to totally surrender her life to Christ and her perceived failure because "I kept part of me for myself." She remembers,

After a long time of discouraging and depressing events, I reached bottom! I was from a family background of religious training in Sunday School . . . I had thought I had surrendered my life to Christ—but in reality it had not been total—I kept part of me for myself—because there were too many decisions *I* wanted to make. Rather it seemed I wanted to do what *I* wanted but did want God's approval on *my* decisions.

But her willful method didn't work,

I met disappointment and unhappiness—nothing worked out as I hoped it would—Until one evening, telling God I had made a mess of *my* way and from that moment on I was His to do with as He saw fit—the commitment was total! And in an instant I became a "new creature" in Christ—my burden was gone—I was liberated with an inner happiness and peace.

This total surrender leads to observable changes in the external world, "Doors opened!" as she enthusiastically reports. New positions become available to her, travel, and marriage at a mature age.

Like the woman whose surrender at first was not complete, another woman shares her temporary failure to totally submit to God's will. She tells us

From the time I was old enough to understand, I was taught about God and Christian principles . . . Daily prayers were a part of my life . . . As a child it seemed all my prayers were answered . . . My life continued to progress very fully and happily through college, marriage, and two beautiful children. I had begun to think that God would always answer my prayers "my way," forgetting my early training of "God's Will be Done."

Her serenity, however, becomes threatened with the illness of her mother.

When my mother became seriously ill, I started bargaining with God in my prayers. I didn't want to face the reality of life without her, nor did I want to leave the outcome of her illness to God's will. When she passed away, it was almost as though I turned my back on God. I felt He had let me down . . . I wanted to punish

> Him. My attitude changed and I was making myself physically ill with my negative thinking.

She escapes this miasma of negativity when,

> One morning, at sunrise, I was standing wide awake watching the sun come up, God came to me in such a glorious and healing way—It was as though a curtain had been lifted and He revealed to me His love and forgiveness. Needless to say I had come home again with a deeper understanding. No longer are my prayers demanding and bargaining. Now I pray for God's will for me and my family and the strength to carry on in a cheerful and loving manner.

She finds peace in total obedience to and acceptance of God's will. Unlike some women, these resolute women neither feel alienated from the traditional male God, nor abused by the demands to relinquish self. They have internalized, as part of their self-conception, the religious ideal of abnegation. Self-consistency is achieved by maintaining this religious ideal.

Mystical Women

So far, we have met women who describe an emerging self, young women in conflict with their desire to satisfy self and their sense of obligation to another, and women resolute in their conviction that their work is to submit themselves to God's higher authority. Still another group of women describe experiences that depict how each was able to accomplish a sophisticated psychological task. Instead of choosing between self or other, self or God, they recast their conceptual and experiential frame of reference, reducing tension between self and other. They speak of a self, not in contradistinction to God, but in relation to, or within. For example, one woman, recounting her "vows of obedience, humility, poverty, purity, and chastity," sees no conflict between her own sense of self-assertion and her desire to be totally obedient to God's will.

She describes how she is able to do this:

I have developed a Communion ceremony (through many meditations and experiential trials) in which I declare I am the Christ
and I accept that through the Communion I will be infused and
transmuted by Light. I do this ceremony every day and every
time I have some sort of spiritual experience.

One night I awoke at 4:30 a.m. I lay there and wondered at why I had wakened, so after trying to resume sleeping
without success, I asked (within) what I needed to do. Rising
seemed to be my guidance. I felt drawn to kneel and once there,
felt a strong inner presence and command to do the Communion ceremony. After repeating 3–5 times I was the Christ, I
proceeded to say the ceremony aloud. Immediately I felt great
power emanate from my solar plexus. It seemed to pulsate and
fill the room. The room became very bright (though no light was
on). Light seemed to emanate from the very cells of all the
objects in the room. Power overwhelmed me. I was virtually in a
sea of enormous power. I continued the ceremony while in the
fetal position. I then sat down. The experience continued to be
beyond my ability to cope with it, so I finally laid down stunned.
After a few moments, I rose and sat down on a couch in the
room. Guidance was to accept that Christ was part of my identity. That I had begun the ceremony stating I was the Christ and
had experienced that reality internally, and physically. I felt very
much commanded and drawn to realize myself as (Sarah) Christ
and to strive to know myself as Christ (Sarah).

I got up, and, being famished, ate breakfast and returned to bed—obediently. I have been realizing more fully, on a
daily basis, the truth, wonder and joy of being Christ.

She may have given up her own will in total obedience
to Christ, but she obtains an awesome power in turn. She has
internalized Christ as part of her own identity.

The women who speak in the language of the mystic,
unlike the self-affirming women, do talk of God. But, unlike the
God, or other, of some women with a will that is sometimes in
opposition to theirs, the mystic finds herself "within a divine
milieu."[7] Blurring distinctions between self and other, she is in
and on God, and God is around and in her. One woman experi-

ences the wholeness of this "divine milieu" as a vacuum or void. Repeating a prayer of self-offering, she suddenly "disappear(s)" as does the "church, time, and everything else except God." Her being is

> buried in a darkness in which I could not see, a vacuum in which I could not hear, in a spaceless-timeless void—I "saw" God, I "heard" God, and I was "in" God. When I again became aware of my surroundings, it was dark outside and my limbs were stiff and strained. But I was "wrapped" in God and carried a sphere of light, warmth, and indescribable peace around me.

In contrast to this specific mystical moment is another woman's description of her spiritual experiences as an integral part of an ongoing process of life, which, she says,

> is strongly felt in my body as energy, which fills my body and redefines me. I have all sorts of agitation, highs and lows, this other energy is continuous, endless, the closest glimpse that I have had to infinite. The energy directs me if I will let it. I often tense and resist and avoid—What do I fear? It seems to point to radical vast change which seems threatening. What is the reality? The change, when I let it come is healing, loving, empowering in the sense of compassionate, sharing, being and caring. So why do I continue to resist? I wish I knew! Just endless replays of the cycle . . . Generally, the world seems to name me as most powerful when I am myself feeling most lost into presence. When the energy flows through me I have courage, clarity, and command. When "I" take charge things are fearful, sporadic, excessive—generally imbalanced.

She doesn't name this energy, but like (Sarah) Christ, when she is at one with this larger presence she, paradoxically, loses herself and at the same time takes "command."

For another woman, a metaphysical understanding of "integration within the universe" and an awareness of how "my own integrity [is derived] from my part of the whole" occurs when she has a vision of human folly. Reading an article in the *New Yorker* about the American involvement in El Salvador, she acknowledges, may "seem rather mundane in its rational component." She tells us,

The writer was making the point that Americans, like the British during the Empire days, seek to impose our will on other peoples—make them want what we want. As I took this in, everything that I believe about spiritual evolution, the progress of all sentience towards a single consciousness rushed to that focal point. I became aware of the folly of this act of political will I was reading about, intensely aware of the alternative it necessarily implied: the concurrence of all wills in God's will. I suddenly found a sort of prayer take place in my mind: "Until the whole universe says with one voice, Thy will be done." I felt dedicated. My hair stood on end . . . I felt enthusiasm—the word means literally, being seized by a spirit—I felt "in the spirit." I felt a kinship with all foolish beings struggling toward release, toward relaxation of will in the universal will.

Each group of women, then, seems to have made different psychological and theological interpretations of her experiences, although all chose to speak of an experience that referred to self. Both the emerging women and the mystical women ignored the demands for self-sacrifice and dimunition; the former group, eschewing traditional religious nomenclature, recognized self-assertion and -definition as a spiritual process and the latter group gave up little power as they identified, or commingled, self with others. These two groups of women seem to have reworked either or both the traditional conception of sin as assertion and pride and their sense of the sex and nature of God, as they arrived at their own understandings. In the two other groups of women, however—the younger struggling women and the resolute—we see women who either have accepted or are struggling with some of the traditional theological categories of sin and of God. Paralleling these theological categories, they also arrive at a different resolution in the psychological balance of self and other, gaining more of their sense of self by their unmodified identification with the other.

Four: The Interpersonal Event

Women lead their lives in relationships—as friends, colleagues, mothers, daughters, lovers, and wives. Very few of us would disagree with this observation, which has both commonsense appeal as well as validation from psychological theory and research. We expect to see women tending to others, whether at home or at work. Women raise children, send birthday cards to relatives, prepare dinner for guests, and water the lawn for a vacationing neighbor. At work, many of the jobs women occupy, such as teacher, nurse, waitress, and service worker, are characterized by a helping relationship to others. While there is an instrinsic interpersonal nature to most female-intensive occupations, women also tend to express interpersonal concerns when they enter occupations not previously associated with affiliation. For example, the women of academe, where intellectual achievement is the currency for advancement, tend to spend more time with their students than their male colleagues do, and they have greater knowledge of the student's personal lives.[1] Not just academic women, but also other working women associate being able to help others as an important source of job satisfaction.[2]

Confirming my own observations of women at home and at work, preliminary research findings on structural stages of ego development have found that females reach an interpersonal stage of development at an earlier age than their male peers do.[3] As we saw in the introduction to the previous chapter, structural stage theorists of ego development may differ in their approaches, in whether they see the ego as mono- or multidimensional, and in the number and defining characteristics of ego stages.[4] Many of the theories of structural developmental stages, however, describe something like an "interpersonal stage." A person in this stage of ego development—labeled "conformist" in Loevinger's schema, "interpersonal" in Kegan's, and "mutual self-other" in Selman's—has the capacity to understand a shared reality with another person, to see another person's point of view. This contrasts, for example, to an earlier reciprocal-instrumental or imperial stage. A person at this earlier stage, with her focus on the control and assertion of self in the self-other relationship, engages in relationships from an instrumental perspective, with its dangers of opportunism, exploitation, and manipulation. The needs and interests of self at this time are not an object of experience and are beyond mediation. At this structural stage of ego development, a person is not capable of mutuality in relationships. But once a person has reached an interpersonal stage of ego development, she is able to construct mutually reciprocal relationships, in fact, her stage of self-other relationship is characterized by her interpersonal world view. With her capacity to objectify, and mediate her own needs, she now can create an intimate interpersonal reality, understand others in the self-other relationship, and coordinate this understanding within a generalized perspective. This, in turn, allows for altruism and the surpassing of narrow self-interests. The limitations of this stage, however, are found in its strengths: someone at this developmental stage may be unable to step out of this shared reality; she may be inclined to overidentify with the other. As a result, she may conform in situations and at times when assertion is demanded or desired, thereby losing or diminishing self.[5]

No one seems to dispute the conclusion that women, more so than men, live in a world governed by the importance of interpersonal relationships. There is fundamental disagreement, however, over which stages of development offer higher forms of human living and expression, both for the individual and for society. In particular, Kohlberg's theory of moral development has been criticized by Gilligan for its assumption that a morality based on individual rights, with its emphasis on separation and its requirement for formal, abstract thinking is superior to moral judgments based on a sense of responsibility to self and others. In Gilligan's more interpersonal context of moral decision making, the emphasis is on connection, not separation, which requires a mode of thinking that uses the context and narrative, i.e., the story of ours and others' lives.[6] As I discussed in an earlier chapter, the value of an interpersonal orientation also is being raised by Carol Ochs, who offers an alternative spiritual paradigm she refers to as "coming into relationship."

Setting aside, for the moment, the debate in psychology and theology over the value and limitations of an interpersonal orientation, the interpersonal matrix in which many women live and work underlines a psychological and ontological essential: we become and express who we are as we are in relationship to one another. Even when we think we are alone, we carry within our psyche not only the early identifications with a loved one, but also those aspects of significant others in our lives we have internalized as essential aspects of our identity. A psychologist might use the language of object relations theory, or of self-theory, to describe this phenomenon, and a theologian might formulate it as "coming into relationship."[7] Both refer to a lifelong process in which we both form, and are formed, by others. Sometimes this other is an actual person, but, as I observed earlier, we also have relationships with symbolic and mythic others, the others of our imagination, and, self-reflexively, with ourselves. All of the women of this study, in one way or another, told of a time of "coming into relationship." For a significant number of them, their experience of "coming into relationship" conveyed an "interpersonal matrix"; they either spoke of an event that occurred in relationship to another, of one that brought them into relationship with another person, or of an experience in which being in the presence of others provided the context for their spiritual moment. The women in these stories talk of a relational spirituality that grows out of the interpersonal matrix of their lives. Unlike traditional religious traditions, which often emphasize withdrawal from the world and a direct relationship with God, these women described a time when they met the divine as they lived in this world and as they made contact and formed relationships with other people in their lives.

Remembering that all of the women of this study

describe a process of coming-into-relationship—for example, with unacknowledged aspects of self or with the internalized values of their parents—we now turn to those women whose stories are set within an interpersonal world, and who speak of a relational spirituality. These women do not necessarily share faith, traditions, age, or race. When speaking of their spiritual event, sometimes their understanding of God was central to their experience, sometimes no God was mentioned. What was central to each, and shared by all, was coming into relationship with another being.

The Parent-Child Relationship

There is, of course, no one way in which we "come into relationship," or in which we "become the I through a You."[8] For some of these women it was within the parent-child relationship that they achieved a deeper understanding about themselves and their relationship to a larger reality. Three women mentioned the birth of a child as a significant spiritual moment; for one of these women it was her most preeminent spiritual experience. Although it occurred over twenty-five years ago, she says,

> I can remember it like it was yesterday, especially the feelings. I felt flooded with love. It was so strong it almost felt like it was overwhelming me. I felt a sense of being a part of creating a wonderful miracle . . . I felt very close to God, closer than I have ever felt before or since, I felt . . . such wonderful feelings of love—both for my baby and for God.

For another woman, her sense that "there seems to be a holy connection" between herself and her children when there are "moments of communication . . . when we have come to an understanding of each other," confirms Ochs' contention that holiness can be found in the everyday world of mothering.

Others who spoke of a parent-child relationship spoke from the other side of the relationship, as the child. It is in this

most primary biological and social relationship with our parents
that we first experience our relationship to being. As infants, we
are first unaware that there is an "I" that is separate from the
world around us. Through contact with our parents we come to
understand that there is an "I" and that this "I" has a unique
identity. Slowly, because of, and through, our relationship to our
parents, we develop a sense of our separateness and our individuality. Separation and individuation are not the only goals of the
parent-child relationship or of human development however. In
addition to recognizing our autonomy and our being as separate,
the parent-child relationship also instructs us in our relationship to
being; we learn affiliation as well as separateness.

One young woman chooses to interpret as spiritual
those moments when she has an intimate connection with her
mother. She tells us,

> My most spiritually enhanced moments have been spent in the
> arms of my Mom. This feeling has occurred a couple of times in
> the last year and one might describe the experience as an ulti-
> mate sense of bondage between two people where the amount of
> love cannot even be put into words. It's as if your souls have been
> elevated above today's mundane . . . When we hug it's like a
> closeness that can't be broken.

Another woman, reporting on a turning point of her
life that occurred when she was twenty-one years old, tells of how
she became estranged and then reunited with her mother. Her
spiritual experience led to a new perspective on self, and a renewed
mother-daughter bond.

> It was late spring; it was '66; it was a month before my
> twenty-first birthday; it was an anxious time—I was five weeks
> pregnant . . . "How could it have happened to me?"—how many
> other young women, countless women, reviewed those same
> words, over and over—and yet, I knew, actually knew, the mo-
> ment it had happened; and it was only the second time we'd been
> together . . . The waiting was painful—praying that it wouldn't
> be true, and yet, it was.
>
> There was no choice. My whole being felt there was
> only one thing to do—abortion, even though it was illegal. I

could not let our irresponsibility impact on my parents—to be humiliated, shamed by their pride and joy, their first-born. I felt miserable knowing that I had let them down, disappointed their trust in me. I wanted to hide, to run, and at the same time, I wanted to tell them. I was feeling so alone . . . I knew I would find the right time to tell them.

As X [the father] and I talked on the phone about what to do, his mother overheard the conversation, and hysterically called my mother to inform her. When I came home that afternoon, and she and I were alone in the kitchen, she asked how I was. I froze momentarily—this was not the time, not the place to tell her, not yet—I didn't have everything worked out yet. I answered fine. She then asked me directly if I thought I might be pregnant. I was stunned; I blanched and answered "I didn't know." She then got angry—not so much at my being pregnant, but that I didn't tell her, and that she had to find out from X's mother. She was deeply hurt—not understanding why—after all the open discussions about all kinds of things—I didn't come to her immediately for help. I admitted that I was pregnant and that I had planned to tell her; not for her to find out this way; I was furious at X for talking on the phone where his mother could have overheard. It felt as if something irreparable had happened to my relationship with my mother.

When my dad came home, the three of us talked. The end result was that he arranged through a friend of his for a gynecologist friend in New York to give me an abortion. I accompanied my dad on a "business trip" to New York a week later and had the abortion. My twenty-first year—that supposed magical year—would begin afresh.

It was a terrible year. X and I got engaged, but fought most of the time. I couldn't forgive him for his carelessness that led to the "felt" unspoken chasm between my mother and I. My mom, dad, and I never talked about what happened. Each of us held it on our own. Actually, I had no one to talk about it with. I couldn't let anyone know about my mistake—it was so unlike me—I had an image to protect. I thoroughly isolated myself. I cried a lot by myself. When I was with people, I acted as if everything was fine, all the while being plagued by feelings of remorse, self-doubt. I was sure everyone could tell what had happened just by looking at me. I became very submissive towards my mother—I guess looking for forgiveness, and yet never asking for it. I wanted the whole thing to have been just a nightmare I could wake up from and not have happened . . .

X and I broke up. I was going to go to Israel in June, but the Six-Day-War broke out and postponed the trip for a year. It was another long, lonely and fearful year. My self-confidence seemed to continue to dwindle.

I looked forward to being in Israel. To get away from all the reminders here at home; as well as go to something very important. Crucial was my visit to the Wailing Wall in Jerusalem. It was a hot day, and my cotton sundress seemed to provide little relief. Much of the perspiration was due to tension, excitement about the visit. I found a spot along the Wall—amidst all the others who were there that Friday afternoon—where I could be by myself—only to be with my best friend. I knew why I had come—I had come to talk with God. I began to tell him of all the events of the past two years, and soon found myself sobbing, oblivious of others. As my story unfolded, I could feel the air around me lighten, I could feel the openness, the acceptance of myself by some otherness, the lack of belittling judgment. Waves of relief began to occur. My body shook and the fear of exposure that I had been living with relaxed. I began to feel lightheaded, that I could breathe, that I had permission to exist, to begin to live again. God was the first person I had been able to talk to, to tell my story to. The apparent forgiveness for my fallibility was reassuring—I could forgive myself—I could live with someone knowing—the burden of shame was gone—now, the new year could begin afresh.

I had a new sense of myself, realizing that the struggle for perfection was hurtful. What happened had happened, and I could now look at it in a new way as part of my experience of growing up. When I returned home, I was able to approach my mother and talk with her about the whole thing. She had long ago forgiven me—something I didn't realize, being so scared and wrapped up in my own feelings. She only wanted to help me and have a solution that was workable for me. She loved me and wanted only the best for me. I was still her shining star—something I thought I had lost long ago. I was able to regain, or renew my relationship with her and my dad on an adult level, no longer needing to be submissive. It has taken time to share this event with others, but it is no longer a skeleton in my life.

One of the lessons we can learn from two women of this study is that the relationship between parent and child does not have to be ideal for a spiritual understanding to be reached. Parents at times have irredeemable flaws, and children, also being human, contribute their inadequacies to the relationship. But one woman's story illustrates how even a tragic figure of a mother can give, perhaps indirectly and unknowingly, some spiritual meaning to her daughter's life. One woman respondent speaks about her mother with no illusions.

> I never saw my mother as up on a pedestal ... Many of her problems which made her life increasingly tragic were brought on by herself. She was a warm, generous person with a sparkling personality ... Brought up to be a socialite, she was cultured, well-traveled and witty ... a magnificent pianist ... from a wealthy family. Although she was given whatever she wanted, she was not snobbish or insensitive to others less fortunate. This was her situation as a younger woman. Over the years, however, the drinking increased and the money disappeared. She was acutely aware that her beauty was fading. My father made a 180 degree change in occupation ... Much of the time he was away from home. She looked for love from others and never found anything more permanent than a fling for a month or so. She wore low-cut dresses, spiked heels, long, painted fingernails, and bleached her hair. Although all of this mortified me, she was never really cheap. By the time I was in high school we lived most of the year together alone. By then she was definitely an alcoholic. My mother was going through menopause and I, through my teens, did not make for a happy combination. We had hopes for each other that neither one of us could fulfill. Although we were aware of this, we never spoke about it.

Even under these sad, conflictual family circumstances, this woman reports feeling loved.

> I always felt that my mother loved me not because she was particularly proud of me—I was not the poised, pretty, witty, or charming daughter that she maybe had hoped for. But we were close. We never wanted to hurt each other, although anger and frustration made us do so upon occasion; we were always sorry afterwards.

Somehow this woman was able to feel loved by her mother, and was able to transform some of the inadequacies in her relationship with her mother into positive contributions. She concludes,

> Mother was not a model for me to grow up by. She was much more important. Living with her helped me to realize at a young age that life was not going to be easy or predictable. She had problems. I had to provide most of the answers and solutions for myself. I was able to draw on my inner resources because her love for me gave me the courage to do so.

Another woman tells of a spiritual experience that also grew out of her mother's weakness and inability to cope with life. Although she does not give the reason for her mother's despair, her mother's suicide attempt clearly signals unendurable pain. And it is her experience with her mother at this painful time of her mother's life that she choses as her spiritual experience. She describes her response to her mother's attempt to end her life;

> I felt a lot of things: guilt, sorrow, anger, resentment, and happiness (that she didn't succeed). When I look back on the incident and myself I see that I have grown up a lot. I had a lot of responsibility (taking care of my mom) that I never expected at nineteen. I am proud of myself in that I helped her overcome her doubts and insufficiencies. I respect her and am glad that she has come so far.

Both this young woman and the woman whose mother was an alcoholic found spiritual meaning as they reached deep within themselves for strengths that their mothers significantly lacked. Using these inner resources to care for their mothers and to make sense of the world, these two women transformed pain and incompleteness into increased understanding.

It is not just in the mother–child relationship that spiritual meaning is found. Two women described how their relationship with their fathers offered possibilities to arrive at spiritual meaning. The relief that one young woman felt when her father responded to her suspected and unwanted pregnancy with love and caring, rather than with the expected recriminations, was a time she remembers as a spiritual moment.

Another woman reports on her relationship with her father, remembering not a time of high drama, "but a general experience that happened regularly during my childhoold," and "which . . . has shaped my world view." She recalls;

> I would walk with my father usually along the beach on Long Island. The times I remember most vividly are in the winter when there were hardly any other people around. I don't remember him saying much, we walked pretty much in silence, finding old Noxzema bottles that had washed up on the shore (which wasn't cleaned during the winter), horseshoe crabs, and even a toilet seat. At these times I began to gain a sense of being connected with something beyond myself, a oneness with nature, an awareness that my being did not end with my body, that everything was interconnected.

Not needing incense, gold, and stained glass to evoke an experience of the transcendent, she finds it in what typically would be seen as an unaesthetic and quite ordinary toilet seat and Noxzema bottle. In the context of being in communion with nature, with her father, and with life, she created an awareness of the absolute from the particular, even mundane, reminders of everyday existence. Carrying out this theme of the holy found in the everyday, it was a stale Fig Newton that was offered as a sacred symbol. Noting this time together,

> It was truly a communion experience . . . we . . . shared stale Fig Newtons before we went home. My father would use these occasions to clean out the bread box since everything tastes good after you've been walking outside for awhile . . . this basic experience of the divine Spirit and energy now is the foundation of my life. It is not something I . . . was taught but it was a fundamental experience that can never be taken away. It has helped me question institutionalized religion and has encouraged me to formulate my own concept of the divine . . . I never internalized what I learned in church, I *knew* there was more!

And, finally, one woman is brought into a spiritual realization as she becomes aware of her family connections and is reminded of her roots and of who she is in history. She finds herself in Dublin.

after some ecumenical jet setting in Europe, I was in the midst of rejecting both church and state as repressive political structures . . . I was exhausted from work and travel . . . Then I was plunked down in Dublin, plane late, baggage lost, and fuel in short supply so my toes were cold when I slept. It was there that I began wandering, exploring the city, only to find myself in front of a Catholic church. I mused pessimistically if they had anything else. But I started to look at the faces of the people—I saw my friends and family as if in processing. Dorothy Ryan was there and Madeline Murphy passed by. A few aunts and my grandmother seemed present in the faces of people who left the church. This was not a drug experience! It was simply a quick and final realization of my roots, and awareness of the fact that having been brought up . . . Irish Catholic . . . I was who I was, and all of these typical Irish people looked like me. They have my hair and fair skin, my body build and walk. There we were fair and dark, tall and healthy. I was there but only because so many of them, my mother's old friends, especially, were there with me.

Influencing Another

Some of the women's stories here tell of a time when as a parent, or in relation to a parent or family member, they experienced some spiritual discernment; they speak of a transformation in self-other, self-world relationships. Another group of women also reports how another influenced their spiritual direction, but in their case this other person was not one with whom they had had a long, intimate family relationship. In fact, one young woman chose to report on her chance meeting with a stranger.

Once on a train trip back to school from spring break, I met a young woman who, in just thirteen hours, made a strong spiritual impression on me. Two years ago I might have labeled her a "Jesus freak" and been completely turned off, but something about her was appealing and magnetic. We just started with small talk, but by the end of the trip, I found myself telling her things that often would take years to get out of me. She was encouraging and kind and not overbearing and forceful. She was simply so confident in her faith and beliefs that actions were the only means necessary to convince me of her sincerity.

Although she has not yet determined how to incorporate what she has learned and experienced with this unnamed train companion, she continues to consider the possibilities.

She didn't convert me overnight to her strong faith and beliefs, but she did show me that such a strong faith can be very appealing and can bring much inner peace. I'm still in the process of deciding whether I can and will make that commitment.

Two other women, instead of describing how another influenced them, tell of their attempt to influence. Both Evangelical Christians, they selected as a memorable spiritual experience an occasion in which their concern was to have another accept their interpretation of faith. Unlike the woman on the train who tried to set a spiritual example, their approach was less subtle. One attempt to influence was successful, the other less so.

The description of the successful attempt to influence another comes from an Asian woman who used her language background to help out the missionaries of her church who "found a Korean lady who just moved in state." She describes how, in addition to trying to decide whether or not to stay with her husband, this Korean woman also was deciding whether or not to end a pregnancy. The explicit help she offers is to teach her "the importance of our Saviour the Jesus Christ and the Repentence and Baptism." The implicit help she seems to offer is the community support that will be available to the "Korean lady" once she accepts her helper's view of reality. The Korean woman accepts the offer and becomes "baptized by immersion of water by missionary."

Another woman's story, somewhat unusual and certainly conflictual, describes her unsuccessful attempt to influence another. She informs us,

I have always been a Christian and have never really doubted that there is an ultimate authority—God and the three persons of

God. When I was confirmed . . . I did "decide" that I would follow Christ.

She reports having had "a few 'memorable experiences,'" but the one she chooses to speak of is about a wrestling match with "an atheist." Although she does not give the living arrangements one infers a college dormitory setting. She tells us that

> The occasion was that an atheist had been picking on my faith, then we had a physical fight, I fell, and hurt my back. I went to my room, cried for a bit, and read Luke. Reading Luke helped to calm me down and the atheist came into the room and apologized to me.

Then her story takes on a somewhat surprising direction. I was expecting to read about some type of reconciliation with the "atheist," instead she reports,

> The next morning I awoke and found the pain in my back to be so strong as to immobilize me. I was bedridden for two weeks and had much time to think about my beliefs and the Bible. It helped me realize that what I had experienced was nothing compared to what Christ had gone through (the crucifixion). I had been so mad when I had gone into my room and reading about Jesus helped make me see the stupidity of my anger.

Admittedly this is a somewhat negative example of how an interpersonal event evoked some spiritual experience; two women literally struggled with one another, yet no reconciliation occurs. Her experience points out that all aspects of life allow opportunities for transformation, for gaining a new perspective. One also wonders how these verbal arguments between her and the "atheist" were maintained and how they broke down into a physical struggle. She is silent on this. It is clear that she felt "picked on," drawing parallels between Christ's crucifixion and her experience with the "atheist." I think, however, that we can infer from her selection of this incident as a spiritual experience that she is trying to understand her inability to see the other person's point of view and to justify her behavior with the atheist. The self-doubting her story implies may be an initial movement in the process of being able to see another person's perspective.

While these three young women have described an interpersonal interaction in which there was an effort to influence or challenge another person's belief system, a fourth woman tells of a more subtle encounter with another person. Also defining this experience as spiritual, she and the other person do not try to challenge or change the other's ideas. Like the mystical women in the chapter "Views of Self," she describes a process in which the two voices of self and other become one. Her experience occurred at a time when

> I was twenty-five . . . a new grad student, and in a period of my life when I was undergoing a conversion of sorts. I had been in tremendous turmoil that resulted in a lingering illness, and as I recuperated I was taking one graduate seminar, *The Dialogue Novel*, it seems worth noting. It was all I could manage, and it was very important to me, partly because I was taking it with my favorite professor, and partly because I had decided that this was the course that would make me or break me as a graduate student. My spiritual investment in this course was tremendous and I seemed to make increments in understanding with each weekly meeting.

Next she draws a description for us so we understand the physical relationship between her and her professor.

> I was sitting at the professor's left. The seminar table was in a T shape, and he always sat at the center of the crossbars, with, essentially, the crossbar as a barrier . . . I usually sat in the first seat on his left.

With the physical arrangements clear, she portrays a time when an "I" and a "You" converge into one.

> As the discussion mounted in intensity, eventually a dialogue took place between the professor and me in which such congruence of thought was operating that I lost all sense of which one of us was speaking. In fact, we seemed suddenly to be operating out of one mind, centered between us at about a 45 degree angle from each body—this was a distinct spatial perception of the experience. We continued in this way in pursuit of the inquiry we were making until we arrived at the words "free will." I do not know which one of us spoke them, but at that point the

"bubble" burst and we each went back to our own individuality. Seven years or so later, when I asked him if he remembered that happening, he said he did.

Within a Group

So far the stories have been of women in a one-on-one relationship with another person, but sometimes the influence of another was felt as a member of a group. Although the spatial field of the relationship included many others, it was, nevertheless, as intense an experience as the more exclusive one-on-one interpersonal relationships.

For one woman it is her relationship as a parishioner with a young, open, and enthusiastic assistant parish priest around the time of Vatican II (1964–65) that she chooses as spiritually significant. She remembers how this young priest's ability to extend himself and to convey the message of Vatican II in "a very spiritual/personal [and] moving way" sets into motion "a series of experiences that added up to a profound 'disclosure' experience— a real Confirmation experience."

Not a priest, but a well-known author, influences another woman. She tells us,

> From the moment I saw him I felt a special connection. He is a very human person with hang-ups and problems familiar to us all. He also is on such a high spiritual level some cannot understand him but I never felt that. Whenever we exchanged ideas a special bond was there.

Her "coming into relationship" was realized not just by her "special bond" with this author, but also as a result of her group experience. She describes "a special spirit present in the place and in the group . . . we were much bonded and sharing at a deep personal level with a sense of trust that all would be received in love and it was . . . I felt like a sample of heaven."

The group experience as an interpersonal context for

becoming transformed in relationship is described by two other women. The first woman recalls,

> I spent a day with a group of strangers in a large ballroom in a hotel. All of us, sixty or so people, were focused on a tiny light of a woman who was the leader of the group. We sat in a circle, then in concentric circles, held hands, laid stretched out on the floor, stood up, looked at strangers in the eye, walked around the room, first in one direction, then another, talked to each other, sent energy to various spots in the room and talked about that . . . For the first part of the morning I wondered if I'd made a mistake in selecting her workshop. I felt hard and judgmental and didn't like the contact I felt forced to make with strangers. When the first break was announced I felt cheated because I felt no different . . . still hard and unyielding and closed. However, when I walked (back) into the hall I could feel a difference in my eyes and I noticed right away that I was noticing eyes . . . I was really looking at people and looking at them with warmth . . . I felt so authentic, and as the afternoon progressed with more of the same centering experiences . . . I certainly knew I felt quite different and the difference was created by feeling created-in-balance, whole . . . the experience of being whole was a transformative one because it was the truth or rather a realization of the truth.

A second woman defines her most memorable spiritual experience as a time

> during a group meditation with twenty-four people whom I was close to. We sat in a circle, I think we held hands. My feelings were of tremendous peace. A lightness and clarity prevailed. It is hard to describe. I felt so light, I hardly needed to breathe. It truly was like being in a beautiful church. I felt very removed from the body, physical sensations, the everyday world. Like a drifting or floating, an effortless being. It felt "higher" like I was in a higher part of the brain. Other than effortless being, there was no thought or sensation.

Other women, in churches, synagogues, mosques, and meeting houses, describe more traditional settings for their spiritual insights. For one woman, it was just "being with these peace-loving people" that is a spiritual experience. Another woman tells of a time she overcomes her sense of estrangement when she becomes a member of a church. She reports, "I didn't feel alone or depressed anymore. I felt I had a place to go where people cared." A third woman, a Jew, recounts two unforgettable times, one celebrating the holiday of Ramadan with Muslims in a Cairo mosque, and the other in a series of synagogues. She remembers,

> Last year I studied in the Mideast—six months in Cairo and six months in Jerusalem. Two experiences stand out in my mind from that year which I would define as spiritual. One took place in a mosque, and the other in a series of visits to different synagogues. During the summer in Egypt the holiday of Ramadan is celebrated by Muslims. While returning to Cairo from a weekend of sun and beach in Alexandria, we (a busload of students) went into a mosque on Friday at a time of prayer. The religious feeling in that building was amazing. In the community of people who, at that time, felt so strong about their spiritual or religious practices, I felt something sparked in me. To see what appeared to be such devout prayer made me feel strong as an individual and strong as a part of humanity. Also, it made me feel strong alongside these people in what I thought was a shared feeling that a greater power pervaded. For there must have been a greater power to elicit the electricity in the air and the strength of feeling in the room. Likewise, in Jerusalem I visited a series of small religious Mid-East and East European synagogues during a holiday that began at 3 a.m. I felt the same strength in relation to those praying as I had in Egypt.

Finally, for one woman, a dramatic realization of a group experience occurs later, while alone. She tells us,

> I was praying to God and I had a vision/feeling of someone putting their hand into my body and holding my heart, pumping and beating. My overwhelming feeling was of trust—that rather than killing me the hand nurtured me and was OK.

When we hear more of her story we understand that this vision/feeling of complete trust she experienced grew out of her work with others in a group.

I had just spent a lot of time working with a group of people to prepare and run a retreat. There was a strong sense of community and closeness to God, a lot of trust and feeling OK. I felt open—to others and myself. I felt happy, lifted up, euphoric. I treasure the moment.

In the Company of Women

One woman's description of how "surely this group of women acted as midwife to each other" suggests what in the group encounter acted as a catalyst for some of the women's spiritual experiencing. It was being in the company of women that created a sacred time and space for four women who, together, represent quite a range of diverse religious traditions. One, belonging to an "unorthodox" Baptist church described how a group of women helped her give birth to a new sense of herself. Another woman, a witch, notes that her first spiritual experience coincided with her first women's gathering, a women's harvest weekend of "workshops, opening up, letting down my guard." Continuing, she remembers,

at the very end we gathered in a circle holding hands and singing a Chris Williamson song, "Song of the Soul." The energy was so high, I was crying and soaring, crying and soaring, so happy, so full, I felt like bursting!

She also describes another time, five years later, this one happening with a smaller group of three female friends, when she experiences a "cone of power" eerily whipping out as she and her friends hold hands before a fire.

I was sitting with three friends in my house before the fire holding hands, enjoying our friendship, silent, unplanned, just happening when I realized that the energy was whipping around—a silverish white band connecting us and whipping around. I got a little scared and realized it was the cone of power, but having no experience with it before, I said "this is the cone of power, let the cone go, ground yourselves." I let it go, [Nancy] and [Sarah] did also but [Wilma] was last and it fluttered up in her and out her head. She was very frightened.

The same woman uses imagery to describe a third experience, also defined by its interpersonal nature. "Making love to my lover and hearing the dance, getting swept up in the dance, visualizing the flowers blooming, the white dam breaking, the dance, the rhythm, the vision, the beauty."

Sharing the harvesting of peanuts with a group of African women and children unfolded into a spiritual moment for an Episcopal woman. She takes us to that time.

We were harvesting peanuts—pulling up the plants and picking off the peanuts. The women were dressed so colorfully in brightly designed Kangos. We were sitting under a gigantic Baobab tree which seems female to me (witch-like in the dry season, fruit-giving in the wet). The little jiho (stove) was roasting corn. I felt utterly in union with the *earth* (the peanuts we were harvesting would really keep us from *starving* the coming year). I was in union with the women who seemed ancient in their ways—rather *timeless*—there was *no* time. It was past, present, and future—all. One of the women present was Mama Forbi who is the closest to the Great Goddess I can imagine. She is huge, solid, sturdy, wise, full of humor, she is beautiful and she was working with us. We'd sing from time to time. I felt utterly present and complete.

Finally, while the manifest content of a Charismatic Catholic woman's spiritual story concerns her relationship to God, the latent message of her story is about the crucial role her women friends play in her spiritual experiences. She tells us,

The most recent "little voice" came to me on April 13. I had read the book *What Happens When Women Pray* by Evelyn Christenson four or five times before, but that morning decided to reread it. After several chapters I put it down to meditate on its beautiful message. Then this small voice said, "Get the neighbor women together for a pray and share time." I . . . argued vehemently, but to no avail. Then I decided to test the validity and played roulette with my Bible. . . . I was happy when it opened to Revelations as

I felt that couldn't verify my voice—didn't that deal with the end times? Here's what I read and it confirmed the voice for me: Rev. 3:2: "Wake up; revive what little you have left; it is dying fast. So far I have failed to notice anything in the way you live that my God would call perfect, and yet do you remember how eager you were when you first heard the message?" And in 3:7, "Here is the message of the holy and faithful one who has the key of David, so that when he opens, nobody can close, and when he closes, nobody can open." Some four months later now, I can finally see why He opened this door to the neighbors: one was preparing for a move and needed help with the garage sale—all six who responded (out of ten invitations) pitched in to help. Recently, this same neighbor had lost her husband and here again the "girls" were invaluable. Another had lost a son two years ago and is dealing with bitterness toward the government for cir- cumstances surrounding it. She is being helped immeasurably! Many friendships are deepening and my heart rejoices that I listened to those words! I was so afraid of rejection and the tag of "religious freak" that I almost rejected HIM who was putting these few words in my head.

She may place more emphasisis on God's intervention than I would, and I might place more stress on the instrumental role her women friends played in this experience than she would, but I think she and I would agree that, in large part, she felt this divine presence because of, and through, her interpersonal rela- tionship with "the girls."

A Relationship with a Ferret

We assume that an interpersonal context signifies a relationship with at least one other person; certainly the "person" in the term interpersonal leads us to this conclusion. But some- times the other with whom we come into relationship is in the being of another order than our own. Buber understood this quite well, observing that we are in relation not only to other human beings, but to nature and animals as well. We are, he exclaimed, "educated by children, by animals!"[9] I close this chapter with one woman's account of a transformative moment, which transpired because of her encounter with a ferret. Her day begins inauspiciously:

> Another day. An important letter, so long postponed, can no longer be delayed. Harried by the pressures of a full agenda, I slip off guiltily to the post office. Rushing in, my mind is on completing the task at hand, when something not quite usual breaks into my consciousness, inviting my attention. I stop short, and see a small furry animal with brown saucer eyes, held protectively in the crook of a young man's arms. To the question in my eyes I heard him answer, "It's a ferret." My whole body had come to rest and I could feel a grin take over my face. I took a brief moment to stroke the slender creature and mumble a few absurdities to its owner—pleased, I like to think, over the encounter—then we both moved on, picking up the beat of our lives. It was a quick moment, trivial even, without purpose or importance. Yet . . . a transforming moment. A moment when "I" was forgotten, my preoccupation with tasks and moods broken through . . . my pace slowed; I felt rich and thankful for having been given a glimpse of creation. My whole being was given an infusion of joy and peace that, while not altering the facts of my life or the state of the world, did alter my attitude and the way I moved through the rest of the day.

I think it is clear that the women's stories here speak of a relational spirituality, and that within this common expression we also find diversity. One describes coming into relationship with a ferret, another wrestles with "an atheist," a woman walks on the beach with her father, or learns lessons from an alcoholic mother. A group provided the context for the spiritual experiences of many women, and for four, it was being in the company of women that was important. But, even within this diversity, for each woman it was within an interpersonal matrix of her contact with another that led to a significant spiritual realization.

Five: On Death and Dying

All of us struggle, with different levels of awareness at different seasons of life, with the fact of
our mortality. We all must die. Some of those among us—of
whom the most notable and successful seems to be Woody Al-
len—consciously ponder the meaning of death. Sometimes we
sublimate the anxiety that the knowledge of our death brings, our
"existential entrapment," with positive and constructive action;
we paint, mother, write, or sail around the world. At other moments we may lapse into neurotic or psychotic "compromise for-
mations,"[1] where we experience the threat of death too intensely
and with too few resources. Too vulnerable, we mimic death with
depression, displace it with phobias, or, if schizophrenic, mal-
adaptively and desperately try to ward off any early loss of self by
having no self to lose.[2] Unable to accept the fact that we must pay
for our life with our death, we try to reduce the price we will
eventually pay by diminishing the value of our existence.[3]

Although we may try to deny or suppress the knowledge of our death, we can never totally succeed. Throughout our
life we confront our own, and others', finitude when we experience the death of a parent or a friend, and, symbolically, as we
watch a sunset, feel the seasons change, or complete a major
project.

Psychological thinking offers varying perspectives on
how to imagine death. Freud insistently linked the ability to
confront the total annihilation of self with maturity, offering no
pacifiers to, as he saw it, this stark reality.[4] Jung, however, advanced the possibility of life beyond death, encouraged by what he
saw in myths and symbols.[5] Coming from a divergent stream but

a common source, existential writers encourage us to confront with courage the eventual fact of our non-being. Understanding the burden this knowledge places on us, they also see how only our awareness of death allows us to fully appreciate the vibrancy of life and that existential courage leads to a life authentically lived.[6]

Yet another position, described as "a formative-symbolizing perspective," is offered by Lifton. He argues that it is essential for us to confront our eventual death. Offering more than the "maturity" required by Freud, or the "courage" needed for the existential position, he believes that "we . . . require symbolization of continuity—imaginative forms of transcending death— in order to confront genuinely the fact that we die." Lifton rejects the idea of a *literal* immortality but sees as vital to the human experience and understanding a *sense* of immortality. Observing that we live on images and that "to grasp our humanity we need to structure these images into metaphors and models," he sees the symbolizing process around death and immortality and our understanding of participation in a collective life-continuity as a fundamental aspect of self.[7] To be fully human, that is, to participate fully in our present, to take our historical stand, and to map our future, requires imagining the dialectic between death and the continuity of life, and constructing meaningful symbols for ourselves.

Lifton describes four modes by which we can achieve a sense of immortality. In the *biological* we continue our life after death through progeny, in the *creative* we live on through our works. The *theological* mode may offer a literal version of an immortal soul or afterlife—as in Christianity—or "death-transcending truths"—as Buddhism and Judaism do. The continuing cycles of life of *nature* offer a fourth possibility for attaining a sense of immortality. All of these four modes—biological, creative, theological, and nature—require an experience of transcendence, the process by which we sense an immortality. Within the transcendent experiencing, "time and death disappear" and the self feels, at once, connected, in movement, integrated, and still.

Transcending experiences evoke a paradox: "the self is both non-existent and most alive."[8]

Arguing that we must confront the negativity and formlessness of death in order to fully experience the vitality of life, Lifton requires "imaginative access to death in its various psychic manifestations."[9] This confrontation with death requires not only imagination, but awareness and courage. A number of the women in this study did speak of a time they found the courage to face death. As they made this confrontation they reordered what they saw as important and how they saw themselves in the world, and they achieved a deep sense of renewal. This process of confrontation, reordering, and renewal also is described by Lifton. These women's experiences with death and dying teach us that there is yet another mode of attaining a sense of immortality, i.e., a connection to life. While one could understand some of the experiences they report on as reflecting a theological orientation, I think their stories reveal another possibility. Expanding on the Lifton categories of biological, theological, creative, or in nature, most of these women speak of feeling a sense of connectedness and of participation in a larger human process through their relationship with another person; in these instances with the near or actual death of another. The women who talk to us of death and dying are showing us how they achieve a sense of immortality by being brought into relationship.

Some are brought into relationship by dreaming of a dead friend or relative, others by feeling the presence of a dead friend, one by having a premonitory dream of her sister's narrow escape from death. A number of women speak of their direct and personal experience with another who is dying—a close relative, a nurse with a patient, and, for one, with a stranger who shared her mother's hospital room. These women give vivid accounts of how their relationship with the dying and death of another open the door to their understanding of a symbolic immortality, of a "principle of life continuity."[10] Through their meeting with another they become aware of a larger human process and, as they do, the other lives on in them.

Dreams and Intuitions of Death

The women's stories, told next, speak of connections with a loved other which remain unbroken by death. We learn from their spiritual stories that even the finality and irrevocability of a physical death does not end the possibility of another bringing us into relationship. Instead of an end, they describe a "continuous symbolic relationship,"[11] with the other.

Two of the women speak of dreams in which a deceased loved one appears to them, and this manifestation in their dream allows them to come to terms with the death.

One woman dreams of her mother, she recalls:

In June 1978, my mother arrived D.O.A. by airplane, in our city. Because of my broken father who had to be driven to our home and four young children to be met there by me, I held back tears and controlled all other emotions. Next came legal matters followed by the arrival of our close relatives, keeping me very occupied, still without tears.

All funeral arrangements completed and relatives returned home, my great preoccupation became one regret: I had not said "goodbye" for the last time to my mother.

About six weeks after Mom's death, she appeared to me during my sleep. She looked healthy and smiled at me. I began to cry, telling her that I loved her very much. She answered that she knew all the time. Then she left, although neither of us touched each other. I awakened crying very hard, but feeling relieved, with no regrets. It seemed that God allowed her to comfort me when I could no longer reach her on my own.

A friend whose life was interrupted by a hit-and-run driver appears to another woman in a dream. She tells us:

A good friend had been murdered in a hit-and-run accident, and I was having a lot of trouble with that. About five months after the murder, I dreamed that I was sitting on a hill at a friend's farm. Richard (the dead friend) came walking over the hill and I was thrilled to see him, but confused at his presence. When I told him he was dead, he smiled and said, "I know, but it's all right." He hugged me and continued down the hill. When I awoke I could still feel his touch and I felt as though a great weight had been lifted.

Informing us that "I had never been to the farm where the dream took place," she next reveals that a year later she does visit a farm, and "it was exactly as it had been in my dream (or whatever)." Initially referring to a dream in her account, she later appears uncertain with her reference to "whatever," about how to name the phenomenon of communicating with her dead friend.

Another woman never thinks of her experience as a dream, but matter of factly reports seeing her dead friend in the doorway of the bedroom in which she was sleeping. Not seeking to explain how this happened, she simply accepts it. Now seventy-one years of age, this woman's story takes us back to 1939, when, at the age of twenty-seven, she reports:

> I experienced the loss of a dear, personal friend. Other than deaths in the family of older ones, this was the first among my peers. At that time it was the custom to hold the two-day period of mourning in one's own home, if feasible and desirable. As a friend of the entire family I spent the night preceding the funeral in the homestead. The night before the services I was wakened from a sound sleep to see my dear friend in her wedding dress (she had become seriously ill a year before her wedding), standing in the doorway, smiling and her arm raised as if in farewell. My grief was intensified the following day but later on I came to believe it was a gesture of friendship and love.

It was not in a dream, or in the middle of the night, but during a day on a Welsh hillside that a dead friend appears to a fourth woman. Setting the scene for her experience, she tells us:

> I was twenty-three . . . living in a small village in Wales . . . spending a good deal of my time reading mystical writings of various religions . . . practicing yoga and meditation and living celibately but with a woman friend. It was a blessed but a difficult time. My emotions were often in a tumult. I wanted only to be exploring my own spiritual leanings but my university was demanding my intellectual rigor on themes I had little interest in. It was as if I was being pulled one way by the

leadings of my heart and intuition another by my intellect and sense of social obligation. It felt as if I was going crazy, the division seemed so great.

What restored my sense of sanity was when I went to a little local market garden and worked with other Welsh women in the garden. One day I was walking to the garden past pastures of sheep and ancient woodlots. Increasingly I became aware of the vibrance of the colors and beauty all around me. The sounds of the birds and the rustling of the leaves sounded exquisite. The smell of the sweet air and damp air was overwhelming. All my five senses were so utterly delighted in what they perceived that they merged. I could not distinguish one from the other and it was difficult to distinguish myself from my surroundings. This experience came with an overpowering sense of being loved. I had no doubt of a divine presence giving me a window into the miraculousness of life. I have no idea how long this lasted, but the sense of blessedness stayed with me a long time after.

There was another rather odd dimension to this experience. I had the distinct impression of another presence there, someone I had loved dearly but who had died. She had been an older woman of great compassion, and humbleness. I had moved the previous summer to be near her when I learned she was dying of cancer.

As I stood in this lovely pastoral setting I really felt she was with me and that she was conveying to me that she always had been with me and always would be. I felt somehow that I would always be able to turn to her for help or guidance after that day.

I suppose the end of this story, which is also a bit odd, is that I got a letter from this woman's husband not long after. I had regretted after her death that I was never able to express to him how much she meant to me and how I loved her. We had hardly spoken since her funeral and certainly never written so it came as a great surprise to me when I received a letter from him, mailed the day of my experience, which contained only a poem by her.

One could explain—or explain away—the dreams of dead loved ones that these three women bring to us with interpretations of them as compensatory psychological processes that allowed the women to accept death, and as their attempts to resolve some aspect of their relationship to an important person in their life. This type of perspective, with its roots in Freudian thought, provides some insight into their experiences. But it seems inadequate and wanting, when set beside Lifton's articulation of the metaphorical image making we create as we seek life continuity. If we view these women's experiences with a "formative-symbolizing perspective," we arrive at a different understanding. The women do not speak of a literal immortality; instead they use their dreams to render their metaphorical imagination, and experience, of immortality. They, like all of us, are trying to understand their relationship to death and to find a way to express their part in a collective life continuity. This imaginative process is not just a compensatory psychological mechanism. It does not explain an adaptation to life; it *defines* our life. Set apart from other life by our awareness, we are driven to find meaning in the most fundamental given of our life: our certain end. And as we seek that meaning from life we create images of death that metaphorically address our teleological striving for continuity, and at the same time create our life.

And, finally, within this group of women who have deceased loved ones appear to them, is a remarkable account of another woman's spiritual experience. The story she tells takes us back to 1965 when, a mother of four young children, she also was the staff nurse in the operating room of a local hospital. She begins:

My sister, a year older than I, was scheduled to have her fifth child by C-section in late May. Because I knew her physician well, I was allowed to be present during the surgery. My sister's pregnancy had been quite normal and uncomplicated. I had no conscious anxiety about her scheduled surgery, although she had expressed some anxiety at the outset of her pregnancy. But as the pregnancy advanced and she felt well, her reservations seemed to disappear.

I went to sleep the night before her delivery date feeling confident that all would go smoothly. My sister was a wonderful patient, cooperative and eager to recover and return to her own young family. During that night I had what I will classify as a precognitive dream, although at the time of the dream I had no knowledge whatsoever of the language of parapsychology. It was this dream which initiated my spiritual search, and thus, I call the event the "initiating" dream.

The dream was in color and incredibly distinct and real. In the dream, I was in the operating room observing my sister's surgical procedure. She was awake and excited about her delivery, and I was standing at the head of the operating field talking softly to her . . . and joking about the sex of the baby about to come into life. The infant was delivered and handed over to a delivery room nurse who walked over to a crib in one corner of the operating room. I followed the nurse (in the dream) and watched while she checked the baby. I did not see the sex of the child but felt delighted because the infant breathed spontaneously and did not require any medical assistance as some C-sections do. Satisfied that all was well, I returned to the operative field and stood to observe the rest of the surgical procedure. When I looked at the field, I saw blood flowing over either side of my sister's abdomen, running down onto the floor.

I awakened in a state of absolute terror. I then did something that was exceptional for me. I awakened my sleeping husband and told him of the dream. Wisely, my husband suggested that the dream was probably premised on my anxiety. This made very good sense at the time. After all, it was quite inconceivable that an event such as the one in my dream would occur. Patients simply don't hemorrhage the way I had seen in the dream. I slept soundly the rest of the night and awakened refreshed and eager to reach the hospital to join my sister for her 8 a.m. surgery. The dream was forgotten completely.

I arrived at the hospital, changed into O.R. garb and went directly to my sister's room. She had been given her pre-op medication, but was alert and excited. We chatted until it was time to take her to the O.R. I stood at the head of the field to watch the surgery. Every now and then I would bend over and tell my sister what the surgeons were doing. At one point I slipped my hand under the sterile drapes and held her hand. She squeezed my hand and I leaned down and kissed her cheek.

Shortly, the baby was delivered, a healthy little girl. The obstetrician handed my new niece to the waiting nurse who carried her over to a crib in the corner of the room. I walked over and observed the initial care and felt a surge of delight because the infant did not require either suctioning or oxygen. I still did not recall my dream despite the exact parallels unfolding in this reality.

Assured of the baby's safe arrival, I then returned to the op field to observe the rest of the procedure, I looked up and witnessed the catastrophic hemorrhage I had seen in my dream. My God, my sister is dying, I thought.

What had transpired was a real obstetrical nightmare. During my sister's pregnancy, unknown to her physicians, the placenta had grown through the musculature of the uterus and attached itself to the wall of the bladder. When the surgeons removed the placenta after the delivery of the infant, an entire wall of the uterus disappeared with it, leaving a large, bleeding area. Another source of this massive bleed was the wall of the bladder which poured out blood from the placental attachments. (I do not want to overwhelm the reader with clinical details, but this explanation validates the perception of a real obstetrical crisis.)

A priest was called to give my sister the last rites for it seemed certain that she would die within minutes. I returned to the head of the table and saw the look of death on my sister's face. In shock myself, I left the room and went to the nurse's lounge to gather my composure. Alone, I prayed "God, let her live." I saw the faces of her family flash before my inner vision. And suddenly I realized I could not let my sister die alone. The strength which came into me in these minutes that allowed me to return to the operating room was surely a gift from God because I am not a courageous person. But I did go back to be with my sister and felt a blessed calmness as I leaned over and whispered to her as she lay there dying and unconscious. There was no doubt in my mind that my words of love reached thru her unconsciousness.

The rest of the story is history . . . very dramatic and medically intricate, strewn with the work of the Spirit, I believe. My sister lived although her recovery was marked with a series of incredible crises.

My major reaction was that of incredulity, terror, and shock. This was followed by an overwhelming sense of peace, confidence that something quite unusual had transpired. As I recall these moments, I reexperience all the emotions I originally felt with the addition of a real sense of awe and thanksgiving for the blessing I had participated in and witnessed.

Months later I reflected on the experience and began to try to conceptualize this event. How could I have known the future so clearly, so accurately, before the future manifested in the present? My curiosity threaded its way through parapsychology in search of understanding . . . and this was the beginning of my very conscious efforts to understand a phenomenal event that could not be explained by rational means. Along this path I discovered the intersections of the spiritual and psychical dimensions. My studies have been cross-cultural and historical and involve world religions over history. Long before healing and holistic medicine became trendy and somewhat legitimated in contemporary disciplines, I gathered a small group of "like-minded" people to study various phenomena including healing. Our study group meets weekly and has a longevity of about thirteen years for a core of our members. We are concerned with emotional growth, psychic development, and what some would call spiritual development, a phrase I am not comfortable in using because it sounds unctuous, I think. Growth in any sphere is pretty natural I think . . . and one can't force teeth to grow any more than one can force other kinds of growth. As other authors have noted, psychic development and experience with various paranormal phenomena are the flowers of an unfolding consciousness. And so it has happened that I have become "psychic" in the process of my studies.

But more important than all else I believe is what has happened to me at a personal level through my exploration of consciousness. Where doubt and confusion has resided, there is an evolving awareness of God's love for the human reality. Although I still burn with the desire to know and understand more, I have great confidence that each of us lives in the presence of his Love. It is all around us and within us, an understanding which has transformed my approach to the world and my relationships with others.

The significance of this sister's premonitory dream, it seems to me, almost defies interpretation. Its natural drama cannot be enhanced by an observer's comments.

Experiences with Dying

We have heard the spiritual stories of women who met with a dead loved one in their imagination, and of one woman who foresaw her sister's near death. The next group of women report how they reached new spiritual understanding because of their participation in the dying process of another. Again, the recurring theme in these women's stories is of a relational spirituality. It was through another person's dying and death—for some a family member, for others a friend or stranger—and their relationship to that process and that person which evoked a sense of symbolic immortality.

Although she cannot quite find words to describe what happened to her, the occasion of her grandfather's death elicits some inchoate understanding of a collective life continuity for one young woman. She says,

> All my life I have been very close to my grandparents/my mother's parents. We lived in an extended family since the day I was born. Because of such close living quarters my grandparents acted as second parents. When I was eighteen my grandfather passed away. He had been very sick for several years (I feel as if there is a God watching over him now.) When he died, my brother and sister sat in my room. This moment of closeness and suffering together was an incredible spiritual experience. We discussed towards the end of remembering everything we did with him . . . God, heaven and earth. This experience has left me with an incredible "spiritual" feeling, unexplainable feeling.

As she sits with her family the death of her grandfather brings them closer together, and, as they remember him, they acknowledge how he remains a part of their life, and with that acknowledgment he achieves some type of immortality.

Another young woman, age twenty-one, also speaks of being brought into relationship with others as she experiences the death of a dear friend. She remembers:

> A friend of mine died of cancer three years ago. It was a very sad and slow death and I went through stages of doubt, encouragement, and disbelief. I doubted my belief and I couldn't figure out

why something so hard and cruel would happen to a contemporary of mine. When he was alive, fortunately he had so much faith that he helped me through. But when he died, I couldn't believe it and I was angry and confused. A few days after his death I found out that the morning he died he spoke of a third presence in his hospital room, when only one doctor and one nurse were present. When they both left and the nurse returned five minutes later, my friend had died. I still do not understand why it happened but I do know that God did not forsake my friend. Part of my faith is believing in the way God works—and I believe that taking my friend did serve some purpose. The good things that I see that came out of it were strengthening my faith and bringing me closer to our mutual friends and to his family.

Contrasted to these two young women's stories, which speak of an intensified bond with others that derives from another's death, is another young woman's account. After hearing about her grandfather's death, instead of seeking comfort and support from others, she goes off by herself. Like her contemporaries, she cannot quite explain the totality of her experience, but she tries to convey to us its import in her life.

When my grandfather died I had the most "spiritual" religious experience I have ever felt. I went to the chapel here at the university and prayed to God. I didn't know exactly how to act, what to think, etc., he was the first person very close to me to die. I felt confused and upset, and being in the church—staring at the stained glass I felt some sort of explanation. It was almost as if being there made things a little clearer. I still was very confused and extremely distraught but I felt a presence there that calmed me in a way. It was a very difficult feeling to handle, and a difficult one to explain. It was a different experience and a memorable one.

These three women, all twenty-one years old or younger, have already had a first confrontation with death. Since they chose this particular experience to illustrate their memorable spiritual moment, we know that their experience with death was a formative one. Like the younger women in the earlier chapter, "Views of Self," who seemed to be actively engaged in the struggle to understand their responsibility to self and other, these young women also do not seem quite able to fully understand or articulate the process they report on. Perhaps still too close to the actual experience, and still too embedded within the subjective experience, they are not quite able to reflect on and observe what the death of the other means to them. But they try. And in their attempt to arrive at meaning, they implicitly address the dialectic of death and continuity through their relationship with a loved one.

Next are the stories of women who, perhaps because they are older, can better observe and comment on their experiences with death. In addition to offering a more developed view of their experiences, they also differ from the younger women who report on how they felt after another died by choosing to tell us, not of how they felt after a loved one died, but of their participation in the death process.

It was simply chance that introduced one woman to one who was to become a significant person in her life. She recalls:

I was visiting my ill mother in the hospital when a woman of thirty-three was brought in to the semi-private room. Her name was Helen and she was from a small town about seventy miles from Buffalo. Her husband and I had coffee while they were readying her for bed. He told me that they had a three-year-old daughter and that she was admitted to the hospital for tests of cervical cancer and was going to have a test the next day when she would be anesthetized and if he couldn't get there in time when she came from surgery, could I be there. I told him I would be there.

When she was returned to her bed the next morning I was there, he wasn't. My mother was asleep. As she was coming out of the anesthetic she put out her hand, I took it and it was then that I experienced a feeling of oneness with a stranger, stronger and more beautiful than words can tell. I knew in that instant that we were one, that her pain was mine and mine hers. It made real for me what I had been hearing all my life that we are one body. Helen and I became close for the three months that she lived, I will never be the same. While it is painful to feel one with others it is also a source of great joy and comfort to

know and really feel part of something or someone—inexplic-
able—but beautiful. Since that time I have felt more strongly and
surely on many occasions a feeling of universality with other
people and everything on God's good earth. My brief encounter
with Helen changed my life for the better, so death does not
scare me as much because I know there is something in the spirit
that never dies.

Just as this woman's participation in Helen's death
allows her to realize she is part of some larger whole and relieves
her fears of death, so does the death of a friend for another
woman. She remembers this period of her friend's dying as "a
moment of beauty and wholeness." She explains:

A dear friend was dying and I was with him. Our communication
at the time was one of deep understanding—a connectedness
which I will cherish the memory of forever. His "giving up" to
his "creator," his God, allowed me to feel the presence of something—someone else in the room. Possibly what I felt was the
non-separateness or absence of what is called a duality. I only
knew that whatever fear I may have had before left at that
moment. I was freed of something, that is hard to explain. A
deep love came over me, for not only my friend, but for myself
and for everyone else. Our imperfect perfection. Our vulnerability and strength. The need of comfort from each other. This
helped me to see myself and my relationship to others—or
rather what I value in my relationships to and from others.

Instead of feeling fear, these women report feelings of
calmness, love, and wholeness as they confront the formlessness
of death. Another woman's account reflects this same theme:

My husband had had the first part of a major heart attack, and I
was awaiting the doctor, trying to make my dear one comfortable, but as he and I looked into each others eyes I knew with
absolute certainty that he was going to die. And he was communicating this message, though without words passing between
us. I cannot adequately describe the feeling of total calm which
came over me. I greeted the doctor and listened to his comforting words—another hour before the massive part would come,
and the ambulance would have delivered him to the hospital

ward by then and all would be well. I *knew* it was not to be. The ambulance was late, it had no heart equipment, and the hour was up just as we drove into the hospital. All the efforts of doctors were no use and I was told nothing more could be done. I had been a Quaker for some fourteen years when this happened, and I am sure that each small experience of God entering my life led me to a more "listening" person. Each day is now a new revelation of the Spirit and I try to live totally within its life and power.

Unlike these women, whose prominent experience was of well-being and wholeness, another woman's participation in the dying and death of another creates inner conflict and a temporary fragmentation of self. Her relationship with a dying friend brings her into such closeness that she loses her own boundaries as she describes not so much experiencing his death as other, but experiencing his dying as him. She eventually recovers a more differentiated and cohesive self and achieves some resolution through a dream of him after his death. She speaks:

In 1973 my colleague on a research team was diagnosed as having a particularly virulent cancer, a melonoma. We were good friends—he was married, as was I, but living apart from his wife. As his fear grew he became more and more dependent on me. Eventually as the cancer spread he was admitted to the hospital. His wife did not even know about him. I was "next of kin." A strange merging of our personalities gradually occured. Before I realized what was happening I was (Jason). I felt his fear—his pain—his regret—his frustration. Worse, when the doctor came around to give him the result of his tests—I stood outside the door in the hall and felt keenly everything that (Jason) must have been undergoing.

When we were alone after that and he knew he only had two to three months to live we were lying side by side in his bed and surely as anything I've ever known, we merged into one unit. I was able at one point to speak out against his wife—a long angry diatribe, stating facts I never knew—going on and on. When I finished I said "I said that for you—you were never able to." "Yes," he said. The communication between us was so acute that I would wake up suddenly at night—knew he needed me—get up and walk over to the hospital. I'd show my ID card and go up to his room. His eyes were on the door—as he watched and knew I'd be there. His wife was finally alerted to his condition and came to the hospital. He had lots of money—she feared, I think, that I wanted it.

Anyway, he had to go home when discharged to get his papers in order, then he was to rejoin me. Instead, he called sobbing—she wouldn't let him go—he was too weak to fight her. Of course this was the only way it could end and it saved my marriage. The link continued however after our separation and I felt his deterioration, his racing pulse, his shortness of breath. I was afraid I would die, too. I began psychotherapy. One night I awoke fighting for breath—but the fear was gone—I had given up and found choking wasn't so bad without fear. Not long after that I heard that he had died. I never felt it—slept right through it. Jason was a strong atheist. About two weeks after he died—I dreamt he came to me—whole and healthy again. We ran across fields and laughed. I said I forgot how much fun it is to be with you. It was more than a dream.

This woman casts in psychological and mystical language her dramatic account of her participation in the dying of a friend and colleague. Another woman, at age eighty-one the oldest in this study, uses a more traditional religious voice to speak of her experience:

In December of 1951 I was summoned to my parents home. My father who had been ill for some months was in a coma. My mother went to pieces and was unable to cope. She called the doctor who said he could not come to the house because he was very busy and just couldn't manage it but would call the hospital to send an ambulance. It was bitter cold and snowing—roads were icy. This entire episode was a nightmare—I had never experienced death at first hand, but had learned to pray and trust my Heavenly Father. I felt His presence and rode in the ambulance to the hospital. It was around 5:30 p.m. I sat in a chair by the bed praying without ceasing. It was then I saw Jesus comforting my father. It was as though Jesus had come to take my father with Him. There was a feeling of peace and gratitude which enveloped me and shortly after he was pronounced dead.

To different degrees, the women whose stories have just been told, convey their intense and emotional relationship with a dying person. They tell us of feeling a "presence," of being "confused and upset," and of emotions so significant and unique that they are "unexplainable." As they participate in the death of another, they describe their emotional realization of a beauty and wholeness, of a connectedness with another, of peace and gratitude, and for one, of living in a psychologically fused state with a dying friend. Other women also report intense and endurably significant relationships with a dying person. While the previous women emphasize more their active emotional participation in the immediate experiencing of another's dying and death, the women presented next reveal more of a sense of being influenced by their observations of another person's dying. These women write about their experiences with dying and death from a reflective remove.

Death Lessons

One woman tells of her relationship, over time, with a young woman who was a fellow graduate student. She explains that this fellow student, "had a very serious progressive disease which required frequent treatment involving hospitalization and surgery." Not acquainted with her at first, she remembers,

> I was intrigued and drawn to this woman because she was such a determined person—she persisted in her studies despite obvious discomfort and she never dwelled upon her obvious ailments, always maintaining a positive outlook. As I got to know her, I learned that a very strong religious faith supported her through her difficulties—it was not an ostentatious thing, but rather a quiet presence within her. The attraction for me was that a person could suffer but still be at peace with herself. With time she developed metastatic carcinoma which her doctors thought might have developed due to thirty-plus years of exposure to x-rays. This meant yet more surgeries and chemotherapy. She went through many crises in attempting to come to terms with this added insult to her body, but her faith was essentially unshattered. She finished graduate school and worked a short while before she died in a nursing home at age forty.

This narrative may sound like *her* spiritual experience, but we were close friends and thus I became very much in touch with her spiritual journey and still, twelve years after her death, view it as the most powerful spiritual experience I've had. When I met her I was in a stage of agnosticism of sorts and initially felt her beliefs totally alien—but the sense of alienation changed to a feeling I cannot exactly describe—a sense that I was in the presence of something stronger than I'd ever known. In my approach-avoidance response to my friend's efforts to share her beliefs with me, there were times when I withdrew because I couldn't accept the *content* of her beliefs, but I always "returned" because of the emotional pull of the remarkable and (to me) unexplainable coping. I should say too that I am sure that her physical suffering which became intense must have been a factor in time of withdrawal.

In writing of her spiritual experience, it becomes clear that this woman continues to try to integrate what she witnessed as her friend lived and died, with courage and faith, with her own ordering of reality.

I've never tried to put the experience into words before and I find myself groping for words and at the same time re-experiencing the awe I felt at the time. In retrospect I feel a sadness, I think, that I could never fully accept or share the content of what she believed because clearly it gave her an ability to somehow rise above physical suffering and to face death without fear. I hope it is clear that this was far more than a respect for another's bravery in the face of suffering—my own emotions were and are too involved in the *process* through which my friend went. It is probably the only time in my life thus far that I have felt in the presence of "something" greater and more powerful than anything or anyone here on earth. My friend wanted to help me get in touch with that "something" (which she, of course, was able to define as a personal relationship with God), I "searched" but never quite found—and until this very minute I didn't realize that perhaps I'm still looking—I hadn't thought that was the case. I find myself without the language to describe all of this and wonder whether the impact comes across.

Although this woman seems to have some doubts about her ability to successfully convey the fundamental influence her friend had, and still has, on her life, I think this is poignantly revealed in her account, with all its searching. Her friend's gift to her was not finding a resolution, but in opening her to questioning and searching.

Her sister's eighteen-month fight against acute leukemia became "one of the most important spiritual experiences in my life" for another woman. She explains:

My younger sister was diagnosed with leukemia (acute). Our family was immediately plunged into a very heavy emotional trial. She had just passed her eighteenth birthday. I did not live with my parents at the time, and being very close to my sister, it was difficult for me not being able to see her as often as I would have liked. Visiting her in the "cancer ward" was a revelation to us all. The extent of human suffering is almost incomprehensible. My sister, however, was not a "whiner." She gritted her teeth and cussed her head off, but I never once heard her ask, "Why me?"

It was humbling to see the amount of determination and defiance she possessed for one so young. Every day was a battle for remission and she fought the battle well. Many of the other patients just lay back, resigned, but my sister never resigned herself to the "fates" as some would say. She embraced life with a fierce passion that awed me. I have never before or since seen anyone *live* so well. Each setback was a heartbreak and each step forward a triumph. In a race for life, she was determined to win and I cheered inside at her unbreaking stride. The value of life became focused on the simplest of things. The beauty of nature, children, sunshine all became magnified through the realization of mortality. An agnostic, my sister never prayed or asked for spiritual guidance, but she unwittingly gave it in abundance. She fought for eighteen months against the disease within her, and finally her heart gave up. Her *mind* did not. She was as determined near the end as she was at the beginning.

She has been gone for two years now, and I often recall her indomitable spirit and love of life against all odds. It helps my perspective of the trivial matters that get me tense. I value the memories of my headstrong sister. She taught me lessons that the church, my parents, school, etc., could not have done. And remarkably enough, she did not know she was teaching and was unaware of the profound effect her courage would have on my life. I thank her often.

Thus far, in all of the stories about a woman's relationship with dying and death, our attention has been focused on the effect this process had on the teller of the story. In the next account, we get a glimmer of how this relationship affected the dying person. Her story begins:

During my second year of nursing school at Georgetown University, we began floor work. My assignment was in general medicine, and we were each assigned patients to "hover" over. One gentleman, Mr. M, whom I remember vividly to this day, was brought in after collapsing and going into a coma while painting his kitchen ceiling. He was in his sixties and had been previously diagnosed as having lung cancer. Tests revealed that the cancer had metastasized to his brain. He wasn't expected to survive past one or two weeks. He remained in a comatose state with his eyes open—but no reaction to movement, voice, or stimulation. I felt then, and still do now to some degree, that there exists a form of life on a plane beyond our comprehension, and there certain events occur which are beyond the realm of explanation scientifically or with the knowledge which we presently have.

Mr. M's family visited him frequently, sitting beside his bed, talking about him, but not acknowledging him. The doctors and family knew that death was imminent, and that for all purposes he was in a vegetative state.

But I was convinced that he was aware of where he was and what was going on. So I became a regular chatterbox, reading the paper to him, talking about all sorts of subjects. I was convinced he could hear me (although there was no indication that the man was conscious at all), and I decided I would give his final days some "quality." Mr. M's wife thought I was crazy. At the same time I was questioning the meaning of life, death, is there a life after death. My philosophy at that time was that without immortality of the soul, life is meaningless. But I wanted to know that something of us exists after death, other than just the memory of us.

It was a pleasant fall afternoon that I decided I would

put Mr. M in a wheelchair and take him out on the terrace. The leaves were turning and it was a beautiful scene. I stood next to Mr. M looking out over the foliage waxing poetic about fall, the change of seasons and likening them to the seasons of life. I turned to look at Mr. M and there were tears coming down his face. I knew at that moment that he had spoken to me.

Several days later Mr. M died without ever having regained consciousness.

An Alternative Approach

In an earlier chapter, I observed that, as a group, the women's spiritual experiences were characterized by variety. This is important to remember because in our eagerness to define and understand the long neglected world of women's experiences, we may be tempted to make an assertion which implies that all women have a certain trait, or attitude. This, of course, is simply not so. While it is true that most of the ninety-four women of this study did describe what I have called a relational spirituality, not all did. And while sixteen of the seventeen women who spoke of death and dying described a time of coming into relationship, one woman did not. In contrast to the other women, she speaks of a moment when she had to face the possibility of her own death, which she chose to do apart from others.

The night before I was to have major surgery, I had no visitors in the hospital. I had made arrangements for my young children to be cared for and friends would look after my husband, who is disabled. Facing a terrifying experience (the surgery), had created a depression for two months prior. Strangely, the night before, with no diversions or distracting company, the depression left. I felt a state of peace and satisfaction: as much as to say, "I have done all that is humanly possible to lead a good and productive life." I had no anxious feelings; no worry about my family; no fear of the pain I knew would surely come; no regrets for things undone; no sadness if I might die. It felt like total preparedness and peace. I cannot recall a time before or since when this complete serenity was mine: not even in fleeting moments. It was not ignorant bliss, because I was fully aware of the possible danger inherent in any surgery and especially in major abdominal surgery. I had gone over my situation in great detail and was able to feel calm and peaceful.

We have a clear sense that she reached an acceptance of her own death. She describes the outcome of a process in which she integrated the fact of her death into her existence. What is not as apparent to us, I think, is the process she went through to achieve this integration, and what type, if any, of symbolic immortality she imagines for herself.

Each of these women speaks of an encounter with death. And in this confrontation, we can see how many of the women construct their experience so that they arrive at some sense of symbolic immortality. A number of the women describe how the harsh finality of death is lessened and reinterpreted as those who have died metaphorically live on in the memory of another. Although dead, they are still very much alive in someone else's memory, and, as memory, they help shape that individual's perspective of self and world. Two of the women do not speak of an actual death of another. One gives a dramatic account of her sister's narrow escape from death, which she had foreseen in a dream, and how her participation in that experience reordered and renewed her own orientation to life. It is as she faces major surgery that another woman imagines and accepts her own death.

The stories of these women's experiences with death convey their attempt to understand what it means to die. They all strive—some with more certainty and clarity than others—to appreciate the mystery that the formlessness and unknowingness of death creates. Using metaphors and images, they imagine the dialectic between death and life continuity.

While I think it essential to keep in mind the one woman who depicted a time when, alone, she confronted and came to accept her own death, I also find it significant that she was the only one of these women who faced death as she stood apart from others. As Ochs has explained, most of us are familiar with the spiritual paradigm that she labels the "desert experience,"[12] in which we imagine ourselves coming into relationship with the divine when we are isolated from others. But, as many of the women's stories illustrate, and as Ochs claims, it is in the world *with* others that many women come into relationship with some larger reality, not when they are apart from others.

Six: Views of God

Our relationship to God, as a symbol of our inquiry into the "more-that-is-possible,"[1] an inquiry that we began in our relationship with our parents, reveals, at once, something about our relationship to the world, to particular others in the world, and to ourselves. By God I do not necessarily mean a supernatural power or entity, although for some that interpretation has significance. When I refer to God, I am referring to a symbol-concept that both captures and refracts the peculiarly human striving to find meaning, and to transform our experiences and our understanding so that the mundane becomes mythic and the mythic informs the mundane. As humans we face the knowledge of our "ultimate limitation and dependency"[2] by fashioning heroines and myths that call our attention to some transcendent truth, and that allows us a "resting place to live in."[3]

It is with our parents, beginning in early infancy that we begin the lifelong process of finding this "resting place to live in." In a landmark psychoanalytic study, of what she calls "The Birth of the Living God," Ana-Maria Rizutto has traced the developmental path that leads to our reliance on our parents to our reliance on a God.[4] I will depend mostly on Rizutto's analysis, integrating it with relevant points made by feminist theologians on the sex and nature of God, to orient us to the next group of stories from women who speak of their views of God.

The origins of how we imagine God and our relationship to God, Rizutto explains, are found in our early involvement with our parents or, in psychoanalytic language, with our primary objects. Memorialized in the form of "imagos," we obtain an enduring emotional inheritance of our childhood experiences which become prototypic for our continuing object relations.

These "imagos," like later representations, are created and recreated as we adaptively and defensively internalize the experiences we have both of ourselves and of the other in our human interactions, and as we seek self-consistency and relationship to the "real world." There is an essential connection between these self- and object-representations in the formation of self; we do not remember an object-representation without also remembering its concomitant self-representation. Since one type of representation is attendant on the other, a change in one produces a conflict and, potentially, a change in the other. In one sense, therapy can be seen as a process that creates this conflict, or disharmony, in the current relationship between self- and object-representations. The relationship between therapist and patient implies the possibility of a new "object relation," with its implications for a reformulated object-representation and, interdependently, a reconstructed self-representation.

In our early years, the internalizations, or "memorial processes," we make will be more visceral and sensorimotor in nature and, as we grow out of childhood we will rely more on conceptual thought. Regardless of the age or mode of internalization—through our organs, skins, senses, with images or thought—these processes always occur within an experiential context of a particular person's needs, fantasies, wishes, and feelings. So, as children we "take in" the memories of our experiences of the smell of our mother's breast, or the soft scratchiness of our father's beard, and in later life we may internalize our experience with our teacher under a conception of "authority." The particular mode used depends on the nature of the interaction, the experiential context, and the individual's developmental capacity at the time to symbolize and represent. When we read the women's stories on the following pages we will find examples of these different modes of remembering our experiences.

Before turning to a discussion of how we create our representation of God, a number of points about the creating of self- and object-representation need to be made. First, representations are not static, isolated entities, but rather complex, memorial processes; each representation we have has had multiple sources of impressions, images, and experiences with a significant person in our life and the potential for multiple meanings. Second, as we synthesize our current self- and object-representations with our past ones, we undergo ever changing relational configurations of our self- and object-representations. This conscious and unconscious reworking of our early memories and representations continues throughout our lifetime in our relationship with others, always at the service of maintaining self-integrity and, if that is established, in realizing our possibilities. Quoting Loewald, who himself sounds inspired by the metaphysics of Whitehead, Rizzuto observes that we "create a history of ourselves." And, finally, these internalizations of others do not simply incorporate some external reality (i.e., a particular experience with our mother) into an internal reality (an intrapsychic image of the event), but rather reflect a process in which there is a simultaneous creation of external and internal reality. Put another way, we co-create self and other, self and world, self and God, where "the area of creation is the intermediate area of illusion and play."[5]

It is in this "intermediate area of illusion and play," created by our first relationship with a significant other, that we develop our representation of God. Already, at one month of life, we seek our parent's gaze, this contact being the first indicator of our capacity to symbolize. Through the reflection of our parent's eyes we gain our first representation of self, ideally we see their delight in our being.

As the "resting state out of which a creative reaching out can take place," the first relationship imprints all future relationships. Given, to use Winnicott's phase, "good enough mothering," we do reach out, seeking a larger reality.[6] An essential of the human condition is our desire for inclusion, most vividly experienced in the early undifferentiated narcissism of early infancy and never entirely forgotten. But we also are compelled by our human nature to separate out into a larger reality and to make contact with a greater world of people, ideas, symbols, and experiences.

To ease our way into this larger world, we rely on a transitional object which evokes the early trust and security we felt. We clutch our teddy bears and blankets, and suck our thumbs. With our transitional object we enter a realm of illusion, an intersectional area where we simultaneously experience both our inner reality and external or shared reality. The transitional object, as symbol, allows us to imagine a larger world away from our early caretaker, and to seek adventure and creation in this larger world by taking our substitute caretaker with us.

As our representational abilities permit, we begin to imagine within this transitional space an assortment of "fascinating creatures—God among others." The representation of our "fascinating creatures," including God, originate in the child's self-representations and primary object-representations. Referring to the ages of two and one-half to five years, when the child first imagines companions, monsters, and heroes, Rizutto describes the child's representational world and God's entrance into it. "Together with this colorful crowd of characters, and amidst intense phallic, vaginal preoccupations, fantasies, wishes and fears, God arrives. At first [God] may seem one more in the procession. Soon, however, [God] acquires a special and superior status on account of multiple sociocultural, religious, ritualistic, familiar and—not least—epigenetic phenomena."[7]

While we may eventually discard particular transitional objects of early childhood—a teddy bear sits on a shelf, a frayed blanket is tossed away, and a child loses interest in sucking her thumb—we do not outlive our need for transitional objects. Instead, we enlarge our capacity by locating these transitional objects throughout the entire cultural field, which in our adult life "is retained in the intense experiencing that belongs to the arts and to religion and to imaginative living, and to creative scientific work."[8]

God, as a transitional object, however, is distinguished from others because God, unlike others, is derived primarily from the representations of our primary objects, typically our mother and father (and sometimes our sisters and brothers). In addition, the child sees the respect and awe accorded to God by her parents and other adults, as well as the special buildings, arts, and celebrations designed as tribute to God. While the adult may scoff at other fictional characters (witches, goblins, and monsters), they do not scoff at God. God, the child hears, is all powerful, all wise, and completely in control of the world. We sing "God Bless America" and engrave our coins with "In God We Trust." And, as the feminists have brought to our attention, the child learns that God is male.

Turning to her past experiences, the only people the young child knows who seem to approach the power and respect of God are her parents. Our early God representation, then, is built on, and reflects, our early object representation of our parents.

Although Rizutto recognizes that our God representation is formed not only in the early interaction with our parents, but also within a larger social, political, and historical context, her studies did not address this larger context. She does, however, provide a useful distinction between a representation, which is built on the process of internalization, with its more affective aspects, and its roots in the early relationship with parents, from an individual's *ideas* about God. The latter relies more on rational thought and is influenced by a wide array of social and cultural forces; in fact, depending on one's circumstances and curiosity, the variety of ideas about God as a concept are quite extensive indeed. She also discusses the interplay between our concepts of God and the formulation of our God representation, but, again, does not elaborate on the significance of the social cultural forces in the acquisition of our concepts of God and, by implication, in the elaboration of our God representation. To understand at least some partial significance of this larger context in the formation of our God concepts, and our object- and self-representations, we need to turn again to the feminist analysis of religion. Feminist theologians and religious activists have not framed their discussion of the importance of our concept of God in the psychological language of self- and object-representation, but all the same they have recognized the vital part our God concept plays in forming our ideas about self and of our place in the world.[9]

They understand that integral to the concept of God is how we name God, whether as father, mother, or otherwise. Implicit in this feminist critique is an awareness of what we have

learned from Rizutto: our concepts of God impinge upon the
elaboration we make of our object-representation of God, and that
all object-representations become associated with a self-representation. We can only guess about the effect a concept of God with a
male gender, with all of the implications that carries, has on a
female's formation of self. We can be confident, however, that
how we think about the sex of God will have a notable influence
on our sense of self. For example, if we think back to the discussion of transitional objects, for females, a male God means that she
must associate an "area of creation" with maleness. It will be a
male figure that will safely take her away from the more intimate
world she enjoys with her first caretaker to the larger world of
"imaginative living and . . . creative work." And for her, it will
be a male figure who creates the transitional space where the full
relevance of others and meaning for self are found.

Living within a world logic that dichtomizes many
human characteristics along gender lines, she learns that she is of a
sex that does not lead others into areas of creation where creative
work is done, and that, ultimately, she cannot rely on her sex for
that "ineffably private side of human experience where we are
irremediably alone."[10] By deduction, the young female may come
to understand that not just her sex lacks these grand capacities, but
that she does as well.

Fortunately, like all of our other concepts and representations, our God concept and representation also faces lifelong
challenges as we have continuing experiences and encounter new
ideas. As we come into contact with different experiences of
others in the present, and as we imagine new possibilities for the
future, we inevitably rework our historical memories and representations.

As McDargh notes, sometimes the accumulated
weight of intellectual evidence about the concept of God dimin-
ishes the significance of a person's God representation.[11] Although
some disharmony will be tolerated for a while between a concept
of God, and one's representation of God and self, eventually we
demand congruence. We may achieve this by discarding our original ideas about God in favor of a new concept of God, and a new

sense of self. Some women, as we have seen in the earlier stories and will continue to observe in the women's stories of this chapter, have left traditional religion behind, finding it impossible to integrate that concept of God with a new self-integrity. Other times, which we also can observe in these women's stories, the conditions allow a reformulation of this object-representation of God that matches the revised concept of God and of self. And, of course, in the face of a conceptual challenge, some women may sacrifice self-development in favor of maintaining their current concept of God.

Whether we have revised, maintained, or discarded our concept of God, and whatever the related God representation is, how we imagine and think about God suggests something about our current resolution with our internalized primary objects and with our relationship to our self and to others in the world.

Seeing and Feeling the Hand of God

The group of women whose stories are told next experience God through their senses—they see God, talk to God, hear God's voice, and are held in God's arms. They do not describe a conception of God as much as they do of perceiving an actual being. Their God is distinct, visible, and embodied.

One woman explains the circumstances that preceded her startling vision of Jesus:

My first husband was an alcoholic. He finally got sober through the Grace of God, and Alcoholics Anonymous nine years before he died five and one-half years ago of pancreatic cancer. However, his disposition didn't change a whole lot even though he was sober. It's known in the fellowship as dry drunks—even though the person hasn't been drinking, he slips back into the drinking personality.

One time during one of his so-called "dry drunks" he was giving me the silent treatment, for what reason I can't remember or maybe never knew the reason. But, being a member of Alanon (the fellowship for families and friends of alcoholics), I had learned to just act as normal (whatever that means) as possible. I was very upset, however, and was laying in bed saying the Serenity Prayer (which is, God grant me the serenity to accept the things I cannot change, courage to change the things I can, and the wisdom to know the difference) over and over as fast as I could, trying to relax enough to go to sleep.

All of a sudden the blackness I was seeing with my eyes shut started to brighten like the sun coming out from the clouds and there stood Jesus (or our modern day impression of Him), just standing there all in white with His hands outstretched at His sides, palms facing me (like all the statues). It was beautiful, but at the same time very frightening. I thought maybe I was dying, but I had no pain anywhere. So I blinked my eyes several times and as soon as I would close them, I'd see the vision again. Then I started praying for Him not to take me yet, I had a small child and two teenagers who I felt needed me, etc. Just as quickly as it appeared, the clouds closed and all was dark again. I blinked several times trying to bring it back but, of course, I couldn't. After lying there a few more minutes a feeling of peace came over me and I realized that everything was going to be all right. I have tried several times to conjure up this vision again but have been unable to.

A second woman experiences her sense of God through touch. She explains:

The weather was beautiful, clear and invigorating, and I had gone to the terrace to look at the moon. The terrace was of concrete and elevated about five feet from the grass. While I was looking at the moon and stars I called to my cousin to join me. I stepped backward and the next moment felt myself falling. I did not know the terrace ended so suddenly or that there was no guard rail. I went across the shrubbery which was thick and landed on the asphalt walk, my head touching. I stood up and remembered at that instant the feeling of being supported by unseen arms. I had not a scratch from the brushes, no injury to my head nor on any part of my body, and even today I am reminded of that special moment in time when I felt The Everlasting Arms supporting me.

One woman's experience is not of a God who saves her from falling, but of one who knocks her to the ground. But she shares with the woman described above, the sense of an actual presence and the view of a God who intervenes on her behalf at a time when she is in need. She speaks of a time when, feeling troubled,

> I had knelt at my bed to pray . . . telling Jesus all. I waited in silence for God to answer me in some way, to ease, lighten or remove the heaviness from my soul. At some point . . . when I gave up my expectations for an answer, I stood up. I was knocked to my knees immediately upon standing. I stayed on my knees for a very long time frightened because of this unexpected response and knowing that God was working in me to ease my worries. The next time I conceived of the idea of arising, I started slowly up on one knee. I waited a while for some sign that it was okay to proceed. I finally decided that I trusted God and I knew He would not hurt me. I also now knew that if He wasn't finished with me, He would let me know. This time I remained standing. I had an inner peace which I had not felt for an extremely long time. The things that were weighing me down had gone away, but they no longer had me depressed. God had taken them over.

As a result of her experience, she recommends, "Pray and trust God, He will always make a way."

Not all women, however, who report being rescued at a time of need describe an embodied God, or even express certainty about attributing the intervention to God. Asked to describe a spiritual moment, one woman responded with,

> The only experience I remember was when I was driving on a bridge in the pouring down rain. Men had been working on the bridge that day and there was about twenty feet where the guard rail had been removed. All of a sudden my windshield wipers stopped. I couldn't see anything at all. My car started swerving and right before I hit the side of the bridge, my wipers came back on and I realized that if they hadn't I probably would have been killed. I felt scared, shocked, totally upset. And then I felt as if

something (God, whatever) might have helped out somewhat in that situation.

She feels saved, but she is not sure how it happened and who or what did it.

And another woman offers a vivid account of her experience of God that combines the sensory with the symbolic. She describes an actual, embodied being, who seems to have a literal presence; at the same time she draws upon the use of metaphor to explain her experience. Describing a process that happened over a period of time, she tells us:

> It began with images of Jesus and me sitting by a stream (which was where we usually met to talk) but this day he asked me to get up and walk in the woods with him. I was surprised and scared a little because we had always stayed by the stream. He told me that we were going to build my house in the woods; it would be the place I could always come back to, where my deepest truest self would live. I was now feeling more bewildered yet excited. He said that first I was to clear the ground before laying the foundation. I had to remove the dead bark and the weeds. It took some long meditation and centering to discover what was the dead bark and weeds. Jesus and I agreed that the bark were those things in life I had let go of but allowed to still clutter my life, such as my need to weigh 100 pounds and my guilt over past relationships. We cleared them away. Now were the weeds which were more vines than weeds. I pulled and pulled but they were so grossly intertwined and rooted, so deep, they would only break and look gone, but grow back thicker the next day. These were the things in my life which on the surface didn't look so bad but the roots were deep and knotted and if I didn't pull them up they would cling to my house and destroy it. Things like materialism, success, control. I told Jesus I could not pull them up, not alone. I felt frustrated. Jesus held me and said I must soak the roots in the Living water everyday until together we could pull and they would slide out of the moist ground. I wept with relief. It was and is an experience I go back to.

She completes her house over the next couple of years, and conclude by saying, "we are still in the process of decorating and cleaning, maintaining and expanding."

In Sickness and in Health

Other women who report on a God whose presence is actively felt in their lives describe a time when they were healed. Their experience is of an active God who can reorder events and change the circumstances of their lives.

After surgery for stomach cancer, one woman turns to God for relief from the pain that she endures. She tells us:

> I had chemotherapy for twelve weeks after which I was given Percodan for pain. These pills worked for a while, when they ceased to provide relief. The doctor advised me that Percodan was the strongest pain medicine he had to offer. He further stated that there was not any medical reason for my constant pain. My doctor also told me that all the remaining cancer was gone, through the use of the chemotherapy treatment. Yet, I was still in constant pain. I prayed to the Lord continually for some relief from the constant pain. My family and church were in constant prayer for me, but my pain continued to persist. Around three in the morning of April 1981, I felt I could no longer live with the constant pain I was having. I asked God if he would just give me five minutes of relief from the pain. If I could be free of pain for just that short period of time. I laid in my bed waiting in my bed, waiting in pain for God's answer to my prayer. Suddenly a bright light filled my darkened room and complete peace came over me. All the pain was gone from my body. I praised and thanked the Lord for answering my prayers. I could sit up without pain. I could drink water without pain. I could press my stomach without pain. I thanked God for his unending mercy to me. After this period of peace from pain passed, my pain returned but never to the intensity it was before.

This woman describes her relationship to a God who can intercede on her behalf. Other women also share this sense of a definitive and active God but, unlike the first woman, they talk about a relationship to God within an interpersonal context.

Recently arrived in Florida after being widowed, one woman responds to an advertised prayer group, partly out of curiosity. She remembers, "I was received with warmth and true brotherly and sisterly love that I had never known before," which leads to her becoming "baptized in the Holy Spirit." Giving us this background, she proceeds to describe a time when she was part of a Charismatic Renewal weekend. She describes a chapel that is "crowded, . . . four rows in the center aisle . . . soft singing, and praising the Lord." A healing service of intercessory prayers is underway. She joins the line of people seeking to be healed. She reaches the front of the line, and then,

> I was asked to step forward to be prayed over; the young lady . . . held my hands straight forward. The gentleman on my left asked what was my request? I told him I had arthritis on my right side of my spine from my neck on down, and severe pain in the lower right area and, then, both men "prayed in tongues" and the young lady quoted from the Bible in English. Suddenly I felt a flutter from my neck near my right shoulder down to the lumbar area and I was "slain in Spirit." I went helpless to the floor, and had a feeling of being on a cloud. I layed still for perhaps a minute or two, semiconscious.

She informs us that an x-ray after her healing indicates that her spine is "almost devoid of calcium deposits," for which, "I will always Praise the Lord until I can thank him face to face."

Like the woman above, this next woman also joins a Charismatic prayer group, being drawn by their warmth and openess to her and others. She recalls,

> I was deeply impressed with how loving, understanding, and happy they all were. They were showing such loving concern for a member whose husband had died just the week before and I marveled at her trust in God and her cheerfulness. I felt if I became a part of this group my terrible depression, fears, lack of sleep and appetite, indecisions from which I'd been suffering for over a year, would be overcome. I was taking five different medications all of which were working against one another but had been prescribed by my doctor. I would get so unnerved, my husband, who had the patience of Job with me during my long illness, would have to rush me to the doctors. On one of these visits my own doctor wasn't in. One of his associates talked to me and recommended a psychiatrist he felt I should see. After

> being hospitalized twice by the psychiatrist and months of visits, he told me there was nothing more he could do for me. If I wanted to get well, I'd have to do it on my own, this at the time when I was at my lowest point, with the fear of never recovering.

The Charismatic prayer group she had recently joined, however, does not give up on her.

> Each week at the meeting they would pray with me and I know they all prayed for me many times during the week. The two ladies who brought me home from the meetings would pray with me just before I'd get out of the car. Each of those nights, I would sleep all night, giving me some much needed rest. Gradually, with the continued prayers, loving help of all the members together with my husband's, I began to overcome my fears, depression, lack of sleep and appetite. I weighed only eighty-five pounds, which even with my small frame (5′) made me look too gaunt. I had never ceased praying or attending Mass during my depression, but, apparently it was without really trusting that God would take care of all my fears, if I'd just put them in His hands.

Completely recovered from the depression for five years now, she understands it as "a miracle from God. It was God, working through these kind people, who restored me to complete good health, on no medication of any kind, able to live a happy life."

The group of people present at one woman's healing were her children, who, living some distance away, had come to the St. Louis Hospital where she was ill with "Lupus Erythematasus: Pneumonia and anemia with a very high temperature." One of her children, a minister, leads prayers at her bedside, with two other ministers. Annointing her with oil, they ask God to heal her. The next day she reports,

> The Doctors told of their amazement at the fact that the blood count came up so fast that they were forced to take it three times, and the temperature was down to normal, so truly this was a miracle.

Expressing her thanks to God for her life, she feels at peace. Although aware of the severity of her illness, she never was afraid.

Instead, she tells about being "so happy that the influence of Holy Spirit is the life of Christ in the soul, and ever abides with me to sustain me in every emergency and under every temptation. Such love is without parallel."

Humans are not the only beneficiaries of God's healing, as one woman tells of a time when God interceded on her dog's behalf. She sets the stage for her account of this time with an incredible, Job-like litany of hardships she had to endure. The time she was describing is "about thirty-three years ago." Her son, safely returned from combat in World War II, develops double pneumonia. Next, her mother has a heart attack which forces her to delay surgery she needed. Her mother recovers and she undergoes the postponed surgery. Then the day after her operation her mother unexpectedly dies. Still not through with afflictions, on the day of her mother's funeral, she had to have her thirteen-year old dog euthanized because of vaginal cancer. Next she reports,

> As soon as I recovered from all this! I acquired a dear little new puppy. Several months after this, due to a freak accident—due to my carelessness, the puppy cut his ear in our garden. Although I took him immediately to the hospital—the vet neglected to give him anti-tetanus, so while still in the hospital he developed tetanus. It was all so terrible that the whole staff insisted we have him "put to sleep" which we did. Then my son's best friend died under mysterious circumstances on the West Coast. All this happened shortly before Christmas, and left me emotionally drained. One day while ironing in the basement club room, which was my custom, I was overwhelmed by it all!—started railing against God. I brought up one by one all the things which had happened and how He did not seem to care about the grief and pain I was suffering, the great loss! Then I concentrated on the recent loss of the little new puppy and said something like "You even took my little dog away. You didn't let me keep my little replacement puppy," and so on. Well, suddenly, inside my head, I suddenly heard a *male* voice—infinitely calm, consoling and peaceful which said "My child! I did not take your dog from you! You gave him up to death! because you did not trust Me enough!" That was all—but it shut me up instantly. It was

absolutely true! The logic of it stunned me! The caring and loving in His voice! I suddenly could not conceive of anything bad ever coming from Him. He was indeed a loving Father, reminding His rebellious child where the blame actually lay. He didn't say another word—He didn't have to. He had opened my eyes.

Not yet through with her story, she says,

This has a sequel. Years later we had an adorable small beagle whom we had had for several years and who had had all his shots. But, somehow, during Holy Week, he suddenly developed distemper and was quite ill. I nursed him at home until Good Friday when the vet told me . . . it would be kinder to put him to sleep. My daughter and I were planning to go to the three hour . . . service . . . , but the dog was too sick to leave. However, remembering God's message to me—we decided to go, after putting the dog under God's healing care and we prayed incessantly for his healing. There were no messages from God, but by the next day the dog was better, and by Easter Sunday he was completely healed. I felt that this strange circumstance was a test from God and that this time I passed! Praise God!

If we think of Rizutto's explication of the development of our God representation, so far we have heard from women whose current representation of God seems to rely on the "memorial processes" of their early years. It is then that we use more visceral and sensorimotor modes to experience and remember others, and that we are more dependent on our parents, seeking their intervention in our behalf.

The next woman who speaks, however, conveys a different understanding of God. Her relationship with God, less emphatic than the previous women's, is based more on a symbolic understanding of a God in her life. Undergoing tests in a hospital for suspected multiple sclerosis, she remembers that time as "an important and memorable spiritual experience." At the time, she recalls,

My life . . . seemed to be in a balance. Many questions crossed my mind as I pondered what my future might be if MS paralyzed me in any way. At present all I knew was that I was experiencing numbness. Personally, I didn't know how I would cope with any sort of debilitating disease, especially MS, but I prayed for the grace to accept whatever I needed to at the moment. Having a friend with MS who was already confined to a wheelchair at my age, as well as knowing several other persons with MS, was no comfort.

At the time I was filled with all kinds of energy. I had a full-time job and was involved with various other activities. Somehow it didn't seem possible to change my activity-filled life, but as I contemplated the meaning of my life, all that previously seemed so important suddenly faded away. I recall feeling very helpless and very uncertain about what the future held for me, but being able to talk about my fears was helpful. I felt very grateful to be able to share my experience with friends as well as community who showed real love, care and concern.

As she ends her story, we are still not certain about the results of her tests for MS. "Today I continue to remember the significance of that time in the hospital. The call to 'let go' of those things which are binding continues to be with me. It seems that struggle will remain with me for life. It is a God-experience—a conversion." She does not emphasize that she was healed; we are not even certain from her account whether she actually was diagnosed as having MS. Instead of healing, and a definitive and intervening God, she describes a less tangible presence.

Two Ways of Knowing God

We all are continually responding to the memories of early experiences, seeking self-integrity as we try to integrate these early experiences with our responses to current people and situations in our lives. We try to make sense of the world and our experience. Sometimes we resolve a discrepancy between a past memory and a current conception or experience by bending the present to fit the shape of the past. At other times and in other situations, we reformulate our memory of an experience and its meaning into a new constellation of increased complexity. We use all of our capacities—visceral, sensory, conceptual—to make these transformations of understanding and self-integrity. In other words, we feel and we think. The women whose stories follow illustrate these two modes of experiencing memory and making sense of current reality. One woman begins her response to recall a memorable spiritual experience by posing some philosophical questions,

> How can I testify to God's existence? How does he play a role in my life? I was brought up a . . . strict Catholic . . . When I came to [college] I fulfilled my theology requirement with a course called "Problem of God." This course presented a true problem for me because I had never thought to question his existence . . . I made a full 180 degree turn away from my religion . . . We studied WW II . . . the destruction of the Jewish population . . . we questioned whether God was all powerful . . . If he was, could He possibly be all good to let a thing like Auschwitz, hell on earth, occur? Perhaps He was not all knowing? I pondered these questions for a year—totally turned off from . . . my Catholic upbringing.

Eventually she resolves her doubts, when

> after much thought and consideration I came to rediscover God. I took a Christian marriage course that explained many precepts of the Catholic church. Because I learned more about my religion, the reasons its doctrine specified certain things, I found I agreed with it. My religion has become very special to me, and something I rely on, not out of fear or need, but look to for strength in my personal life.

A second woman also describes a process in which she relies on reason to understand who God is for her. She recalls:

> Many years ago, in a Bible class . . . I was asked what I thought was our soul. My explanation was a "seed" in us that since we believe in a Supreme power, that it enables us to put our lives in the hands of that Supreme Being. To me this hope or belief in immortality helps to steady us in the journey through life. This, I hope, has helped me to work toward a moral order in my life— or simply expressed, trying to live by the Golden Rule. This also makes me realize that religion is a practical thing, which draws

its inspiration from God and expresses itself in everyday life, lived according to a reasonable creed.

The spiritual accounts of other women are characterized by their describing how they felt, rather than what they thought at a particular time and place. For example, one woman talks about the time she cried in church as "the choir was singing and light was streaming through the window . . . At the moment my whole body seemed very excited as if I were sexually aroused." While another remarks, "I have experienced the presence of God with me (at prayer, before the Eucharist). I have felt this inner peace and affirmation of faith." Yet another woman describes how "I feel at home when I'm at Mass. It feels warm to me and I feel that Jesus and God are right in there to listen or help me."

Until now, all of the women's spiritual experiences occurred in the context of a traditional religious setting. The next woman's story illustrates the integration of her old religion with new philosophical thought and practice, and a sophisticated sense of her feelings that is at once vividly real and richly metaphorical.

While making a five-day Zen retreat at a Benedictine Monastery located in the heart of Osage Indian land, I experienced the God who is the source of life in me for the "first" time in a very profound way. I had been "studying" Buddhism and Hinduism for six months and had begun the practice of regular meditation. My "experience" occurred while walking on the monastery road and the experience stayed with me the rest of the day. The experience is difficult to put words around—but the God whom I "met" was the person of Jesus—I laughed because I would have expected Buddha in light of my recent studies. When I "met," the experience was not visual—there were no visions or concrete details. I felt full of light and peace and very open. I am convinced that Jesus touched my entire being—I was very conscious of "knowing" Jesus for the first time—the knowing is not an intellectual knowing—but a meeting of hearts/souls; I have had several other "experiences" since that time—and carry since that time always a new awareness of the universe—a cosmic Christ that is infinitely greater than all the "facts" I had learned. In Zen language, I *tasted* Him for the first time.

Like the woman who "tasted Jesus," the next woman—musician, writer, peace activist, and "Christian Buddhist"—has reformulated her previous memories. With her inquiry into philosophy and music, she actively seeks out new understanding and transformation. She explains,

> My experience extends over a number of years. At college I majored in Greek, but was left with a feeling of inadequacy. Later I worked with a Jungian analyst . . . while also studying musical composition with a private teacher . . . and singing in the Dessoff Choir in New York City. I had dreams about numbers which neither my analyst nor I could understand. Meanwhile my music teacher died and I did not know where to turn to pursue my musical studies. Then came a message from a dream: Go to Boston. Boston? I had no connection there. But soon Ernest Levy came . . . to rehearse the choir in his cantata which we were to perform. I asked him if he would accept me as a pupil and he told me he taught . . . [in] Boston. So I went to Boston and studied Pythagorean philosophy, which is the science of qualitative (tonal) numbers. All the dreams I'd had about numbers were thus explained. . . . One episode in the course of all this took place as I practiced meditation alone in my house on a summer's day. It was very quiet. Suddenly I heard loud chords being played on an organ—and I saw the organ pipes go up and down like stamping feet—although there was no organ remotely near—It was an auditory and visual "hallucination," to be technical, but I liked to think of it as revelation of the spirit.

The experiences described by the next two women evoke the hazy outline of an image from an early age. But, here, too, we can see that a new relationship has been established between the memory of the past experience and the current sense of self in the world. Integral to this reordering of associations between past and present understandings, we see suggested in their stories a transformation of the feelings that surround and bring alive these early "memorial processes." Both stand in the midst of an awesome power, with the potential to destroy, but, instead of shrinking back, they acknowledge their own power to create and their desire to participate in creation.

While at a workship, one woman was directed to draw

or write her experience with Kali, the fierce Mother Goddess of India. She tells us,

I went outside into the hot sun and sat on the pavement with pen and paper. All in a hot flash . . . I wrote my Medusa poem. The poem came out in a great rush of words and images—in almost perfect rhyme and meter. It was almost as if it were written from without except for the exhaustion I felt at its conclusion. When it was finished, I was sweating and hot, and hot not only from the sun. I wandered inside as if in a trance . . . When it was my turn to share, I trembled as I spoke. They didn't know how to respond. My emotion was greater by far than the poem. This same feeling and experience was repeated when I wrote the poem for [my stepdaughter].

Not all of the women describe unexpected responses. One woman seems to have conjured up her spiritual experience, which she speaks of in vivid detail. On a small island for a religious conference, she notes, "I had been planning to do a (pagan) ritual in the beautiful stone chapel that crowns the island." She waits for a time when she can be alone, "so that I could sing and speak and meditate to invoke the Goddess in solitude, but I found that there were always people around. Finally, on the last night of the conference I decided that in one way or another, the time was ripe, and went up to the chapel."

Explaining that the chapel is two hundred years old and the site considerably older, she reports:

I am not alone in sensing them (ghosts and spirits) in the chapel, which has been a holy place for so many down the years. I felt very uncomfortable—somewhat fearful, but mostly just sensing non-acceptance all around me—almost tangibly in the empty space. I sat down gingerly, up near the pulpit. Flashing my light around the space seeking the people whose presence I felt so strongly—no one visible—I lit two candles hastily, put out my flash light, took out a guitar . . . and tried to play a bit. A woman came in, oblivious of the others and read some poetry to me and herself. They listened unconvinced. Some of the women's friends came in, listened, and then took the woman away.

Silence now. The resistance to my presence has

weakened. I still sense them watching me though. I strum a few more chords—no, this isn't right. Silence. Then my mouth opens and I'm singing, no words, just a powerful melody that floats and hovers and soars and flies out the many windows to meet the gulls, and the moon and the ocean. My eyes close, and words form in my mind, framed by the music. I sing "Ahhhh" but inwardly think, "Oh moon, come bless me. Goddess be with me." I feel them waiting—felt presence is like a constant background noise, like the constant cries of the gulls outside, like the constant, irregular harbor buoys ringing, like the pure sound of moonlight pouring steadily onto the window pane, into this holy space. These sounds fill me, lift me, connect me to them. I inwardly invoke the Goddess of the four directions . . . I am so full of life and love. Everything I think of I am part of, as it (or he or she) is part of me. The birds, the plants, my conference friends, the children I work with, even the rocks have a life that intertwines with mine. I embrace these things, drawing mental circles around them and me together. I draw a circle around everyone who is in the chapel with me, feeling their presence, and some measure of love with them, too. We are all here for the same reason, I acknowledge inwardly to them. No matter who we pray to . . . I continue my ritual, naming things for the love they represent, feeling my power, which comes for Her, through the elements and my own being. I who am here to enjoy all the love and beauty that she has created for no reason other than that it "pleases" her to create such joy. My inner tumult, my grief at knowing that I must leave this island, fell away. What is left is a floating, peaceful silence as my singing ends. I inwardly open my circle, bid farewell to the Goddess(es) and open my eyes. To the invisible souls who have listened and heard and now bid me peace as I acknowledge them, take my candle, and circle down the hill to bed.

Finding God in Nature and the Everyday

As we "create a history of ourselves," advancing out into a larger reality we find our creative space not only in arts, religion, and science, as Winnicott suggested, but, I think, in nature and the everyday as well. Next we hear women speak of the connection they feel, not to a particular person but to the earth, and who become inspired by the pristine significance of the mundane.

One woman recalls,

> I walked from my home into spring as I opened my front door. As I moved along my route to work, life seemed to surge and vibrate all around me. I felt high excitement and an intimate connection to the earth, to the color of the sky, to nature. I composed haiku poetry to life. I was feeling open to everything beautiful and a part of it. My skin felt bathed with color and every hair, an antenna. I kept breathing deeply so that mother nature could enter my body.

Nature allows another woman to gain a new perspective. She explains:

> I was walking across the park, which takes about thirty minutes. It was a moderate spring morning, and I was thinking about my life and feeling a lump and cry in my chest and I just let it go, accepted it and the sadness and pain attached to it. And at the same time I was aware of the good things in my life, especially those presently surrounding me in the park. I saw a large elm tree next to me and stopped for a minute and touched the coarse bark and looked up into its spreading branches high above me, and started making up a poem about needing a tree for a friend at forty; and I kept walking, making up the poem. And within a few minutes I was caught up in awe of the beauty and larger goodness of life and felt very happy and full and grateful and aware of God's presence in my life then and always.

The next woman also describes how her reflections, as she contemplates a tree, bring her into a larger reality of relationships.

> I was on vacation at the shore spending a relaxing few days. Much about life's meaning and purpose and my place in the universe had been on my mind. I was laying on my bed looking out the window, and my gaze settled on the leaves of a tree outside. It suddenly became clear to me that human lives were

like those of leaves. That people are born seemingly as separate distinct people, functioning in the world on their own—some are whole and perfect—some have physical defects, some are plucked out of life early—some live through all of the natural stages of evolution from youth to old age with accompanying physical changes. But leaves (and likewise people), are not separate, they are all connected to a central system for life support as well as connected to each other. Each leaf is a whole entity but is also part of a larger living being that supplies its life force and supports it with necessary nutrients. This analogy of human beings to leaves made a distinct impression on my mind and my spirit. My feeling was that peace was possible, that support and connection is everywhere and that our lives are a part of the divine infinity. Oneness with God and the universe is possible to experience and possible to believe.

Her reflections on the leaves of a tree lead her to an affirmation of faith in the oneness and interconnectedness of the universe. For another woman it was sitting in an open jeep at the marshy edge of a village in Sri Lanka. She sees

species after species of beautifully colored birds all minding their sunset business. I was transfixed. All of a sudden a rather unattractive marsh had been transformed into a tropical bird feeding ground. We saw bright blue kingfishers, green parakeets, herons—even ordinary birds that I had never noticed before became interesting; I was ecstatic. I had never bird watched before and I felt this incredible awakening to life around me . . . somehow, I felt God far more keenly than I ever had before. God was everywhere!—in those birds walking around, in the reeds, in the water—in the way the whole thing fit together.

Again, we are reminded by one woman's story that no categorical statements can be made about how nature brings women into relationship. For her, nature provides the space she needs to stand in awe at the wonder of life. She explains that she had left a boarding school that "I felt was stultifying" for her home on a farm on the Eastern Shore. Reaching home:

I dropped my bag on the outside steps and walked around the back, moving down toward the water. The grass shimmered, the evening was settling in. I walked down to the edge of the water and sat cross-legged. The sun set with eruptions of purples and blues and hard reds. The water reflected this transformation and a wind rose. Finally, a silence descended and the moon was above. Strange clouds like handkerchiefs floated above. The stars were brilliant. I was alone with "God" and free.

There are spectacular moments when we are reminded of the awesomeness of nature—tornadoes, floods, earthquakes. But, mostly, nature quietly does her work, an integral and often unnoticed part of our everyday existence. It is coming into relationship with the ordinary, everydayness of the life surrounding us that attains spiritual significance for some women: the woman who became reminded of the interconnectedness of life as she walked on the beach with her father at winter and gazed at washed up Noxzema bottles and a toilet seat, and the woman who steps outside her door to breathe in the life of a spring day. Another woman, explaining how she experiences something of the divine, observes, "The cutting edge for me seems to be discovering God and my own faith and spiritual nature through the commonplace." One such time, she remembers, came when walking in an early morning mist.

Along the way finding treasures . . . a dead butterfly, one wing torn. Further along the way I spied and picked up a couple of small bones . . . one the jawbone of some small creature, with teeth. Walking along still further, came upon another butterfly, this one very much alive—large—brown velvet wings, dipped in white. Open to bathe in the morning sunshine, closed, then pointing to heaven in prayer. I felt a sudden emotion—a filling up . . . a welling of tears, but a joyous kind of emotion . . . my lungs expanding. *I am ready to take wing again . . . I can fly now.* A feeling of letting go . . . and suddenly aware of what I held in my hand . . . a butterfly wing and a jawbone with sharp teeth. Paradox again. A knowledge, first-hand and deep, deep within the paradox that is me—*live the questions.* Like Thomas Merton *I* wanted to burst into laughter. Even now I smile.

I close with this sprightly account of an articulate young woman's experience with God.

My earmuffs are burgundy and I really like them. They add some fun to the cold of winter and protect my protruding lobes from the whipping wind as I cycle to my job each day. I love biking to work. Sure, it gets a bit chilly at times, but it also fills me with a simple joy and freedom which permeates my soul and sends me soaring.

It's tempting to try to conjure images of myself effortlessly gliding along, carelessly breezing by the congested traffic and arriving, fresh as a proverbial daisy, to my destination a few short miles away. Hardly. The roads are busy, impatient motorists honk frequently, and I really have to pump to get up those hills. Yet often, everyday even, I get a special thrill from riding my bike which I can best describe as spiritual.

My thoughts often begin with gratitude. I am so thankful that I can even ride a bike, because, for me, it's such a source of happiness. Then these feelings tumble into an avalanche of reflection on how much God has given me: my family, my friends, my job, I guess my very life. I realize that I am so infinitely blessed and inside my head I thank God.

I like remembering that God is there with me on Wisconsin Avenue as I slow down to stop for the traffic light. Too often, I think we, albeit subconsciously, push God into the corner of today's world. More or less, we imagine that God took care of the major business with creation and the Israelites and has now adopted a lax position while perched peacefully somewhere above. Although I doubt that we could articulate it as such, we picture God as viewing us from an ethereal shelf, and we let God get dusty.

But, as my gloved hands grip the handlebars, God is there pedaling right along with me and we spurn the dust on the road. Softly I sing hymns of praise to God as we rejoice in each other. The people on the sidewalk don't hear me, I think, but I hear me, and God hears me just fine. You can sing louder at night. People don't notice as much. You can sing loudest at night when the wind whips along in burgundy earmuff weather.

Seven: Stepping Back: Moving Between Relationship and Relatedness

Being-in-Relationship

As we listened to the women speak of moments in which they sought meaning, we learned, I think, about the pervasiveness of relationships in human living. We also discovered, through these women's stories, that not only interpersonal relationships are significant, but also self-reflexive, intrapsychic, and symbolic relationships.

Although I have distinguished between relationships with self, internalized others, actual others, and symbolic others, these distinctions do not, of course, neatly occur in the course of human events. To be human is to be in all of these relationships. We are never, for example, only in relationship to self, since our self is formed by our internalized past relationships that we hold in memory, by our current encounters with others, and by mythic possibilities that we can imagine. With this caution in mind, we can see examples of all of these types of relationships in the women's stories.

We heard of coming into relationship with self in the story of the woman who recognized and then acknowledged a masculine presence as an integral part of herself. She re-elaborated her relationship with self, that was at once more differentiated and integrated, offering her more possibilities. Similar experiences of reformulating a perspective on self are described by the woman whose experiences with Judy Chicago's art allowed her to identify with her femaleness and enlarge her view of self, and the woman who, after a process of many years, located the Kairos/Goddess within herself.

For another woman, the experience of writing a poem at the Kali workshop seemed to evoke powerful memories—probably from her very early years as well as more recent times—of her intrapsychic relationship with her mother. As we learn from her poems, presented in part 2, "Portraits of Six Women," she is struggling to reestablish her relationship with these internalized memories of another, now part of herself. Two adolescent women, whose stories appeared in the chapter "Views of Self," also depict experiences in which an internalized representation of another seemed to be evoked. One seemed to identify with her parents' values for her social conduct, after an initial conflict with them. The other young woman, juggling the need to satisfy herself with what she had been taught about serving others, presumably by her parents, had not yet achieved a satisfactory relationship between her sense of self and these internalized values. Because of their ages, the relationship outcomes for both these younger women can be understood as part of a developmental process; in time they may achieve a more integrated conclusion.

As I noted earlier, many described a relational spirituality, in which they were in relationship with an actual other. The women spoke of an interpersonal encounter in which one held the hand of a dying woman who shared her mother's hospital room, one walked along the beach with her father, another wrestled with an atheistic college roommate, and one looked into the eyes of a ferret. For each woman, this encounter with another brought her into a new relationship with herself and the world.

Finally, many women spoke with particular emphasis about their relationship with symbolic others, most notably God and nature. Women spoke to Jesus, felt the "everlasting arms of the Eternal Father," saw Jesus stand before them and were healed by His interventions. Other women described coming into relationship with a larger human process as they felt the presence of spring, reflected on a tree, or stood in the marshes of a bird sanctuary in Sri Lanka. Each narrative of a moment in a woman's life allows us an opportunity to comprehend how she, and each of us also, lives her life in relationship, both real and imaginary, current and memoralized, with self and other.

Being-in-Relatedness

Now, I want to step back and reflect on the significance of this understanding we have gained from the women's stories about the significance of relationships in our lives.[1] By gaining perspective and expanding our intellectual horizons, I believe that we can find a theme of relatedness, not just relationships, throughout these women's experiences. If we widen our focus beyond the everyday world of relationships, we then see that these human ways of being-in-relationship occur in, and because of, the context of an enduring and fundamental reality. This fundamental reality is one of relatedness, in which all things—past, present, and future—exist interdependently. It requires the craft of a poet, I think, to adequately express the concept I am trying to convey. The poet-philosopher Alfred North Whitehead devoted a great deal of his work to elucidating this concept. He boldly asserts, "Every actual entity in its relationship to other actual entities is in this sense somewhere in the continuum . . . But in another sense, it is everywhere throughout the continuum . . . the continuum is present in each actual entity and each actual entity pervades the continuum."[2]

I should also make explicit here that when I speak of this reality of relatedness—this unity of existence where wholeness, truth, and beauty abide—that it includes not only the good, but also evil, destruction, and decay.[3] Both lightness and darkness make up the day, our world, and any ultimate reality. I distinguish, then, between a world of relationships—intrapsychic, interpersonal, and symbolic—which occur in the temporal world of everyday human living, and the enduring, fundamental and ultimate reality of relatedness. These two worlds—the temporal world of relationships and the enduring world of relatedness—depend on each other. The everyday world of human relationships rests within this fundamental reality of relatedness, both reflecting it and adding to its continuing value.

Those of us living in the Western world, however, have been presented with a reality in which unnecessary and detrimental separation is made between entities that have an inherent relatedness or interdependence. Our world view is not of a reality of relatedness, but is one of distinctions. I am not, of course, the only or first person who has made this assertion. Feminist theologians, who trace the origins of a dualistic world view to patriarchy, have challenged this construction of reality, seeing the harm that comes from separating death from life, nature from culture, and body from spirit. It seems that the division of reality into polar opposites does not incur a separate but equal outcome. Instead, the side of the duality associated with femaleness—such as nature, darkness, and matter—becomes the other. As an alternative to seeing opposition and otherness, feminist religious writers propose that we understand the interdependence of all aspects of reality and the actuality of wholeness and unity.[4] Also, there are psychological theorists, such as Kegan, Noam, Lifton, and Rizzuto who, to different degrees, emphasize the importance of relationships in human development.[5] Their theoretical perspectives imply an acknowledgement of a fundamental reality of interdependency and relatedness.

A Metaphor for Relatedness

Continuing in the direction that feminist theologians and some psychological theorists suggest, I claim that the psychology of these ninety-four women implicitly requires a recognition of the integrity of existence and of a reality of relatedness. I have chosen *Women's Psyche, Women's Spirit: The Reality of Relationships* as the title and focus of this work to illustrate this central point of the unity of existence. I have chosen psyche and spirit, in particular, because as a psychologist I am concerned that the concept of the word "psyche," with its disconnection from spirit, has had its full value diminished. Psyche, also was known as soul, or spirit, that ineffable, intangible process that is the "breath of life." In fact, the word "psyche" comes from the Latin, which, in turn, derives from the Greek *psukhe,* meaning breath of life, or soul. The word "spirit," denoted as that unseen, vital principle or animating force within living beings, has its origins in the Latin, *spirare,* meaning to breathe, and its derivative, *spiritus,* or breath.[6]

In current usage, however, the concept of the word "psychology," whose roots are found in psyche, is associated with our mind, our thoughts, and, perhaps, our emotions. A psychologist studies mental processes and behavior. For the more biologically oriented psychologist, a definition of psyche can be further reduced to brain functions and chemicals, and for the behaviorist, only quantifiable and observable pieces of behavior comprise a definition of psychology. The definition of the American Psychological Association—"psychology is the science of behavior"[7]—illustrates the current trend in psychology to study only those phenomena that are available to objective methods. This position, of course, fails to consider spirit within a definition of psyche.

The actual meaning of psyche, however, has always embraced more than just those phenomena available to scientific scrutiny. By stripping the concept of the word "psyche" so that it refers only to that which can be objectively verified, we have suffered a loss of wholeness. When we remove spirit from psyche we expunge meaning from our lives. A concept of psyche that lends itself to scientific study may provide important facts, but we will know and understand less about the essential value of our existence and of our place in the universe. We may collect information, but we will never achieve wisdom.

I also chose *Women's Psyche, Women's Spirit: The Reality of Relationships* as a central theme because I understood that the interdependence of psyche and spirit also translates, as metaphor, into a more fundamental truth. The synonymy of psyche and spirit testifies to the relational actuality of our world. Not only are psyche and spirit interrelated and derived from a larger unity, but also, metaphorically, facts and value, knowledge and wisdom.[8]

The imperative to understand the actual and metaphorical relationship between psyche and spirit became poignantly apparent to me recently in a way it never had before, as I talked and grieved with a friend, Alice. Her sister, also a friend of mine, had just died a violent death. How, Alice wonders, can she accept the fact of her sister's absence from her life and at the same time maintain the value of her sister's existence? As Alice attempts to extract some meaning out of the horror and loss she is experiencing, she passionately longs to have more than thoughts and images of her sister. She wants more than psychological memory. Searching for words to describe her desire, Alice hopes that one day she will be able to sense her sister's presence, that she will be aware of her spirit.

Alice understands that the psychological memory of the facts of her sister's life—as a devoted daughter and aunt, loving sister, committed friend, creative artist, and contributing citizen—is not enough. She is reaching, I think, for an understanding of a genetic memory that would contain more than the sum total of the facts of her sister's existence, but also the value that she added to the world and that endures. Right now, Alice knows more than she can express, and this knowing arises out of her relationship with her sister, which, through the transformation of tragedy, implies a continued connection to her sister within a fundamental reality of relatedness. Alice is searching for a framework from which to articulate this knowledge that her sister's spirit, as value, continues and adds to our existence.

For both Alice and me, the tragedy of her sister's death gives a dramatic urgency to the need to comprehend a reality in which we understand the interrelationship of all that exists in our universe. Only by holding this view of a unified, interdependent life will it be possible to intellectually grasp, and emotionally experience, the mutual necessity that exists between the facts and value of an individual's life and, metaphorically, psyche and spirit. Without the facts, of course, there could be no value, and it is value of spirit that endures. Whitehead notes that: "The World of Value exhibits the essential unification of the universe . . . the immortal side . . . it also involves the unification of personality." The facts provide a structure to the value given, "saving it from the mere futility of abstract hypothesis."9 Conversely, facts depend on value. Mere facts, lacking any essentiality in the absence of value, would, like T. S. Eliot's "Hollow Men," be "shape without form, shade without colour/Paralysed force, gesture without motion."10 Facts and value, however, and, analogously, psyche and spirit, are never divorced from one another in actuality. It is only, I contend, our misperception that causes us to conclude that psyche without spirit, or facts without value, could be possible.

Alice's search for meaning in the context of her sister's death explains the need to acknowledge the indivisibility of a fundamental reality. Using the same philosophical stance, I would like to shift our attention from this fundamental and enduring reality to which I have been referring to a more focused examination of the temporal world of human living in relationships to examine some implications for the interpretation of psychological theory and practice.

A Dialogue: Relationships and Relatedness

I have tried to demonstrate that the significance of relationships for these women implies a fundamental reality of relatedness that is an essential fact of existence. I also have noted that the conceptual foundations of modern Western culture do not promote this view of reality. Instead, as Oliver has argued, a nonrelational personhood "conceived as subjectivity has been the prevailing paradigm of Western culture; individualism, its prevailing psychosocial manifestation."[11]

Psychological theory, of course, operates within this "prevailing paradigm." However, as I noted earlier, there are now a number of psychological theories that articulate an understanding of the importance of relationships in human development, and by implication the reality of relatedness. This was not always the case, however. For Freudian psychology the unit of study was the individual (with the notable exception of the triangular relationship of the oedipal period). It was Winnicott and other object relations theorists,[12] and then Kohut and other self theorists,[13] who shifted our attention from the individual to the relationship. Erikson then expanded the development context to include the psycho-social historical field.[14] Recent neo-Piagetian theorists, like Noam and Kegan,[15] maintain and further this understanding with their postulation that the process of development arises out of the dialogue between organism and environment, and by defining self as the subject-object relationship.

Those who have studied the psychology of women also have contributed to this change in focus. The discussion of a self-in-relation by Jean Baker Miller and others reminds us that we are formed through our relationships to others,[16] and the awareness we now have from Carol Gilligan about the interpersonal matrix of many women's lives also contributes to the shift from the individual only to the individual in relationship.[17] I do not agree, however, with their proposal that women have a greater orientation to relationships. Instead, I contend that to exist is to be in relationship, and to live in a fundamental reality of relatedness.

The feminist critique of psychology has made critical contributions to both theory and practice, and it has drawn needed attention to the importance of studying the lives of women. To assert, however, that women have a greater orientation toward relationships—and by implication that men are independent of relationships—is to use interpretative categories that mislead us and perpetuate a myth of individualism that distorts our human nature and detracts from all of us. The difference we find in women's and men's relationships are derived, I believe, from the conceptual foundations of Western culture that emphasize the individual apart from relationship and from a patriarchal political process by which some types of relationship are assigned higher status than others.

Both women and men live their lives in relationships; it is the *nature* of these relationships, and the style of being in relationship, that varies. Although we stereotypically (and falsely) assume that men are more independent of relationships than women, I suspect that the Western focus on individualism has been applied more to explain men's behavior and capacities, because men are the originators and heirs of modern Western culture. So the male in our culture, for the most part, is given the myth of the lone hero to live out. Some remnants of a relational understanding can be found in the ascription to women of dependency on relationships, and to the recognition that a nexus of interpersonal relationships structures many women's lives. Legitimacy and value, however, are given to the individual, apart from the relationship. Myths of individualism—whether propounded by mainstream thinking or by feminist writers who claim that females have a greater capacity for relationships, thereby implying a male tendency to stand apart from relationships—maintain the misrepresentation of a divided reality.

As a group, women and men do differ, of course, in the nature of their relationships, in their relationship style and, most significantly, in the value accorded to the types of relationships they enjoy. For example, we know from the observations of others, and from our own, that the care of others has been assigned to women. It is mostly women who raise the young, nurse the sick, tend to the old, and sit with the dying, whether at home as mothers, daughters, sisters, and wives, or at work as teachers and nurses. The societal task of maintaining private, intimate connections to others has been assigned almost exclusively to women.

Many men, of course, do care for others and show concern for their interpersonal relationships, although many would say: not enough! Men, more than women, however, tend to be oriented to other types of relationships, and in different ways. Men's relationships, more public in nature, carry a different set of compensations. The relationships that men enter typically receive greater financial reward, more recognition, and higher status. The world of women's relationships—found in the inner concentric circles of home and community—have a more private nature and less prestige. Even when women's private caretaking relationships are given a public function—secretary, teacher, nurse—they receive fewer rewards.[18]

Women and men differ not only in the private-public dimensions of their relationships, but also in their relationship style. Noam, who proposes two general styles of being in relationship, refers to one as relational and the other as boundary.[19] When using a relational style, the focus is on the establishment and maintenance of the tie with the other. In its pathological form, a relational orientation overvalues the other and loses self definition. (The danger found in the extremes of a relational style mimics the nature of women's sin, as defined by Saiving, i.e., self abnegation, the failure to take responsibility for self.)[20] The boundary style of relating, as its name implies, accentuates self-control and distance from the other. In extreme form, the boundary style of relating reflects a self "consumed with its own interests and wishes [that] ceases to orient to other except as they relate to the self's needs."[21] (Note, also, that the extremes of a boundary style parallel the description of the Christian conception of (male) sin as the "imperialistic will to power.")

Each of us uses both a relational and boundary style at different stages of our life, depending on the circumstances in which we find ourselves, our socialization, and individual predisposition. Although it has not been empiricaly demonstrated, it seems reasonable to observe that more women than men rely on a relational style of being-in-relationship, and more men than women depend on a boundary style of relating. One moves toward the other, the second moves away, distinguishing itself from the other. Both, however, are ways of being-a-self-in relation. Women and men, then, do not differ on the essential fact that both are being-in-relationship, and both live within an interdependent reality of relatedness. Where they differ is in how they live out their relationships, departing perhaps in which relationships they find more salient, in their style of being-in-relationship, and in the status, recognition, and compensations achieved by their relationships.

The Power of Our Vision

As I have talked about the types of our relationships in the daily world of individual human living, and of how they reflect a fundamental reality of relatedness, I have based my discussion on what I learned from the women of this study. By listening to them describe moments of seeking meaning in relationships, which I propose also indicates a larger, fundamental context of relatedness, I think we observed the potential of collective experience to reveal value and truth. The question is, what power shall decide truth: the power of the current world view, derived from the patriarchal origins of Western thought, which further separation and exclusion? Or will it be decided by the power of individuals, who, in the living of their ordinary lives, include all of us in the mythic quest to comprehend the unifying interdependence in which we all live. In this inclusive reality, we will understand that psyche and spirit both require and enrich one another—as do facts and value, and knowledge and wisdom. We also will be able to understand that this necessity for mutuality provides a beauty and wholeness not otherwise available. The question, or opportunity, that remains is how in the living of our lives with ourselves, with one another, and with the world, we can hold open our vision so that we can include all of us—and all of reality—within it.

Part II
Portraits of Six Women

Although the women's stories have much to teach us, too often we don't find out as much as we would like about who they are, what they think, and how they got to where they are now. So that we could become better acquainted with at least some of these ninety-four women, I asked six if they would consent to a taped, in-depth interview with me. All graciously agreed. I am indebted to each one of these women for her willingness to help and I continue to admire all for the courage it took to engage in a self-analysis that would become public.

The interviews were unstructured; mostly I tried to be guided by the natural flow of the conversation between us, and, as much as I could, to listen. As a psychologist, I was interested in their development, so I asked questions about their family and their childhood experiences. I also was interested in their current relationships. Mostly, however, I simply listened to these women tell me what was important in their lives, how they interpreted their experiences, and how they constructed meaning out of their world. My goal in interviewing them was to obtain at least a moment of understanding the phenomenology of their experience of the world and to gain some sense of how each constructed herself and her relationship to others, whether the other is an other in memory, a symbolic other, or an actual other in her life.

After the interviews were transcribed, I then organized each one into topic areas, deleting irrelevant or redundant material. Next I sent each of the six women a typed version of the interview with her. She then corrected it for factual errors, removed dialogue she thought might reveal her or a family member's identity, and sometimes added new information. In each case, I think, this review process improved not only the factual correctness of the interview, but also allowed clearer insights into each woman's character.

I chose these particular six women because I found their stories compelling. Some of their accounts are more dramatic than others, and they diverge from one another greatly in their philosophical orientations and their current resolutions of their relationships to the world. As a group of six women, however, they offer us, by their example, a vivid reminder that each woman, in her own way, is unique in how she chooses to live her life. At the same time, the portrait of each of these six women offers testimony to the unending human desire to transform experience, to create meaning and, in so doing, to construct self and our relationship to one another.

The portraits of six women, with all that they have to teach us about ourselves and of what it means to be human, are presented next. I tried to let the women speak for themselves, in their own words, as much as possible. Consequently, I did not use any psychological theories of self-development or of faith development to interpret their comments. I have tried to stand aside and let you meet each woman, drawing your own conclusions about how her life might instruct you on the human condition. Each has been given a fictitious name, chosen by her, to protect her particular identity.

Barbara
Reference: Views of Self pp. 42–43

Barbara, a minister with some psychological training, describes a series of formative relationships in her life. At the age of twelve, a minister's acceptance of her introduces her to religion in a new way. After that formative experience, she encounters a number of other people—charismatic teachers, hapless ministers, strong mountain women. She gives vivid accounts of how she uses her experiences with all of these people in her own development. Describing a process of integrating what she would call her feminine and masculine aspects, she has a continuing concern for the role of women in religion, as ministers and as the ministered.

Barbara lives with her husband, also a minister, and their young son in a suburb of a city in the mid–Atlantic region. In her current ministry, she works mostly with young people, and is involved in women's issues, peace issues, and her own writing.

A Childhood of Narcissistic Abuse

Barbara and I began the discussion by noting our common interest and training. Since I am a psychologist and practicing clinician and Barbara has had a great deal of psychological training, we agreed that our interview would focus on psychological issues. Within this context, Barbara began by explaining that, as she worked with the young people in her ministry, she saw that they displayed profound self-alienation, that they had narcissistic disturbances. And as she cried with them, she realized that she felt their pain because she, too, was narcissistically disturbed.

I've had several years of therapy because as a child I was narcissistically "abused" by my parents. This means that they lacked understanding and empathy for my emotional needs. Consequently, as my needs weren't met, I shut down on my own awareness of my needs. I don't remember my childhood . . . My first real memories of life came from my experiences in a church youth group when I encountered a pastor who unconditionally accepted me and hugged me a lot. And I was born anew to myself, as well as to God. I remember how the group would gather in the chapel for a meditation period before going down to dinner. I vividly recall sitting there on my knees praying in front of slides of Jesus that would flash on a screen. I just really got into that. I would be the last to trail down to dinner. But more importantly I remember my relationships with the kids and the leaders of the youth group. Before that I recall only snippets of things and places, but no people—no relationships.

I tell Barbara I am impressed by her lack of memory for her early childhood. As we talk about this, she associates having no clear memory of the first twelve years of her life because of a series of losses she suffered as a child.

I had approximately eleven major losses of family pets and friends and relatives through death, about one each year. My grief for each loss remained unresolved. My parents were the self-appointed caretakers for our entire extended family system and were too busy to attend to my grief, or *any* of my emotions at all for that matter. I don't expect to get my childhood back. My current growth stems from my mourning the loss of the vitality of my *own* life in the midst of all the other losses.

If you'd asked me three years ago, "How was your childhood?" I'd have said, "Normal as possible . . . just like anybody else's." I didn't realize that most people remember large portions of their childhood. I just assumed everyone forgot their childhood. A few years ago as I started gathering data from other family members, I was awestruck by the number of violent events which went on around me—family violence—that I didn't even know about. My father's sister and her husband both died early deaths. They say my uncle "killed" his wife. He was an alcoholic, so I don't know what that means. They left two chil-

dren and my paternal grandmother for my parents to take care
of. My grandmother moved in with us and took over my bedroom until she died. My parents slept on the couch in the living
room. Throughout it all, my parents were basically saying
"None of this is unusual. We're a normal family." The image
was important to them.

I ask Barbara to tell me more about her mother and father, to
describe their relationship, their background, whatever she found
important.

My father is quite elderly and has a Victorian men-
tality . . . He lives with a lot of guilt about the fact that he left his
first wife back in the days when people just didn't divorce. But I
found out that he hung in almost twenty years with a woman
who had a violent temper. She abused him, but he stayed because of their children—only leaving when, I believe, his father
died. My father can't really talk about his life. My mother has
been the one to fill in a lot of details. Everything seems to be a bit
mythological. Fact and image-protecting fantasies are always
mixed. It's hard to tell which of my parents is more "stunted" in
terms of their own narcissistic injury; both of them are extremely
emotionally infantile. They are totally dependent on each other
right now. One can't go out of the house without the other.
They probably have always been symbiotic. Their overinvolve-
ment with each other may be part of the reason they took little
notice of me. It's rather confusing.

Together they make one "normal" entity. Because of
my father's "woundedness," my masculine personality traits are
my mother's, not my father's. When I've tried to draw pictures of
my masculine archetype they look just like my mother. It's
interesting . . . he's a Greek male in a toga, but he has a face like
my mother's. My mother always was a "tomboy." Her father
wanted her to be a male. She was the family protector after her
father's violent death in the line of duty as a police officer. She
was the savior, she was the strong one. She saved my father from
his first marriage, sort of. And his pain . . . she wanted to protect
him. He was sensitive . . . a musician and highly intuitive.

Shortly after my parents were married my father had
a premonition that my mother shouldn't take a particular flight

to New York. He asked her to take the train. She did, and that night while on the train, she had a dream that her best friend was burning to death. In fact, the plane had crashed. All her friends—all the buyers for the store for which she worked—were killed.

Our conversation turns to Barbara's mother. I ask Barbara about her mother's professional life. Barbara notes that her mother had the potential to be "quite a good executive." She handled people and liked to play with power a lot, but soon after the plane crash she quit her career." Barbara then begins to discuss some of the consequences for her of her mother's retirement from a career.

> I recently said to my mother, "Where do you suppose all that went when you stayed home and just had me? What did you do with all that power?" When I suggested I might have gotten a bit too much of her power manipulations, she admitted "Yeah, I suppose you did." She focused everything on me, except for empathy and emotional responsiveness.
> My mother, being obsessed with appearances, thoughtlessly berated me. For example, she took pictures of me from the back to show me how ugly I was in pants, so I'd never wear them. But, of course, I did . . . to this day I am more than a little bit self-conscious about it. But what I guess was sick about it, in my opinion, was the fact that she could tear me down but never said go get some exercise. It was just, "You're ugly, and you've got to hide it." I really have to work at what I'm going to make of myself now. I'm still a fairly sedentary person, but I've joined a spa and I work out. It's very difficult, but very important to me to do it.

I ask Barbara how close she felt to her mother while growing up. She gives some vivid examples of her relationship with both of her parents during her adolescence.

> I basically thought Mom and I were buddies, you know. The few times I had encounters with boys, I talked to her about them in detail. I went to a party once where there was a disgusting kissing contest. My date was a football player with braces on his teeth. And I told her everything . . . I had no secrets from her. But throughout my adolescence I was put on a pedestal. I might as well have been a mannequin in a store window to

be dressed at my mother's whim. My father also put me on a pedestal. He wouldn't let me wear make-up because only "whores" wore make-up. I was my father's untouched and untouchable "angel."

Early Religious Experiences: Dream Images and the Church

Our conversation shifts from a focus on Barbara's relationship with her parents and their influences on her to the development of Barbara's religious imagination. Here again, though, we see her parent's influence. Barbara's father figures prominently in a recurring childhood dream she has, which she identifies as an important religious experience.

Religiously, the one thing I do remember from my childhood is a dream that I had. It was a repetitive dream and it gradually became a "half-waking" dream. The image is saving my father—or some male figure—hung on a tree. I had to cut him down before he died, soothe his head, clean him off, and take care of him. I don't remember how old I was exactly when I first had it, but I almost looked forward to going to bed at night to be able to dream it. Over the years, various figures—movie stars—took the place of the father figure. But the point of it seems to me that maybe by going into the ministry I was somehow trying to save my father. As it turns out, I *have* been a mediatrix, spiritual guide for a number of men, but I've never been able to redeem my relationship with my father . . . or the lack thereof.

I ask Barbara about her experiences with church while growing up. She talks about the church she attended that became so important to her at the age of twelve, when its pastor unconditionally accepted her. She then describes how she lost this critical base of support.

The church where my parents sent me was convenient. It was a very liberal church, and I don't think they realized it. Its teachings really conflicted with their superstitious, quasi-Victorian conservative faith. And again I think that's why the church was so freeing for me. So it became my enclave—my escape. I went there several times a week in junior high. When I was in seventh grade, actually at the beginning of seventh grade, my parents and I were in a car accident, in which we were almost killed. My father never drove again, and by the end of that year they had determined they were going to leave the area. They wouldn't go through that intersection again. They didn't want to face all of the fear that they had. The ensuing move to the West Coast was probably the most "memorably" unhappy event of my school years because I had just found this church group. I even was dating a guy in the fellowship . . . having a fairly normal sexual beginning, and all of it was cut right off. Strangely enough, when they were choosing a new church . . . my parents chose a very conservative church. It was a small, struggling blue-collar church, with a very fire and brimstone type of pastor. And they had to drive quite a ways to go there—out of our own social, economic area. They were running scared and they wanted to pay their dues. We had spent the previous summer touring abroad and I recall a suspicion in the air that we hadn't prayed enough on the trip . . . and that's why we had the car accident. It was our punishment.

I ask Barbara how she adapted to the new, and different, church. She describes how her religious development occurs, almost in spite of the church.

I automatically became the leader of the youth group—and my parents became very active in the church. Because it was small, it needed us. And I felt very displaced with both the conservative style as well as the whole group of kids who weren't intellectual at all. I was quickly becoming a bookworm, and retreating into intellectual stimulation.

But somehow my religion persisted in a rather tormented personal faith. I recall spending hours crying at night and praying for the hungry, the sick, and the homeless people in the world. I remember at some point during those high school years offering myself to God, saying "If what you want is for me to walk across the street and get hit by a truck, I'll do it, if it would bring one more soul to Christ." My only important relationship was with God.

       I didn't date again until my senior year in high school . . . and then the one fellow I dated was a cynic who assumed that I used him just to go to the prom, so he dropped me right after that. Jesus was really my lover in high school. That was what I call my "St. Teresa phase." While I don't think I felt orgasmic, I felt quite swept off my feet by my religious experiences. I dialogued with Jesus a lot. And curiously enough, the one place that I found integration of my body with my mind and spirit was through modern dance. Dance has remained a primary mode of religious expression for me.

By high school, Barbara stopped going to church. Dance, however, remained important in her life.

       Except for modern dance, high school was a bummer . . . just a place to achieve good grades and membership in the right service clubs, so I could get into a good college. My parent's church folded down after they kicked out the pastor . . . and my folks didn't go anywhere. I didn't go to church when I was in college either, because my religion professor became my minister and mentor.

College, Seminary, and More Significant Relationships

Barbara and I then begin talking about her experiences in college and, later, the seminary. Just as the pastor in her church when she was twelve years old had a significant influence on her development, Barbara recalls other women and men throughout her life who contributed to her formation. She met one of these men, whom she describes as one of her mentors, in college. His charismatic personality attracted a following wherever he was. Barbara tells me of some specific example of his Charismatic influence on her, which is profound, with both negative as well as positive aspects.

       He was flaunting himself, using the women students as an audience . . . and I called him on it. And I said, "Look, you're supposed to be teaching religion. You say you're here as a minister and that this is the gospel for you." I said, "How do you feel about the fact that half the women that are here in your class are here 'cause they think you're sexy, and you've got bedroom eyes, which you use to undress them all the time?" Probably half unconsciously, he "psychologically" attacked me for the entire school year. Eventually, I felt I was bordering on suicide because he had just driven me to acute despair. He brought God and my academic performance into it. My study of the New Testament was exciting but confusing to me and I had many questions. Basically . . . he came back at me with the Socratic method of asking me a question for every question I asked him. And I asked him all the big questions of my faith. I laid my faith in his hands, and he didn't handle it (or me) very well. So I hauled him into the dean, who we called "The Great White Mother." She was my first female protectress . . . and I love her for it to this day. I said, "I'm suicidal, and he's the reason." She brought him in and said "What the hell are you doing this for?" He said, "I am trying to teach her the theology of the cross. Her faith is too Johannine (doubting)." He didn't know what he was asking of me when he wanted me to face suffering—my own or Jesus. After that, he walked me around campus and told me, "Oh, you can do anything you want. You know I love you. You know I care about you. You know I wouldn't want to hurt you." The words were not really believable. I most vividly recall the consolation given me that night as I read two "dark night of the soul" poems given me by the dean.

I am struck by the psychological pressure from this professor that Barbara had to withstand, and her ability to handle it at a young age. I comment that he sounds quite horrible, to use his authority in such a way. Barbara is able to sort out his strengths and weaknesses. Even though he treated her unfairly, she also remembers that in other ways he was a good teacher.

My relationship with him was a mixed blessing. He was emotionally immature and psychologically ignorant, but he took my mind quite seriously. He'd spend hours and hours with his students after class. And the wisdom of the cross did become clear to me through his courses in the Pauline gospels. The concept of Christian is "freedom," which is the main thing in Paul that turned me on. In Galatians, the word freedom, you know, involves transcending the forces that are pulling in different directions inside of you, and by opening to the love of Christ . . . which accepts and transcends them.

When my mentor left at the end of my sophomore year, I went into psychology as a second major. I started to study James, Freud, and Jung on religion . . . moral development in children and social psychology and all that kind of stuff and then did a thesis, a "double" thesis, on psychology and religion.

As we shall soon see, she crossed paths with this "mixed blessing" of a mentor again. Meanwhile, after he left, she became engaged in writing her thesis, working with a woman who came to mean a lot to her.

I think my identification with the woman I worked with on my thesis became important to me because she lived alone in a gorgeous house in the mountains. At that time I thought, "Why in God's name would anyone want to live alone in the mountains?" And now she's a very powerful image for me . . . I want to be *able* to live like that. Not that I'm going to leave my husband tomorrow and go do it, but if he dies or I end up alone in life, I want to be like that. That's a symbol for my liberation. So you see, my college years were a time of real probing, working a lot against my environment, with some kind of critical eye to it.

I observe that a number of relationships seem to have played a distinct and formative role in Barbara's life. Also, noteworthy to me is that Barbara seems aware of their significance, not only now, but also at the time. Barbara begins talking about another crucial relationship. She describes becoming reacquainted with, and then marrying her first husband.

Just before my professor left, I reengaged in conversation with the fellow who had dumped me after my senior prom. He happened to be at a college near to mine. I found him in a pit of isolation and hatred (self-hatred and other hatred). He was walking around with his hands in fists . . . and I had to "save" him. And I basically did. I married him the day after my graduation. It was like an exercise in exorcism that I performed on him. One day I said, "I will marry you only if you become a Christian." He shook and shook and shook and cried for hours and said, "Yes, I'll become a Christian." Stupid me. But he still is a Christian; he's very active in the church. He had not been loved in his family . . . He knew nothing of love, and now I realize I knew precious little more about it, but in the relationship I moved out and away from both my mother and my mentor. Our "love" was the clinging of children to their teddy bears—as transitional objects away from destructive mothers.

She moved to another part of the state so that her husband can go to graduate school, and she began working as program director of a women's organization. Here, again, she engaged a woman who is the head of the board, who strangely enough also lived alone in a gorgeous house in the mountains. I express my amazement, not only about the similarity between this woman and her thesis adviser, but also by the prominence of relationships in Barbara's development. Barbara describes this woman as a "wise woman and a Jungian," who calls her attention to the beauty of her inner journey toward individuation. Barbara remembers, "I began to keep a journal and record my dreams because of her influence." Then Barbara's thoughts turn to another relationship, the return of her mentor into her life.

> Here's the strange thing. Within that year, my mentor was hired at the university where my husband was studying. His arrival signaled the end of my marriage. He raised a lot of hatred among the women at the university and I found myself constantly interceding to smooth over the waters. The minute he got there, he kicked the representative of the gay student union out of a meeting and said, "You are not welcome." I educated him about local attitudes and politics and suggested a course of reconcilitory action. Then he started worshiping me as a "wisdom giver" and a colleague. I suppose when he called me a "wise woman" that he gave me the status I always wanted with my father. At the end of the year I left and went to seminary, with renewed zeal for my "call" to serve God in some special way. But in the process of this I lost touch with my husband. My mentor's style of Christian freedom was still a little on the "wild

side" . . . immature . . . and my seminary associates were of the
same ilk. I enjoyed the company of several "counter-culture"
Christians. My husband's corporate success values changed with
those of my new found friends, among whom were, for the first
time, feminists.

Barbara explains that she continued with her seminary studies and
then, shortly after her divorce, meets another man who also
influences her life. I ask her if this is the man she describes in her
spiritual experience, who refused to accept the power she was
projecting onto him. She says he is, and talks about what he was
like.

I met this fellow who basically had the same intro-
verted personality as my father and I was intensely drawn to him.
Fortunately, he was a feminist and had at hand a certain amount
of psychological knowledge gained from recent Jungian analysis.
He was probably the first man in my life who didn't use me to
bolster his ego. While he continuted to dialogue with me as a
friend, he kept me at a distance physically. This puzzled me, but
gave me a chance to turn inward and study his presence in my
psyche over and above his presence externally. It turned out he
was impotent with me, which he didn't tell me until the end of
the relationship. He'd just come out of divorce, and I reminded
him of his wife . . . So there was probably some ambivalence in
him but it worked for my purposes. For two years he basically let
the projection hold until I managed to grow out of it. It ended
when I had a dream one night where I walked into a cemetery
with him and sat down and wrote in my journal. He kept walking further into the cemetery. After I wrote awhile, I looked up
and called for him, and my father walked out. It became very
clear to me then, how creative it is to be held by someone, but at
a slight distance. But to do so requires a strength of self which is
rare. It is my observation that women seem to be more aware of
the search for self and its importance. We women who are
finding our "selves" must learn to hold each other as a community.

We begin to talk about the importance of feminism in our lives;
we mention the names of the different women whose work we
have read, or whom we have met, who have guided our thinking.

My feminist consciousness started burgeoning and I was thrown into a group of fairly radical women. There were lesbian women who were going to be ministers to the gay community, and there were bisexual women who were involved in the "liberation church" on the campus. As a Jungian, I found myself in a more conservative place than most of them, but I took it all in, and I feel a certain solidarity with them now. And we have some really great "published" women from that area—creative, bold, older women . . . great role models.

Next Barbara begins to recall the next phase in her life. She describes a time spent living in a desert community, where she spent much of the time alone, in "a kind of strange, desert spirituality . . . beginning to get a sense of God in nature." While there she remembered two people who have significance for her life then. One is a retiring male pastor who gets her in touch with her artistic side, the other is a strong business woman who is an elder in the church. After her desert experience Barbara returned to the seminary where she has, as she describes it, some "strange" religious experiences as a chaplain in a women's prison. She tells me she had experienced speaking in tongues earlier and now she uses this gift again with her prison ministry. Interested, I ask her to tell me more about this.

I was supervising this Charismatic prayer group when one of the women, who had been a member of a notorious cult, kind of went into an extreme fit because they were praying for the children that they had to leave "on the outside." She just started crying and screaming . . . and she shouted, "God, give me your peace." And she fell on the ground. I walked up to her with the leader of the group. We laid our hands on her and started praying in tongues. God gave the "Charismatic prophecy," the wisdom of which is fairly obvious if you think about it: "My daughter, you already have my peace." Then she "swooned" in my arms, and when she got up, she was composed and quiet. Afterwards she was very sweet and loving to me. But one day she abruptly broke off her relationship with me, saying, "I know you've been divorced. Go back to your husband. This is a sin." Apparently, she had been engaged to be married but some "outside" pastor told her that it was a sin to marry because he had been divorced . . . she would be committing adultery. Oh these poor weak-egoed women. She had no ego. She just bounced between male authority figures.

I'm still entranced by the phenomena of speaking in tongues, and I ask Barbara to help me understand what that is about.

> I see speaking in tongues as something probably to do with the brain or the "collective unconscious" bubbling through and circumventing channels of cognitive awareness. But to me it doesn't need to be explained. [Referring to her fellow ministers, she says:] Most of them ignore it . . . think it'll go away. That's when it becomes divisive. Again, I think that the reason a lot more women are involved in this is because it circumvents other modes of authority. And I suspect it did in the early church too. We can't measure it. We don't have evidence. But I'm sure . . . it was there as a vital force which was squelched because in the end it was threatening to the developing patriarchy of the church.

After the Seminary: Marriage, Motherhood, and Ministry

Feeling we have explored her early development as completely as time allows, we begin talking about her more recent experiences. Barbara recalls her first position after the seminary.

> It was a bomb. It was a complete wipe-out . . . only lasting three months. The pastor treated me like a child. I consulted with his actual daughter and found that she had never done *anything* except what he said because "He had a weak ego." And I said, "Have you ever told him that he has a weak ego and that you never disagreed with him because you didn't think he could stand it?" When she said, "No," I knew then and there that I had to tell him. I told him; and I quit. Living with my own weak-egoed father had been enough for me of that sort of thing. After I submitted my resignation, he came to me with tears in his eyes and said, "If what you say to me is true, I shouldn't be in the parish ministry." And he got out of parish ministry within a couple of years. Is such a thing being "prophetic" or "wise?" I don't know. I only knew I couldn't keep my mouth shut!

So, I taught religion in a Catholic high school for a year. I really came into contact with religious women for the first time there . . . to know what that meant. I shared pretty heavily the experience of one woman who had just left the convent, and was coming out as a lesbian. She had left her lover behind, because she couldn't make up her mind whether to come out of the convent or not. That's one side of the whole Catholic religious scene I had not imagined. I've learned a lot more about it since. It's not the homosexuality, but the acquiescence to authority that I don't understand. But I survived [that year] pretty well and got married in the middle of it.

When I met my husband he was living in a student house in the middle of an orange grove. He had nothing but a mattress and an orange crate to his name. He was getting his Ph.D. Basically he was really mellow, combining many contrasting images and values. He really admired my mind and yet was sensitive to my tender heart. He saw the best in me and wanted to give more than he took. I ate it up. I also was aware of how he treated his dog. I was interviewed in a newspaper recently here and they put that in the article, right at the front—that I chose to marry him because I saw how well he treated his dog and I wanted to be a mother. The summer after my prison ministry I'd been to a workshop where I'd discovered through a dream that I wanted to be a mother. And I had basically started looking around for men who were nurturing and would be good fathers. My husband's an excellent father and a really nurturing man.

We begin to talk about their life together. Shortly after their marriage, when they both had a chance to go to the mountains to do a youth ministry for the summer, Barbara describes a moment when she was looking down from the mountain at the smog where she lived. She thought:

This is crazy. I'm not that masochistic. I'm not going to live down there. So I just quit my job at the high school and we headed out for Arizona. We each took church jobs and [Tom] proceeded to fill ordination requirements after his Ph.D. We found a church, we found a house and got a baby. [Tom] picked up on some of my duties when I was pregnant, but I did most of them. We were looking for a joint ministry after the baby. We found jobs that were separate, but which allowed us to work together in ministry informally.

I ask Barbara what it was like for her to be a minister, and a mother.

>My spiritual life as a mother? Now that I know that I was narcissistically abused, I wonder how much of it I unconsciously passed along to my child. But when I had my child in my arms and was in the church working—either attending board meetings and sitting there nursing the baby—that first year I felt uniquely content and fulfilled. Someone told me afterward, "Well, don't you realize, you are a madonna." The madonna image transcends the whore and virgin. That's a middle image. And that's what I was enacting and so I was more acceptable. Indeed, people viewed me as the madonna with the child, even though I was baring my breast. It was an asexual experience. I wasn't the subject of "dirty old men" type of comments. It was a unique time in my life, and I look back on it longingly. I would like to have another child.

The Philosophy of Sophia and Barbara's Continuing Development

We realize that the time to end the interview is closing in, and Barbara begins to talk about a book she is working on about Sophia, Goddess of Wisdom. She describes how she now sees that this interest of hers came to her through her problematic mentor. Unbeknown to her, he was writing a book on the wisdom tradition in the Bible as he taught courses in other subjects. Only later does she realize his work on wisdom laid the foundation for her own work.

>He gave me the book. I started reading it and started seeing, basically, he was making the correlation between the Son of Man—which is a concept applied to Jesus—and God's wisdom, Sophia. That was the leaping off point for me intellectually for all the other work that I have done since then. Other scholars

have since validated the presence of a Sophia Christology or Sophiaology in the theology of the earliest Christian community.

Sophia of wisdom metaphors, parables, symbols, and sign-actions . . . potentially including mime and dance . . . sets up a new structure . . . a new reality of "grace-full" existence by aesthetically breaking through, or reversing, conventional expectations. I myself experienced that structure as the radical openness of opportunity to explore and to be my true, deeply hidden self. The primary truth that Sophia speaks is that the text alone is not the vehicle for conversion into freedom. The truth must be incarnated in the lives of wisdom givers who mediate the world of grace through intentionally open, nonassuming, and authentic structures of caring. Intimacy is not as much required as empathy. Sophia speaks her truth in the unique revelation of God found in each individual's life.

But I don't want to outline my book here. I think what I'm saying is that God's wisdom has been with me from the beginning. She was with me during my childhood, preserving in the darkness the seed of my fragile true self. And now she gives me light and life . . . she nurtures me everyday . . . as I now struggle to send out roots and leaves . . . someday to blossom in wisdom's beauty. I have a certain trust that God is ultimately this creative process, bringing harmony and beauty to life amidst the worst discord and ugliness. It is important to me that my sense of self has been gained through pastoral counseling . . . in response to my facing the void . . . the dark, terrible emptiness of my being, naming and accepting it. All my years of psychological and spiritual ladder climbing were to no avail without it. My mentor was right about my need to learn the theology of the cross. I understand the Light of God's truth so much more now that Sophia has shown me the true darkness within me . . . and, she, incarnate in the person of my female pastoral counselor, has stood by me and helped me to name it. I can only hope to continue to be in dialogue with this process . . . and for this I believe I must always search out a community of Sophia sisters . . . and brothers.

I note that Barbara has been through considerable self-examination. She begins to speak of her current work in her continuous search of self-awareness.

I feel radically open, yet structured, like a good parable, to God's wisdom. I feel patient to see what unfolds in my life. So many of my expectations have been reversed. I trust the "deep mystery" within me. I simmer before I get out of bed . . . I sort of percolate intentionally before I get out of bed, and also when I go to bed at night. And I am chanting daily. I am slowly finding a new authenticity to my values and commitments. While my consciousness of sinning is increased, I am not guilt-ridden. And even when I sin, I do it with a positive consciousness of God's wisdom being with me. I say "sin" boldly, knowing that my past "goodness" was only a facade . . . a false image of self-righteousness inherited from narcissistic parents. But I have a sense that slowly, but surely, there will be integration even as I sin, because there always has been in the past.

My happiest moments these days are spent singing and chanting . . . my voice teacher integrates vocal instruction with spiritual direction. We're doing the 23rd Psalm, which I have changed to, "she leads me beside the still waters." Anyway, as I sang it yesterday, it was one of the most integrated experiences I've had with her. At first she asked me to get my soft palate relaxed and that took me months. Now I can often get this open, connected, deep tone that resonates an "earth Mother" sound. As I approach each phrase, she stops me and says, "Now feel what this is saying. You're singing Sophia's praise." This is really making me be what I believe . . . to not push on each phrase, and not come at it too hard because as I do, then there's a withdrawal and a self-defeating push in my throat that closes off the sound.

We end our conversation by once again talking about the importance of women getting together with one another, of helping one another search for our own meaning in life.

Because of my need for maternal nurturing . . . I need to be with women more. I want to learn significant ways to mediate spiritual growth to and with women—and not just men. I would like to figure out what evil is . . . both in my own life and in terms of a general pattern for women. Certainly evil has been in and around my life. I'd like to figure out the evils of narcissism in family systems and in institutions such as the church.

Emily
Reference: The Interpersonal Event pp. 61–62

From the age of four, Emily came to realize that the direction of her life must be found within herself. This lesson was learned as she perservered through many difficulties while growing up. Her family suffered financial reversals, which contributed to her mother's problems with alcohol and her parents' estrangement from each other, and at age seven Emily spent a year in bed with tuberculosis. She was able to transform these experiences, however, and gain something of value.

Emily's father was a businessman, and her mother, a housewife, came from a socialite background. Her paternal grandmother, with whom she was close, lived with her family until her death, when Emily was four years old. She also has two sisters; one sister, who has died, was four years older and the other sister is eight years older. Today, Emily lives in a quiet suburban community with her husband, a teenage daughter, who is a senior in high school, and a fifteen-year-old son. She teaches chemistry in a private high school and actively participates in refugee resettlement.

Early Experiences with Grandmother, Church, and God

I begin the interview by asking Emily who influenced her religious development. Emily first thinks of her grandmother. Although Emily has only a dim memory of her grandmother who died when she was four years old, she has a clear understanding of her formative influence on her development. Realizing that she acquired many of her values and attitudes from her grandmother, Emily remembers:

> I've been thinking about what I was going to say to you . . . but one thing that really had an effect on me is my grandmother. She only lived until I was four, but she lived with us until then. She was a very religious person. She was a Christian Scientist and she read to me daily from the book of *Science and Health*. Of course, I don't remember much about it, because I was only four, but I do remember her warmth, the fact that she always looked after me, read to me, and cared about that kind of growth in me. Somehow I think that all took hold. Even though it was only till I was four.
>
> I don't remember how much I actually learned from my grandmother about the Christian Science religion as opposed to what I realized later when I went to the Christian Science Church. The Christian Science Church was in some respects like a Quaker meeting in the sense that the individual approach was very important, what the individual saw of God . . . You had to find your way—having confidence in yourself. A silly thing I remember—typical of the child—was that if you lost something, you were supposed to sit down and really concentrate on it, so that an image of its locations would come to you. Well, I used to try it. Whether I thoroughly believed in that method is another matter. I often tried it, as a first attempt, even now sometimes. The idea that stuck with me at that early age was the importance of trusting yourself. My father had a tremendous respect for his mother. That helped to make me value my grandmother's guidance long after she was dead. And so I went to the Christian Science Church when I was little. It was the closest church to our home, and you could walk to it. I think Dad was pleased when we went to church . . . although I can't remember him talking about it.

After her grandmother died, Emily was the only member of her family who attended church. Her parents and oldest sister stayed at home, and her other sister strayed, finding the local drugstore more interesting than church.

> I never saw my parents go to church except for a funeral or wedding or when we were being tourists. It always

amazes me that attending church became important to me when it wasn't to them.

> Dad never talked about religion, but he had a strong sense of right and wrong, which he tried to transmit to us. My mother was driven more by love than sense of duty, or right or wrong. This made her charming, impetuous, sometimes irresponsbile, and often unpredictable. One thing really good about my mother was that she was never prejudiced, although my parents didn't have Jewish friends. That was something that I wondered about. There were never negative remarks about other groups of people—not even blacks. Of course, that was in an era when people never associated outside their own type of people. I must say that I never heard my parents make any negative remarks about any groups—which I have always been grateful for. Not that they jumped to the defense of any group if the topic came up; they didn't necessarily do that. But, they were never negative.

Our conversation shifts to the times, as a child, that Emily and her sister would walk to the Christian Science church near their home. I ask Emily about her sister's interest in religion. Emily talks about her older sister's lack of enthusiasm for religion, which was evidenced in childhood.

> She was a complete atheist right from the beginning. Why she became so firm about this at such an early age I never understood. She was always cynical. She cared very much about justice and became a social worker later in her life. She was very moral, but had little inner peace. She was supposed to go to church with me and rarely did . . . she would often walk with me to church, but then she went on to the drugstore to read comic books. She would go to the drugstore, and use her money that she was supposed to donate at collection time for comic books . . . she was a very honest person. It was not in her character to be sneaky like that. I think she didn't want to displease my parents by revealing to them that she thought going to church "was for the birds."

Emily continues to talk about her sister.

> She had a very strong conscience . . . she was a philosophy major in college but she was a die-hard atheist until she

died—about four or five years ago—of cancer. I saw her mellowing that last year. We lived 3,000 miles away from each other at that point, so our discussions on religion were few. But she made some comments in that last year that implied she was not so certain of atheism. And she developed an inner peace that made the process of her dying over that year seem beautiful.

I remark that for some reason the idea of religion seems to have left an enduring impression on Emily, even when it was rejected by her older sister. I ask Emily about what her religious ideas were as a young child. She remembers these early ideas about God and religion.

> I always had trouble with the concept of God being the creator. I even have trouble with the concept of God . . . even today. I loved the humbleness of Christianity. That really appealed to me . . . the fact that Christ went and helped every person, no matter what their station in life. I always thought it was important and I loved that aspect of Christianity. I guess I always had my sister nagging at me, saying, "You don't believe that." I don't know if I am just remembering how I thought in college or in high school. I can't remember for sure how I thought way back then. What I am sure of was that the quest— the search—was always important to me.

Parents' Lessons About Life

Emily talks about her mother and father, and as she does, she recognizes both their strengths and weaknesses. We begin to talk about the spiritual experience Emily chose to report on as memorable, which was based on her relationship with her mother. I remark to Emily that I continue to admire her capacity to convert some of her parents' inadequacies into lessons for her own life. She achieves some balance so she can still appreciate her parents' positive qualities. Emily begins to talk about her mother's and father's backgrounds, which she describes as being very different from each other's.

My father came from an entirely different background from my mother. I feel mother's background was superficial, whereas father's background was different. He was very plain, hard-working, serious, very honest, not very exciting and charming like my mother was. The problem was that Mother had been brought up in this very elegant way of living and she handled that beautifully, but she had not been prepared to live another kind of life. She was forced into it at a rather late time. Unfortunately, her background was such that she wasn't given other kinds of values that would have helped sustain herself in what appeared to her as troubled times.

First of all, she just didn't know how to handle money. Money was something you played around with. As soon as you had some, you used it for something fun. She became more responsible after Dad died, but then so much had been lost. She could have taken what wasn't a hard situation financially, made ends meet, and helped Dad, but her background stressed home decor, culture, entertainment, foreign travel, socializing. That is where a large part of her money went. She had inherited a lot of money. It was her money, but Dad's business really could have used it as it was faltering. Mom rarely saw the need of adjusting her life style to circumstances. I was aware of the fact that her values made her ill-equipped. She often told stories of the elegant things that her parents had done. The stories embarrassed me. For example, her father and uncle belonged to hunt clubs. They bragged about the number of birds they killed in a day.

My parents' honeymoon also embarrassed me. They traveled around the world for a year and a half. My mother took twenty-one pieces of luggage! It was incredibly excessive. Have you ever read the books by P. G. Wodehouse? Well, my mother was a "Bertie Wooster" of sorts. She also was a lively, charming person—really quite a lot of fun. She had a spark about her. It's hard for me to describe it. She had interesting ideas. She loved to read and discuss things and was always game to try something new, even if she couldn't afford it.

And my father was a good person. He wouldn't do anything that he didn't feel was right, honest, and fair to people. Sometimes he lost advantages in business transactions, just because he insisted on doing what was "proper," the fair way, and all that . . . when even the values of the day would have allowed him to bend a little. In a way it was helpful to have parents that were so different from each other. I could see how both types of personalities had advantages.

After Emily referred to her family's tough financial times, I ask her to describe in detail how her family's financial hardships came about and how it affected them. She explains that her family suffered a financial reversal when her father's business failed, about the time she was in the fifth grade. It was at this time that her mother developed a drinking problem.

It was all very gradual. At first everything was fine. It's just that Dad overextended himself in developing the cranberry bogs in Wisconsin—just at the end of World War II. Cranberries had been a "war crop." Cranberry growers had been highly supported by the government during the war. Dad lost that support at the very time he was expanding his business. When I was about in fifth grade I first became aware of the change in our financial situation. We bottomed out by the time I was a sophomore or junior in high school. According to my mother, it was certainly drastic. Now looking back on it, and being exposed to people like refugees, I think, how could I bother even complaining about it. It was nothing.

We had to sell our house. We didn't have much left compared to what we had. We always had food. There wasn't any money particularly to buy clothes or anything like that . . . just the basics. One thing, though, I still continued to go to private school. It was very hard for my parents to send me. You see, I shouldn't complain about it. I shouldn't mention a reversal. I always had the feeling that my parents were tremendously in debt, however, because the creditors would often call us. My father didn't want me to go to private schools. He thought it was silly. But my mother had social aspirations for us. She insisted on us going to private schools. Then we were living in Chicago and the public schools were very rough, even then. My mother, just to be honest, was an intellectual person in many ways. She wanted us to have a good education. My father I don't think was so intellectual. He valued hard work and being honest. "If you can't afford something, don't pretend you can." They were separated by the time I was in junior high school. It wasn't a formal separation, but Dad spent most of his time up in Wisconsin tending the bogs and Mother would go up over the summer for a month. In the winter we—just Mom and myself—stayed in Chicago, so that I could go to school. When I was in college, they had to get back together because neither one of them had any money, and that was the cheapest way to live. They lived up in the Wisconsin home, which was not meant for winter living . . . no insulation and often −30° F in the winter. They did their best. They began to go to Mexico over the winter where living was easier and much cheaper. Eventually they were able to sell the family bogs that were always losing money. They then had enough money to manage. They were financially comfortable then, but not happy together. The fought a lot.

I remember from Emily's spiritual experience that she learned a lot of valuable lessons from her mother. I ask her how she was able to do that, again expressing how unusual this seemed to me. Emily, however, doesn't see what she did as particularly noteworthy. Next, she talks about her mother's difficulties, and also what she gained from her mother.

> My mother deteriorated because of the alcohol. And I don't know when that started. I remember in the fourth grade hearing my parents talk about divorce. The heavy drinking coincided with the financial problems. What caused what, I'll never be able to figure out.
>
> Underlying all that, I really loved my mother. I wanted to see what was good in her because I loved her. Now I can't explain that, why she was such an unusual person. She had so much charm. I knew she always cared about me, too. She was always interested in me. For example, when I called from college, she always wanted to know everything that was going on, and she didn't spend her time talking to me about what she was doing. She wanted to know about me.
>
> When I heard someone at Meeting speak about their mother, referring to the glorious things that their mother did, I realized that I had the same feelings about my mother. But she didn't have all those accomplishments that I could refer to and say, "This is why I loved her."

She has been a mystery to me, too. I never really understood how they got married, although I loved them both and they both had some wonderful things about themselves. So it's not that I can't see why people aren't attracted to either one of them. It's just that they seem to be such a mismatch. I guess that whole experience was what drove me to look at myself, to look inward. My upbringing has been my most significant spiritual experience. Mother is the focal point because she received so much of the blame for what was going on. I'm not sure that that was deserved. Certainly if she could have stopped drinking, things would have been a lot better. Certainly if she could have handled money better—at least she had tremendous resources of money until she used them all up—she could have helped Dad out with his problems. On the other hand, I could say, why wasn't Dad more forceful? He couldn't face her drinking problem and he left her . . . or is she at fault for not following him to the bogs of northern Wisconsin during winter months? I loved her and wanted to help her, and yet she was the one who seemed to cause so many of the problems—it was a tremendous dilemma. I guess it is something I have always tried to figure out, and work out in my mind. When I was that age, a teenager, I hadn't been exposed to anything else. Now, if I had the typical refugee type of background, such problems would seem minor. But that was my little world and that was all I had to work on. It was this background that caused me to search for what was important to me. It helped me guide myself. I realized that no one life style was a ticket to success. There was something more important than material things.

A Theology of the Inward Search and Acceptance

I wonder how Emily translated the lessons she learned from her experiences with her parents into her ideas about religion. She explains how she has worked this out.

I could never work out the theology, even as a child. I gave up on it because it just didn't seem important compared to the other things. One thing I always appreciated was different types of people. I found I liked everybody everywhere I went. That sounds very insipid, but when I was in school, everybody was my friend. I'm sure there were a few people that weren't, but, you know, I really liked everybody. I wasn't in a group. It was never important to me to be in one. I enjoyed being friendly with everybody. That has been true all my life. I really try to enjoy other people and I find I can. It means a lot to me. I guess that is part of the process. It doesn't sound very significant . . . I never looked for a group to belong to because I have always known I could get along and find lots of people very interesting to me.

It's not theology that draws me to Quakerism at all. I don't feel myself a Christian. But it is kind of the inward process and kind of looking inward and the acceptance of other people. It is looking for God in other people. I don't feel any guilt for not relating everything I want to do to the Bible or to Jesus or to Christianity. I don't have to explain evil. I don't have the guilt. That was the real reason why I couldn't go for God being the creator. I never could justify what happens. How could evil and unhappiness be created by a God of love? That is unanswered— to me. So then I began to say, why is it that important? Just look for what's good and go after that.

Emily turns to her thoughts of death.

I could die anytime. I mean . . . that doesn't horrify me. It is just that I don't want to leave the people I love because they would be unhappy.

In terms of there being nothing afterwards, that is hard to accept, but I don't see anything else. I'm not convinced there is anything else. Maybe it would be great if there were. Maybe it wouldn't. I just feel that we are so fortunate to have had any kind of experience of life. When you think of the whole universe . . . life is such a freaky thing, that even if it doesn't go on forever, we are very lucky to have what we think we have.

I ask Emily how her training as a scientist has guided her theological thinking. Emily explains that she originally earned a degree in mathematics, but then realized that she had missed a lot of science courses. After teaching math for many years, she took one course in chemistry and "fell in love with it." We end our discussion with

Emily talking of her love for chemistry and science, and how they influenced her metaphysics.

Chemistry met my intellectual need: it's quantitative, logical, and mysterious. I loved it. I began to take chemistry course after chemistry course in my late thirties. A year or so later I was in graduate school . . . in chemistry. I found my niche. I think that science helps to keep giving us fresh ways of looking at things and helps us to realize our position in the universe. It is very exciting, the fact that there could be other worlds out there. In fact, it's kind of ironic. Scientists who have been accused of destroying God, so to speak, might be able to prove that there is a grand scheme of communication within the universe. This may be what God is.

Beth

Reference: The Interpersonal Event pp. 72–73

Beth is a Charismatic Catholic with an unwaver-ing conviction that God directs her life. Before her conversion ten years ago at the age of fifty-four, she was a more traditional Roman Catholic. The second oldest of four children, she grew up in a home with a devout mother and grand-mother, both of whom attended daily mass. She married and, with her husband, raised a daughter and two sons; her oldest son was the person who initially introduced her to the Charismatic movement. Once her youngest child was in the sixth grade, she worked many years as a secretary. She and her husband retired and moved to Florida where they live in a neatly kept middle-class neighborhood of a small city on the west coast of Florida. Beth, active in the Charismatic movement, takes care of the Charismatic library at her church, occasionally types for the group or for the priest, and regularly attends prayer group. She and her husband also volunteer at a local hospital.

Growing Up

Beth's outstanding characteristic is her devout faith in God. Im-pressed by her certainty, I asked her if she had been as religiously convinced as a child and young adult as she was now.

> I wouldn't say I was religious. As a kid, I looked on Jesus as somebody wonderful. You knew He was there. I knew He died on the Cross for me, but He was just somebody I didn't feel that close to. I went to mass on Sunday . . . and as kids we went to confession every Saturday. In fact, I even got hit by a car

rushing home one Saturday morning because I was almost too late for confession. I just had a good strong religious mother. She had had a very, very strong . . . both my mother and my grandmother went to daily mass and made litanies and novenas and all sorts of things.

I ask her if her father also was religious. Her father, Beth explains, was not religious when she was a child and "did not even attend church." Three years before his death, however, he converted to Catholicism, an event she describes as "one of the highlights of my life." Next she describes how she thought of God as a child, compared to now, and draws a comparison between her sense of God and her feelings for her father.

Well . . . God was just kind of a stern, good person that I was afraid of. I think there was a lot of fear of Him in those days where now I can call Him Abba, Father, and feel like He's almost my own father. I can feel the closeness that I had to my own dad whom I loved so deeply. And for years I couldn't even talk about him without crying. I still can't. I didn't have that closeness with my mother that I had with my dad. And yet we didn't really talk about it . . . I didn't go to him with problems really . . . I just had a deep love for him. He couldn't put it in words and I couldn't either. But it was there. And I imagine that's something like the way the Holy Father, I mean God, the Father . . . that's similar to my feelings about him.

I can't help but notice that there are tears in Beth's eyes as she talks about her father, who died in 1953. I mention that it seems that memories of her father still move her deeply. She explains:

And I really don't very often cry about him at this stage, but I guess this brings a lot of things back.

I ask Beth, who feels so close to her father, if she takes after him. We begin to talk about similarities between her and her mother and how she is different from her siblings.

I think I was more of an emotional person all my life . . . more like my mother. My father didn't express emotion too much . . . and yet I knew he was right there for me. My mother . . . she cried fairly easily I think. Funny, I was more like her and yet I was closer to my father.

She recalls other ways that she resembled her mother:

> Of course, every time I walked out of the house, somebody would say "You're the spitting image of your mother." I got a lot of reminders . . . she liked people and she liked to be with other women a lot and I did, too. My sister, I think, was different. She had one good friend. That was all she wanted. Mother liked pretty clothes and I liked pretty clothes. My sister didn't give a darn. Any old thing would do.

I ask Beth if she thinks she was different than her sister.

> Yes, I probably was the most sensitive of the family. I cried a lot if things didn't go right . . . I'd get hurt over things, where my younger sister didn't seem to, she still doesn't. She rarely cries.

Beth also has an older and a younger brother. I ask her if her brothers share her religious interests. She explains that her younger brother has "pulled away from the church completely," and her older brother and younger sister, still religious, do not have any interest in the type of Charismatic religious life that she leads. I ask her about her older brother. Beth describes him as "the most religious" in the family during their childhood.

> In his younger years he went to daily mass, he served the priest as an altar boy even after he was married and had six kids of his own, but he probably goes less now than he did when he was younger . . . He's still very religious, I think, but he's just not going to daily mass like he used to. And he can't understand what this is [the Charismatic movement], but he won't give himself a chance. He won't go to a prayer meeting and try it. And my sister doesn't believe in it [the Charismatic movement]. She's a good Catholic, Sunday church, gives her money—that's it.

I ask Beth how she has changed as a Roman Catholic since she was a child. Beth explains that although she is active in the Charismatic movement, she still doesn't attend daily mass, like her mother did.

And even though she has moved from a more traditional Roman Catholicism to a Charismatic, she never questioned that she would always be a Roman Catholic.

> For example, I knew my children had to go to Catholic school. It was just something ingrained in me from my mother that there was no other religion. Right. I knew that I wanted to marry a Catholic . . . I went with my husband and he wasn't anything. I had about three dates, and I said I don't see any point in pursuing this because I will never marry anyone but a Catholic and he said, "Well, what makes you think I wouldn't become a Catholic?" And I said, "Well, in that case, . . . I'll keep seeing you."

He does convert, and they do marry, enjoying a happy life together. Beth remembers, however, that before she married she had wanted to go to college, a dream she never realized. I ask Beth what she wanted to study in college. She begins to wonder about this "road not taken."

> I'd love to have gone to college. I loved shorthand and typing and I wanted to teach them but it was right at the heart of the Depression and Dad couldn't afford to send me and in those years you didn't hear too much about working your way through college like the kids do now.
>
> And then once I got started in the business world, I got what I thought was a very good job working at our local utility company right out of high school. Then I got over the college idea right away. I just didn't have the desire to work and put the money aside to go to school. I decided I had as good a job as any girl in our class had, so why not skip college.
>
> And I knew that eventually I'd rather get married and have a family anyway . . . but it sticks in my mind . . . about what I might have done.

Being Baptized by the "Holy Spirit"

Beth describes her life before her conversion experience as being qualitatively different from the way it is now that she has been "baptized by the holy spirit." I observe that her conversion experience seems to have been a significant turning point in her life. She explains, "Until I received the baptism in the Holy Spirit, my life was just nothing. I base everything now on whether it was before the baptism or after." She recalls life before her conversion experience:

> I think my whole life has done such an about face. At times I used to get depressed, when the children were growing up. I had wanted children, I loved children, and yet there were times when I questioned whether I should have been a mother or not. And this youngest son about drove me to distraction during his teenage years. And I think so often now, if I had only been as close to the Lord then, as I am now, I think I would have made a better mother . . . yet I know that the Lord had it all timed, that this is when I was to get into it and thank God I got it when I did.

Beth explains that she went back to work when her youngest child was in the sixth grade and the oldest in the eighth grade. I remark that having to juggle work and family is difficult for many women, and I wonder if this contributed to her depression. Beth responds:

> Oh, I had a lot of times when I was depressed without really a reason. We didn't have problems with any of their health. I think we had one broken arm and one fractured skull, which healed beautifully. There wasn't any problem compared to other families. Yet I would have times when I was so depressed I just didn't know where I was going. The least little thing . . . I could go to pieces and cry. Like I wanted to hide from the world. I couldn't talk to my husband. Now it just seems like a whole different world.

I ask Beth what else in her life might have been putting pressure on her. She says that in addition to her responsibilities at home with three teenage children, one of whom caused her some problems, she recalls having difficulties at work.

> And there always was competition in a big company and I think I probably always felt a little inferior because I didn't get a college education like I wanted. I don't know what the

actual difficulty was. There's always competition in a large office and I felt like the young girl under me would like to have my job and I wasn't ready to retire for quite a while yet. I was having trouble getting along with some of the girls I worked with. I didn't approve of the things they were doing. I had started reading about that time this book, *I'm OK, You're OK*, because I kept feeling that I wanted to study some kind of psychology and try to figure out why I couldn't get along with some of these people. Competition . . . and I just felt like I needed to get in better touch with my own feelings before I could do anything about my feelings for others. And deep down I kept feeling it was *my* own fault and I wanted to find some books that would try to change *me*. And at that time I had no idea that it was a religious thing that I was looking for. I just wanted to study some psychology. I only had a high school education and I was probably meeting a lot of people that had a lot more education than I did and I felt like I would even have taken a college course if I had a chance. But I came across this book, *I'm OK, You're OK*, and I didn't really understand it. I didn't really approve of it, and then I tried something by Elizabeth Kubler Ross—something about dying . . . *Death and Dying*. I don't know why, whether someone just handed it to me or why I picked that particular book. I remember reading that at the time, and not getting too much out of it.

I ask Beth how she was introduced to the Charismatic movement, an event which she sees as changing her life. She describes a visit to her son and his family, who live in another state.

This one particular trip I'll never forget because we got in late at night, but we sat around the table and talked for probably an hour or two before we went to bed. He came into our bedroom as we were going to go to bed. I had noticed how every few words he was saying, "Praise the Lord, Praise the Lord," and I thought, "What is this with [Tom]?" . . . something's different. I couldn't figure out what it was.

So he read my mind, and he said, "Mom, you probably can see there's something very, very different about us." And I said, "Yes, I haven't been able to put my finger on it, son." And he said, "Well, I know you're tired and you don't want to start thinking about it tonight, but I've got a lot of things to tell you."

He said, "[Sally] and I have gotten into what's called the Charismatic movement. Have you heard about it?" And I said, "No." I hadn't heard of it back in our area at all.

He then said, "Well, I don't want you to get keyed up tonight, but in the morning I want to talk to you about it." So the next morning, bright and early, he started telling us that somehow or other he had gotten into a group, and it was through the Catholic church. He didn't want me to think that he was doing anything that was away from the Catholic church. But within a year he had pulled away from the Catholic church and joined the Nazarene church. But he supplied me with books that to this day are very, very near and dear to my heart, and I recommend them to all newcomers to our own prayer group.

At first, I was hesitant . . . I wondered, "Have I got time for this, I'm working forty hours a week at a job and I want to do this, and I want to do that . . . have I got time for any more religion?" But after I started reading a few of the books, I developed that hunger for what these people have. If they had what these books said they had, then I wanted it. He started feeding me these books, *Clap Your Hands,* and, gosh, I can't remember all of the others. I took four or five books and read them in the car, on the way home.

I ask Beth what happened when she got home, if she found a way to use this new information in her life there. She recalls that as soon as she got home, she checked on Charismatic groups with her local parish priest who said, "Oh yes, I've heard of it, but I don't believe in it." Although he disapproved, he tells her of a Charismatic group at a nearby parish. She immediately went, and she also joined a women's prayer group called AGLOW. She explains how her involvement with this women's prayer group leads to her participation in a weekend retreat and her conversion.

I went quite a distance to get to AGLOW . . . ten or fifteen miles away from home after working all day, to join these women because I did get such an uplift from them. They were going to have a conference quite a distance from my home and one of my dearest friends and I decided to go to this particular weekend. Being a strong Catholic, it struck me very peculiar that the wife of a Baptist minister would be the leader of our little group. I very much respected and loved [Karen] and yet I had a certain hesitancy about being in her group because of her being Baptist—I had the feeling that she might try to pull me away from my church, which I didn't even want to think of doing.

[Karen], in this little get-together with a half a dozen women present, asked if there were any there who would like to receive the baptism. Now, I had been attending prayer meetings for possibly a year and had heard the term so many times, but didn't really know what the baptism was. And so I naturally said yes, I wanted to receive anything there was to offer. But I didn't really know what it was and she said, 'Well, you just give yourself completely to the Lord. Jesus Christ becomes the complete center of your life. And every thought, every action you will ever have, is centered around Jesus Christ." And I said, "That sounds like what I want, [Karen]." So she prayed over me with her hands on my head and she prayed in tongues and I remember praying as hard in English as she prayed in tongues and the tears just running down my face. Suddenly a warm sensation came over me and I just felt like Jesus was right there in the room with His arms right around me and I *knew* that He was there. And He was what I wanted for the rest of my life. Well, then we went on to other little meetings and I remember particularly the group walking up to a confectionery store that night and having ice cream and how happy all of these perfect strangers were . . . I'd never met them . . . but we shared our love for Jesus Christ.

Remembering her mother's strong religious practice, I ask Beth if her mother was alive when she had her conversion.

Mother had just passed away not too long before that. And I had a strange thing happen there. The first few months that I got into it, I kept wondering what Mom would think of all this. As religious as Mom was, I sort of had a hesitancy about it. I wondered if Mom would really approve. So one day after I'd gotten in all the prayer meetings and had received my own baptism, I ran into an old friend of Mother's, who was a neighbor of mine. I was trying to tell her about the movement, and she was just not interested at all . . . so we went on talking about different things. She said, "You know, I always remember your mother and stepdad." You see, Mother had been alone about

eight years after Dad died and then she remarried. She married a
rough and tough old railroad man who never came anywhere
near matching my dad . . . and, of course, nobody ever could
have . . . anyway, that doesn't matter. [Hal] took very sick and
Mother had to go to the hospital with him—for months and
months on end she went to the hospital every day to be with him.
So this friend is reminding me that this one particular day just
shortly before [Hal] passed away, Mom told her that she sat there
one morning. She put her elbows down on the kitchen table and
she just said, "Lord, I absolutely cannot go on another day. I
have come to the end of my limit. Now there's nothing more I
can do. It's up to you." And you know when Mary told me that,
that's exactly the baptism in the Holy Spirit. Mother received the
baptism right then and there the day that she gave her whole
life—she couldn't go on alone—she gave it up to the Lord. She
went on to the hospital that day and every day until he died. She
did it because Jesus was with her. And I got my answer. I know
now Mom approves.

I ask Beth how her husband and other children responded to her
involvement with the Charismatic movement. She responds:

> And then, of course, the minute I started getting all
> these good feelings about it, then I wanted everyone in my
> family to feel that way and have the opportunity. I pushed books
> at them . . . everything a person shouldn't do, I did. My hus-
> band . . . he was interested, and he *is* interested, but not to the
> extent that I am. He goes with me every week to the meetings
> and he prays, but he can't raise his hands in prayer to the Lord
> like I do. He goes to Charismatic meeting with me and he'll
> approve of my going anywhere I want to go to a big conference.
> He tells me to go. But he doesn't always want to go with me.
> He's gone to Notre Dame three or four times to the big con-
> ferences, but it's because he loves Notre Dame's football team.

Beth switches the topic of conversation to her two sons. To her
sorrow, about a year after her oldest son introduced her to the
Charismatic movment, he left the Roman Catholic church to
attend a Protestant one. Her son continues to investigate different
churches, and she continues to hope he'll return to Catholicism.

He's been transferred now to Texas and he's going to a Baptist church there. For a while they were going to a Presbyterian church because his wife had been Presbyterian before she married him. For a while they each went different directions. She'd take one of the children and he'd take the other and they'd go to their own churches. They felt, I think, that when they got into the Charismatics that they could be together. And I really thought this was good too. It helped to take the edge off their leaving our church. At least I felt they were a family together at the Church of the Nazarene. And I felt good about that. I just know that eventually they'll be back. I pray the good Lord will help me keep my mouth shut until they do! The only thing I had ever said to him was "Son, how can you give up the blessed eucharist?" Because they don't have the daily Communion that we do. We can have it every day of the week if we want. And I know he'll be back. Believe it or not, our relationship is the same. We have only one part that hurts and that is that he doesn't approve of the blessed Mother. I mean, he thinks we shouldn't spend as much time praying to her as we do to Jesus. And I think he doesn't understand it thoroughly and that's the reason he feels that way. We honor her as the Mother of our Lord, but we don't worship her or give her undue credit. We had a few words on that one time, so that's one subject that I do try to stay away from.

Her younger son, she explains, has never been religious and still isn't.

We had to fight to get him to go to church all through high school. Of course the minute he left home, that was the end of his going to church. He just didn't even bother anymore. We could see from the time he was in high school, he was just harder to talk to than the older boy had been. He wanted a car at sixteen and the older boy didn't even want to lean to drive until he was eighteen.

He's had three wives already and three divorces and now he's living with the fourth gal, and yet I've learned to laugh about it. Ten or fifteen years ago it broke my heart; I couldn't talk about it. Now the strange part is we love the little girl he's living with now more than any of the three wives. We wish he would make it legal because we think so much of her. But if anyone had told me fifteen years ago I could ever laugh about my son doing what he's done, I would have called them a liar.

And for years I felt like it was my fault . . . an error in *my* judgment. Somehow *I* had failed *him*. And it's only been in the last few years I've had any peace about it at all. That I feel I did the best I could and if it wasn't good enough, well, it's all I had then to work with. But if I had then what I have now, I think I could have done something different. But I feel like the Lord's going to understand. It's going to come out OK in the end, so I'm not worried.

I just had this heaviness of heart over both boys. And every book I would pick up I'd find this same scripture. But each time that I would worry about the boys, Acts 16:31 would come up in a book I was reading, or somebody would mention it, or it would be part of Father's sermon that day: "You and your household will be saved." I just claim that scripture. I just know this is a promise.

I ask her if her daughter shares her sentiments. Speaking of her daughter, Beth says:

She's a good Catholic and works with her daughter in the young people's group and is a very good wife and mother and a wonderful neighbor. If anybody in her neighborhood needs anything, she's the first one there. I'm really proud of her. And she respects the way I feel, but she doesn't want any part of it, so I respect her feelings there, too.

Views of God

I mention to Beth that it seems as though she experiences a God who is very active in her life. I note that examples of what she sees as God giving her signs to direct her life are interwoven in our conversation. She agrees, and begins to talk about how her and her husband's decision to buy a house in Florida and move there for their retirement was an important event for them. She talks about this time when they were deciding whether to buy a particular house they had just seen.

> We drove around and got up by the beach and it was getting along towards supper time so we decided to look around for a place to eat. [Bill] said, "Well, here's a place right here that has an eating place." I was so excited at that time I didn't think I cared for food, and for me not to want food, that's something else. So we pulled into the marina parking lot, and all this time I'd been praying. I don't know how hard [Bill] prayed, but I kept praying, "Lord, send me a sign if we are to buy this house. Send me your sign." And we pulled up to park at the marina and the first little boat I saw in the harbor was named "Praise the Lord." And of course that's the slogan for our Charismatic people. Anything we are excited about, happy about, "Praise the Lord."
>
> I knew that was *my* sign. My husband agreed. That was the nice part. He didn't always go along on all my theories, but he did agree that was our sign.

Still speaking of how she sees signs from God, Beth talks about the special bond between the women in her prayer group, and how God speaks to them through prayer.

> Matter of fact, I even called one of them this morning and asked her to hold me up in prayer so that I would say what the Lord wanted me to say, rather than what I wanted to say. And she assured me that she would hold me up in prayer. We just have a bond between us. We all pray of one mind if we're praying for one particular person in the prayer group. We all pray together in tongues, or if somebody wants to say something in English, we say it in English. There's just a bond between the five of us that I've just never had anything like before.
>
> And sometimes someone will come up with a request. Recently, one of the girls was led to pray for some children in our town. But she got the word from the Lord and we all felt sure it was from the Lord that the children we were to pray for were bruised and battered children. Many times we have prayers come up like that and . . . something is told to us so we know we got the word from the Lord. And it's just beyond description.

I ask Beth how she can distinguish between her own ideas and God's voice. She explains:

> Well, I think the time that I really felt so positive was when He told me about getting this neighbor group together and then I said, "Well, Lord, if it's really you, then I'm going to open this Bible and you've got to show me." That's when He showed me the scripture . . . that to me was a go ahead that I had to do it. And that usually happens if I go to the Bible and open it up without any idea of where it's going to open; there will be something on that page that will tell me that was His voice.

Next we begin to talk about some of her beliefs. I ask her if she thinks about what the purpose of her life is. She replies:

> Not so much that, but I think often of how could I have ever been so fortunate as to have been born in America. You know, when you look at the rest of the world and the starving people, and when you think what we have compared to some of those people . . . I think "Lord, how could I have been so chosen." I feel very fortunate, blessed, just blessed, because with me nothing is luck. I feel like it's a blessing from the Lord. I don't believe it's by chance. It's funny . . . before I got into the movement, I loved to get the morning paper and see what Aquarius was for that day, and I was so shocked when I got into the movement to find that we did not believe in signs of the zodiac any more. Lady luck does not enter into it at all. It's what the Lord has in store for us, in His master plan.

I ask Beth about her ideas on an afterlife, then. She replies:

> Well, I don't believe in reincarnation at all, but I think we have a heaven, a hell, and purgatory, and I think we don't hear too much about purgatory any more like we did when we were kids. But it's still there . . . Well, since my five years in Florida I feel like this is almost heaven. I can't think of it as being too much better than what I have now. No stress, no pushing, no worries, just the Lord sitting there for us to worship and adore.
>
> Yes, I just don't think of it too often, to be truthful. I think lately of that Gospel story of the fellow trying to trap the Lord . . . the wife whose first husband died, and she was left without any children so she married the second brother . . . It

goes on down the line, she's been married to the seven brothers. When she gets to heaven, whose wife is she supposed to be? And the Lord said when you get to heaven there will be no wives and husbands. You're just all there for the glory of God. So I get to thinking about that and wondering what is it really going to be like? It makes me wonder.

Hell, she explains, she thinks of "as burning fire. But the real Hell I guess is supposed to be not seeing the glory of God." I say to Beth that it seems to me that compared to her childhood notion her concept of God as an adult has become more benevolent. She agrees, saying that her idea has changed from a God who is stern and "unapproachable" to a God who is more accepting and who would "forgive me no matter what I had done." However, she talks about how she still thinks of God, as she did as a child, as being up in the sky.

> And yet I don't think I ever look up into the sky and see these beautiful mounds of clouds but what I think, one of those clouds is God, or His holy spirit. If I could just look right into the middle of the cloud, I feel like He'd be right there. And the more beautiful the day, the more I feel like He's right there.

We agree that we have come to the end of our interview. Beth ends, as she began, by emphasizing her complete faith and trust in God.

> If a situation came up that I couldn't handle, I would just pray and say, "Lord, I don't know what's right or wrong here, you tell me." And it seemed like, in those early years of the renewal, before I even had a chance to ask the Lord for what I wanted, He'd give me answers . . . before I got the question. That was one of my favorite remarks in the early part of it I remember. I just know that when things are going wrong that I can just take it to the Lord and say, "Here, take over Lord, I've done all I can do and I give it all to you."

Ellen

Reference: On Death and Dying pp. 81–82

Ellen personifies the New England spirit. An inquisitive and independent thinker, she has a no-nonsense approach to life that provides the basis for her inquiry into the paranormal or into those other realities with which we are not as familiar. Brought up in the Roman Catholic tradition, Ellen grew up in a New England family of four children; her mother was a schoolteacher and her father, who worked for G.E., had frail health. She married her husband when she was twenty-two years of age and, with him, raised her two daughters and two sons while she worked as a nurse. In 1981 she returned to school to earn a Master's degree in Pastoral Counseling, which she uses with her current work in hospice and counseling. Now fifty-three years old, Ellen continues to integrate her spiritual development with the rest of her life, and lives with her husband in a middle-class neighborhood of a New England city.

Childhood Experiences

I begin our discussion by telling Ellen how moved I was by the precognitive dream she described as a memorable spiritual experience and, although I wasn't sure why, everytime I read her account I was strongly affected. I wondered if it wasn't because her story seemed to capture the human struggle to find courage, as it also showed the triumph of love. I add that her experience made an allegorical statement about the power of sisterhood. We talk about this for a while and about how vivid and accurate her precognitive dream had been. I ask Ellen what her childhood had been like and if there had been any precursory experiences that suggested she might have some sort of sensitivity.

> I just can't see any correlation, from my own point of view, between my own personal developmental process and what happened in that precognitive dream. These spontaneous events often occur around states of illness . . . emotional states, or states of high arousal. This is important to note, I think, because traditional religious practices elicit those emotional states by appealing to our sensory awareness. In the case of my sister's impending Caesarian, I felt no anxiety . . . I was not in an emotional state. If I had been in a state of high arousal, then I would have written it off . . . I would have attributed the precognitive dream to a high arousal state.

I ask if I understood her correctly, that the fact that Ellen was not in a high arousal state made the precognitive dream even more significant. She confirms my understanding. Next our conversation turns to Ellen's childhood. I ask her to discuss the role religion played in her life as a child.

> As a child it [religion] was my whole life. My socialization was as a Catholic child. It was our entertainment when I grew up. I was a child of the depression period and we went to church on Sunday morning and then we went back in the afternoon . . . We followed the liturgical calendar and, as kids, we were involved in every opportunity that the church offered. But, I don't even count that. My experience growing up Catholic was more of a socialization process, of conforming to family norms. That's just religiosity. It has almost nothing to do with spirituality.

I'm still interested in whether or not she felt any different in any way as a child. I ask her about this and she replies:

> Oh, I don't know. Yes, I think probably that I am different, and I was different as a kid growing up, although I never really understood it at the time. Well, looking back I think I was probably more self-aware as a child . . . I seemed to have an objective awareness. I've met other people who have talked in that same way about their childhood, that they felt different in this way. I wasn't treated any differently as a member of the

family, however. [One of four children, Ellen has a sister who is a year older, a twin brother, and a younger brother.] I don't think there was anything remarkable about me . . . It was subtle. . . . I wasn't as interested in the typical things children are involved in . . .

I ask her to explain what she means by "objective awareness." She responds:

> An objective awareness is like an observing ego . . . but with a neutrality. It's like some part of me knew more than the me who was a kid. I didn't feel uncomfortable. It was as though a part of me could reflect on things from another perspective . . . this other perspective contained some wisdom and understanding that I hadn't earned, but which was very much there . . . and it was completely nonjudgmental.
>
> I still experience this "objective awareness." It's hard to capture and put into words, but it's something I trust because of my experience with it. It's similar to what traditional religions refer to when they talk about "the spirit moving me."
>
> Maybe all kids have that capacity—to reflect on something and at the same time to participate in it. I don't know—I suppose I thought that everybody had that capacity.

Ellen then begins to describe how her avid interest in reading as a child laid a foundation for her investigation into the paranormal as an adult.

> As a young kid I was a reader, but I probably read without great discrimination. I read a lot of fiction . . . nothing unusual. I read mostly for entertainment. In high school, though, my reading habits shifted. When I was in high school I worked at a library, so I had access to all stacks . . . that was a great experience for me. Well, I had to read the stacks, to put them in order and there's nothing more tedious than reading stacks. So if I saw a title I'd just pull it out. And because the library system was old and very large, there were a number of books on the paranormal. This was an area that I had never heard of. And I looked at it and I don't even remember being incredibly interested in it at that time. I didn't even appreciate what a rich source of information it was. It was only when I went back as an adult and began a library search of the paranormal

that I realized that I had read this material before. In high school
I hadn't understood it; as an adult I did.

Next I ask Ellen to talk about what her family was like when she
was growing up.

> My father had fairly poor health and my mother is a
> schoolteacher and went back to work and this meant that I
> assumed some of the responsibility in the house. Today I guess
> you'd call me a parentified child; but I didn't mind it. Growing
> up the only big concern would have been my father's health. I
> had a lot of nice relatives; a very close, cohesive family. My uncle
> was a priest and having a priest in the family turned out to be a
> very positive thing. He was an uncle, brother, and son before he
> was a priest. And I think having that experience with him did
> something to my sense of my Catholicism. My sense of the
> Catholic church was very much linked to my uncle. And I really
> liked him. He was super. I listen to other people and hear their
> anger at the church and I have my own agenda of anger . . . but
> it's very different. Because the church and my uncle are one.
> They both were like family, and my relationship with my uncle
> made the church more human.
>
> I didn't realize this until an occasion with a close
> friend of mine, who had grown up in the same community as
> me. She was talking about her anger at the church with great
> passion. Although I thought we had common experiences, I
> didn't have the same anger and hostility as she did. Then she
> pointed out to me that my experience was different because of
> my uncle . . . the traditional Catholic socialization didn't take.
> So I had no fear of the church. It's fear that motivates people to
> grab onto a belief and to hang onto it and it chokes them. And
> fear can turn into anger. My uncle was very human, and very
> understanding and I associated the church with him. He didn't
> instill fear, so neither did the church.

Current Family Life

Next, our conversation turns to what her life was like before the
turning point of the precognitive dream.

At one level my family and I are very ordinary. I was mothering, working, busy—family involved—a practicing Roman Catholic, but not running to novenas. My family is fairly conventional people. They're used to me. So when I became involved in paranormal research, they were used to me doing things that other mothers didn't do.

I ask Ellen to elaborate on that.

Oh, for example, I was involved in anti-Vietnam activities early on, and I belonged to a feminist book club. My husband never had any objections whatsoever into my research into the paranormal. He was interested and would periodically become more involved and then he would lose interest. Football is more important to him.

My kids were very interested and when my youngest child was three years old, she was phenomenally psychic. I was able to notice this because by this time I understood psychic phenomena. And then I saw that because of socialization she sort of tuned out of that kind of reality. She also is a very spiritually oriented kind of person although if you met her you'd never notice it because she's really quite regular. She went to a parochial school and the sisters would say to me, "Are you aware of how spiritually minded this child is?" I didn't see it because at the time I didn't see a link between psychic sensibility and spirituality . . . it's still an unanswered question I have.

I ask Ellen what made her realize her youngest child had psychic capacities.

I think the first thing that I noticed was one day I was washing dishes at the sink, and I had run out of dishwashing soap. The kids used to play downstairs in the cellar. My husband is an elementary school principal and we had some old desks in the cellar and they used to play school. As I went to the door to call for my daughter to bring up some soap, I opened the door and she was standing there with a box of Tide. And I said "How did you know?" She was only three and she couldn't answer me. But there were a series of minor things like that . . . When she was six, she was running in the woods across the street. She saw a log ahead of her and saw herself tripping over the log, so she slowed down and when she got to the log she wasn't injured. Now that she's and adult she tells me that she had that faculty all the time, but she thought everybody did as a child. And then it stopped. And I can't tell you at what age it did stop, but it did stop. I'm theorizing now about why it stopped. I think probably in order for consciousness to function in this reality, I think you've got to tune into a consensual reality. And there's a strong pull from the culture to tug people in to the way reality is organized for most people. The kids all accepted the psychic ground, and the spiritual dimension, quite naturally. They had no problem with it.

I knew she was psychic, but I didn't encourage her to develop it. I just let the normal developmental processes occur. I didn't want her to be any different than any other child . . . I just let her be a normal child.

Spiritual Development

Our conversation turns to how Ellen's precognitive dream became a turning point in her life. I ask her how this dramatic experience affected her life. She begins to talk about her need for an intellectual as well as an emotional comprehension of what she experienced, and her determination to arrive at her own independent conclusions about what had happened.

I did approach my experiences after that with a fairly open-minded, but scientific frame of reference. I guess I had conversion of the heart—if you can call it that—but not of the mind. I knew that something extraordinary had happened, but I couldn't explain it, so I had to go through a process of looking for the explanations. And that's where I think a scientific background was extremely helpful. I kept open-minded . . . I didn't settle for just one explanation. I wasn't vulnerable to someone else's interpretation of that experience . . . (I was) always . . . very objective. But simultaneously I was very respectful toward what had happened. And that was really an incredibly opening up experience. I did a lot of reading in the area of parapsychology. I went back into the old literature, written around the turn of the century in Boston. I did read about the experiences of some very famous people and their understanding of it. And I went back to the roots of spiritualism, but that was unsatisfactory. I was delighted to find that some very famous people with very bright minds were involved in the same kind of a search. At about this time I started attending a spiritualist church.

She explains that Spiritualists do not accept the divinity of Christ and also do not use the Bible. Basically they believe "that all people are spirit, and their ministers, acting as mediums, give readings and preach automatically."

I was very concerned and interested in what these people were like. I have a phenomenal curiosity and I wanted to understand how they could allow a discordant voice speaking through a medium to direct their lives. And then I wanted to know about the mediums—what the impact of their messages were, the content of the messages, what help they gave to the people who received their messages to deal with grief and loss and that type of thing. And I went every week for ten years. Everytime I had one set of questions answered, the next series would come up. In the meantime, I had begun to do my own sort of psychic development—I guess that's the only way to call it. I was determined not to be contaminated with other people's belief systems or to use them to interpret what I was experiencing. I wanted to do the exploration . . . I thought of it as an exploration of consciousness.

During this time I had a few other equally startling events that occurred like my sister's episode, but they were far more connected to dream states; some were in an actual awake state. I remember that, as a culture, we were just beginning to look at states of consciousness. It is fascinating to me how the things that I was doing then were also being paralleled in the culture. This is discussed in the psi literature . . . how there are times of increased activity or interest in psi phenomena.

I express my amazement to Ellen that her curiosity led her to going to the Spiritualist church for ten years. She remembers, "I had a lot to work through . . . I wanted to talk to them, to see why they came and why the left. I just have a lot of curiosity." I ask her what she learned from this experience.

One thing I learned . . . it was an observational learning . . . was that the message you got from a medium was a
reflection of the personality of the medium. What bothered me
was that their belief in the content of their messages was absolute. They never questioned whether they influenced the content
at all . . . they never thought to question whether their unconscious was at a party.

And I wondered if the mediums cultivated a hallucinatory image, or a mental image.

I ask her to explain this, and she responds:

A hallucinatory image is one that is projected out . . . it's external, whereas a mental image is internal. It's an inner mental
image. At first the mediums were reluctant to talk about this. But
eventually I determined that the younger mediums were inclined
to use mental images, but none were particularly psychologically
sophisticated. They had no understanding of the paranormal. I
did learn a lot of interesting things from the Spiritualist church,
such as Catholics make wonderful mediums. You know what
our liturgy is like. Any kind of repetitive action, like the recita-
tion of the rosary, brings you into a transcendent reality. That's
the purpose of these rituals in any tradition. Anyway . . . I came
to understand through the paranormal the richness of our own
tradition. For example . . . the use of incense, the twentieth
vows, and the grand chants, all these can lead to an altered state.
And then I decided that the church had some special place where
they had all this information in a catalog. I started trying to get
information from seminaries and from priests but, of course,
they didn't have it. Then I ran across a really wonderful priest at
a workshop. He also is a psychologist, and he had been in Brazil.
He had been working in the same tradition, but instead of calling
it Spiritualist, in Brazil they referred to it as spiritists. What he
was doing was very similar to what I had been doing. He started
to process his own beliefs while looking at these other things and
he did a pretty nice synthesis. He pointed out how aspects of the
liturgy were evoking a transcendent state. Now this seems obvious and simple to understand, but at the time studies of consciousness were not being done.

I went through a very lonely process. I have one close
friend who's very bright and she also was involved in this same
kind of research. But you couldn't really talk about this to a lot of

> people. Some people were interested in psychic reality but they were into it for other reasons . . . they were interested more in the sensational, the bizarre . . . for their own personal gain. That wasn't why we were interested.

I wonder how this process of her investigation into the paranormal was lonely for her. I ask Ellen to talk about this. She describes two premonitions to illustrate the burden she felt at times, because of her psychic abilities. One involved a time when she persuaded her brother not to drive his own car after she had an image of his death in that car, and another had to do with a precognitive dream of a child's death (who, in fact, did die as she had dreamed). She continues:

> And the thing that was so disturbing about that is that I didn't want that information. I had to function in this reality and I didn't want to get information that I couldn't do anything about, and that was going to in any way disrupt me . . . So I actually did some programming of my own mind and just said that I will not accept any information that will disrupt the natural flow in my life, or the lives of other people. In effect, I shut down a lot of spontaneous images. That was good for me. It forced me to make priorities and to discipline myself; it had an impact on a lot of other areas of my life.

She goes on to explain that other people with psychic power get into trouble when they don't learn how to moderate their psychic awareness, and how part of her work has been in trying to help them.

> They don't shut down. They're into something that they really don't understand. They follow and interpret these images but they don't try to differentiate the content or the meaning. They don't look at the symbolic meaning, because they don't have enough background in psychology to work with this type of thing . . . So, I've dealt with people who do get into trouble in this area. In fact, the priest I referred to will often send me people who are really limping from getting into the area. A psychologist friend of mine has done the same thing.

I ask Ellen to explain how she works with these people who have gotten into trouble with their psychic abilities.

I use an extraordinarily rational approach, because I want to disrupt their system. They're into something with no objectivity whatsoever. We had one woman here that I spent about five hours with . . . This woman had a dream in which she was on an airline that went down over Europe someplace. She wasn't speaking lucidly, but she talked about how her consciousness was on the plane—or her astral body—I think that's how she phrased it—was on the plane. All the people on the plane died, so that meant that she must be dead. Or her astral body was dead. So she was kind of wandering around without her astral body, and she was off the wall. Part of her motivation for getting her astral body back had to do with money. She was working with the police on cases, and she was charging them, except psychics aren't supposed to charge money or you'll lose your power, so to speak. So she was charging astral flight time if you can imagine that, and she needed her astral body back so she could begin charging again. She also needed it to be alive.

See, she adopted this system and didn't understand it. But it was a tidy system she could work with, because it allowed her to take money for her services. I said to her, "Who said there is an astral body? You know, that's just someone else's belief system. If you want to work with it, that's fine, but that concept is really strangling you, so you'd better get rid of it." I never knew what happened to her after our visit; she worked with a case in our area on the kidnapping of a child. She also worked with local police on a couple of murders. She was a real novice . . . unsophisticated. She had reached the point where she no longer spoke with her children, instead she was communicating with them psychically. When she would go out to dinner with her husband she would sit there and tune in to other people's conversations or believe that she did. I told her, "You're going to have a break if you don't get hold of this." I gave her three months from that point, but I never heard what happened to her. What surprises me is that she isn't the exception. A lot of people are interested in psychic phenomena because they're eager to make money, to gain some authority or personal power. I wanted some sort of conceptualization before working with a group of people.

Our conversation shifts to a discussion of a group she formed of people with similar interests, who would look into psychic phenomena. She explains that she began the group about five years after the precognitive dream of her sister's near-death experience.

I spent about five years after my precognitive dream of my sister's operation researching this area. One of the things I've insisted upon is that the people who come in are either fairly psychologically sophisticated, or have fairly strong religious systems that they work with. You have to have one or the other. Because if you don't, you're going to go far afield. And it's been a very interesting process.

My experience is that most people are looking for a tight belief system into which they can tuck their experience, whether it is a religious system or the paranormal. There's an extraordinary amount of tension associated with letting something float. I think the impulse is to tie it down, and it is very strong. So I think I am exceptional in that regard. When we work in a group, one of the things that we talk about is making sure that no one imposes a belief. You can believe anything you want, but you're not going to be free to dump your stuff on anybody else. And you can talk about your system, and argue it, and debate it, but you're not to get offended if people don't accept it.

People with a strong need for a tight and tidy religious structure . . . or a tight psychological system . . . don't stay with the group. A lot of people self-select out of the group because that's a hard one to handle—the ambiguity, constant questioning, and never settling on a definitive answer. We are not socialized to that, and those who hold fast to that principle have some remarkable changes that occur at a psychological level. They become much more tolerant, and they look at situations from multiple perspectives. One of the principles we use in exploration of our consciousness is to look for alternate explanations for phenomena, not to settle in. If you can put it into a tidy explanation, beware of that. I don't care where you put it as long as you know that there are other competing explanations.

We have a healing ritual that we do every week and it's really very lovely. Everybody gets into an altered state. One of the experiences—and it's so beautiful—that we have is one of a sense of unity that really transcends all of the differences in our personalities. We can be in a hot and heavy argument about something, and when we get into that altered state, that's what counts . . . that sense of unity that's experienced.

I ask Ellen to explain what she means by an altered state.

> The altered state is a focused consciousness, or fo-
> cused awareness; there's also this detachment that would allow
> images to come . . . I think the fastest way to get into the state
> that I'm talking about, which is one of receptivity, is the condi-
> tioning that would come through hypnosis . . . I have had a lot of
> experience with healing, which is also wonderful. Once you are
> conditioned, it doesn't take a long time to achieve or retrieve an
> altered state.

Ellen's Personal Philosophy

I ask Ellen if she still considers herself to be Catholic. She explains
that she attends Roman Catholic services now, but that she isn't
active in parish life, saying "I'm really very anormative in terms of
being a Catholic." I ask her how she would characterize her beliefs
now. She continues the discussion, in which she describes her own
personal theology.

> It's really very beautiful, what I believe, because I just
> believe that we live in the presence of love and that love is a
> creative energy. God is love and a creative energy, and we live
> within that presence at all times—if we could only get to that
> point of knowing it and experiencing it. I have a totally different
> understanding of sin and evil than I was socialized to believe. I
> think of sin and evil as unreflected consciousness . . . a lack of
> awareness. I am perfectly capable of dealing with the propensity
> to do evil or sin in the individual. I think it's important for us to
> come to terms with our humanness and to acknowledge what, I
> guess, is called our dark side. I believe that thought is energy,
> and the thoughts that we send out have a life of their own. If, in
> fact, I call myself a Christian, then I have to monitor myself in a
> new way, so that what I send out is good and positive and
> healthy. One of the side effects of going through the process of
> studying and experiencing the paranormal was that I felt even
> more responsible for my thoughts. What else do I believe? I
> guess I believe that the energy of God exists within each of us. As

far as a real theological view of God, God is not male to me and God is not female to me.

When she remarks that, to her, God is not male or female, I wonder if she thinks of God as embodied. She responds:

> Personified? Not really, again, because of the paranormal, I can work with the concept of a creative energy with consciousness . . . a disembodied energy with consciousness. I have no problem with that. I struggle with the Eastern view of being embraced in nirvana and that used to be very disturbing to me because of my orientation to the Western notion of individuated consciousness. I really struggled with that. Now I guess I believe that we are individuated bits of consciousness but we are all part of, or becoming part of . . . a collective consciousness. That's really kind of a neat thing. If I believe that, and that collective consciousness impacts on us, then it switches my theology around so that I even wonder if, in fact, God as an energy is evolving, itself, himself, herself. And this causes me to feel more responsible in my own behavior. As a result of a lot of these beliefs, I am more concerned about empowering the individual.

I ask Ellen how she explains the figure of Christ in her philosophical system. She talks about her own interpretation of the meaning of Christ, and describes how it came to her as she participated in Holy Saturday liturgy.

> I suddenly understood experientially . . . for myself . . . what the Christ consciousness was all about. It was a moment of insight. We talk about sleeping in the peace of Christ. Have you ever heard that phrase? I think of the Christ consciousness as a locus of consciousness. It's a kind of a neat idea because when you get into the literature, and the experience of . . . little bits of consciousness wandering around, disembodied energies . . . then I get the idea of Christ as a locus. Other beliefs would have another figure as the locus, for example, Buddha. It's a centering of consciousness . . . It's not magnetic. It may have a magnetic component. It might be able to be explained in some form to satisfy a scientific perspective . . . What is central to me is that beliefs shape experience. So, according to my understanding, what a believer sees or experiences . . . for

example, Christ . . . will be central to their experience after death. And for those who don't believe, or who have rejected their original beliefs . . . I think that the original belief is still present in some form and that it will shape that person's experience. So, a lot of the things that I had been exposed to in our tradition were understood in new ways, and because they were understood in new ways, then they had much, much deeper meaning.

How do you work with Christ? Well, he was a man, obviously. That's one thing that we do know, that historically he existed. We don't know, though, from the actual content of scripture of the New Testament what he actually said. I guess you could put what we know on the back of a postage stamp. And to the degree to which the attempts to depict Christ reflect actuality is an entire other matter. But I don't even think that matters, because there are certain elements of his life that have their own kind of appeal . . . the idea of discipleship. You gain a certain sense of justice, and pluralism, love, healing, and service. I use the Christ qualities and the style of his life to work with the Christ figure. I would go to that to use as my model, and I don't have to believe that he was divine. You know, we're all divine. That's how I understand it.

Ellen goes on to speak about her views of death, evil, and forgiveness.

I think my belief is that we do survive physical death. That consciousness is something that can't be destroyed, because it is an energy, and I think energy can be transformed after death. I've read systems where there are seven planes and eight steps in an after-death world. I always get a boot out of those things. It's all so well ordered. I think there's probably a system there but I haven't been convinced by anybody's writings that their system has more validity than another. Death . . . it's just a transformation from my point of view. It doesn't mean that I am any more comfortable with the thought of my own death. To be totally honest, I like the normal reality very much, as much as I've diddled around in the other reality, and it certainly has been a wonderful experience. You know, I'm still stuck here . . . very much earth bound, because it is what I know and what I have experienced.

Then she remembers what she learned when members of her group regressed to previous lives. Commenting on that time, Ellen explains:

> One thing I have discovered is that there's no emotion. When you are in a "regressed" state . . . when you are brought to an "in-between" life state, there is an absence of emotion. For example, people were alone, but not lonely. Those in that state found it to be peaceful and calm. Since there's no body, there's no way of having emotion. There's a memory process of emotion, but one of the characteristics of that state of being was emotionless. When you work with that principle life itself becomes precious. We have the physical vehicle to experience life in its fullest. That in itself is a real gift, so that's one insight or belief that I have. Each person who regressed back to a previous life was asked the meaning and purpose of a life. Each of them mentioned some positive quality, like patience. There was a purpose to living, and part of the evolutionary process was to learn certain things in our lifetime. Our group, however, doesn't necessarily believe in the reality of past lives . . . but we use these experiences to explore those possibilities.

Our conversation drifts into talking about evil and sin, and how to understand these concepts. Ellen begins to talk about evil:

> We come into experience without a lot of choices, and we're shaped by that experience . . . by the social system, culture, the economy. I wouldn't label an individual evil, although there are evil acts. When we talk about evil what disturbs me is that we don't take into account the context in which the evil act occurs. If we separate evil out from its context, we are not owning our own human capacity for evil . . . we are denying it.
> I just don't feel that sense of needing a terrible amount of forgiveness. That may sound horrible to say, but God would understand.

Her ideas about forgiveness remind Ellen of a time she worked with a friend who had tried to commit suicide after her daughter's accidental death. When Ellen visited her friend in an intensive care unit, she found that her friend's greatest concern was that she had committed a sin with her suicide attempt.

I was just appalled. Here is religion adding pain to her pain. It was horrible. I was furious at the church for planting that idea in her head. This was what I mean about working with a sense of sin. And, boy, do I believe in grace. Because there's an awful lot that I've done with people . . . I really feel that I am guided in working with people. And working with her became a religious experience because we got right down to her relationship with God. If God could speak to you right this minute, what would God say? Would he understand your pain? And there was no need for forgiveness per se. She understood that. And I wish we had more of that. I just think that the world needs a lot more understanding.

I ask Ellen if how she worked with her friend was smilar to how she works as a pastoral counselor. Ellen explains that her motivation for becoming a pastoral counselor was to assist people in finding their own belief systems as she did.

One of the reasons I went into the program that I went into was because I feel that most people are socialized to a religious tradition, and then they play out their lives according to those principles and really choke on it in many ways. And that was one of the things that I wanted to get into because of the professional counseling that I do. I think you're socialized to religious traditions when very young, before you're even verbal. It's a structuring experience that shapes your whole world view. I thought it was very important to get back to those early roots in order to get effective counseling done. You can work with a person using a psychological process and language, but I really was very interested in moving back into the original religious socialization. I start working with a person at a psychological level, but I also use an awareness of religious socialization.

I don't mean to sound glib, but one's view of one's theology, one's personal theology, gives you a lot of information about where the person is psychologically . . . This is a very critical point when working with clients, particularly with women and their view of God as male . . . and what that does to them psychologically. A woman must come to her own beliefs, her own theology and view of God. As long as a woman attaches herself to a patriarchal religious tradition, she'll be fragmented.

We end our conversation by agreeing that our talk could go on for years. Ellen observes:

> The search for spiritual understanding is a process of discovery and dialogue. I have questions about my own experiences and observations, but beyond that I don't have all the answers. I don't even have the questions.

Lilli
Reference: Views of God, pp. 116–117

Lilli, who finds meaning in literature, art, my-thology, and living, practices psychotherapy in the Washington, D.C. area. Although she speaks of despair, struggle, and of existential truths, she is full of passion and vitality. The mother-daughter relationship is a recurring theme in our discussion, as it is in her professional work. Her dissertation, for example, articulated patterns of the mother-daughter relationship as depicted in literature written by women. The mother-daughter relationship also is the subject of the poems "Medusa's Legacy" and "The Naming of Laura-Athene." (Both poems appear at the end of this chapter.) She wrote "Medusa's Legacy" at a workshop, discussed in our conversation, which became the moment she wrote about as a spiritual experience. The second poem she wrote on the occasion of her stepdaughter's marriage.

The oldest of five children, Lilli grew up in a working-class Italian family in Buffalo. She attended Roman Catholic schools until graduate school. Lilli, now forty-two years old, lives with her husband, a poet and eccentric. Her daughter is studying anthropology at a college in another state and her stepdaughter, an artist, lives nearby.

The Mother Church and the Mother

In response to my opening request to talk about the development of her ideas about God and spirituality, Lilli discusses the origins of her ideas about religion, making an association between her relationship with her mother and her relationship with the church and religion.

I was raised Catholic and went to Catholic schools through undergraduate school. I don't know that my ideas of God can be separated from my experiences with Catholic schools and my family. From the beginning I didn't fit. From the moment I walked into kindergarten until I walked out of Catholic college, the overwhelming notion I had of myself was that I was too much. I was too emotional—too much showed on my face—the nuns said it; my mother said it. I was too smart alecky. I asked too many questions. I wanted too much. I was not sufficiently hidden, restrained, or self effacing.

I then ask Lilli if she can recall how she thought of God as a child. She responds:

God owns you. The first thing I remember the nuns saying when I was a little tiny kid was, "You do not treat me as if I am a person. It doesn't matter if you like me or not. It is my habit that you relate to; I am a representative of God." And the nuns run your whole life. They tell you who you are and what you should be. They judge you and so does God. Your self belongs to the nuns and to God. Your self is not—as it is—OK. You must be molded until you fit what God wants—a meek and obedient self that belongs to God and the nuns and your parents. You have two choices—your self goes underground or you are in constant rebellion and you feel alone and unlovable. I chose the latter, and in the process, came to believe that religion—spirituality—God—was a thief of my self. I felt they all wanted to own me, to engulf me. From the beginning I was resistant. I didn't want to give over. Let me tell you about my first communion. First communion is a very big deal—all those rehearsals—confessions, telling a priest how truly bad you are, all those little kids in white clothes with crucifixes around their necks. This is it. How you'll really belong. Well, I received the body of Christ. I went back to my seat trying to look holy and wanting to feel holy, and I felt nothing . . . nothing happened. The body of Christ tasted like scotch tape. This was my conscious thinking, but obviously something else was going on with my unconscious. I fainted and had to be carried out of church. My parents were embarrassed. There I was again . . . being too dramatic. I guess it was dramatic. I guess I really believed that now God owned me and I was terrified and preferred death.

I comment on how intense Lilli's early experiences with religion were. Lilli agrees, explaining how what she learned about love from religion became intertwined with the expectations for her love she felt from her mother. Next she offers an example, that occurred as an adult, of a time when she needed to protect herself from this fused image of mother and church.

> You know, they're always telling you that God is love—that God loves you. My mother said the same thing over and over again—"I love you." Of course, I believe it, but I didn't think very much of love. I interpreted love as obedience—as service to another. You know that one of the first questions in the Baltimore catechism was: "Why did God make you?" The answer is: "To know Him, to serve Him, and to love Him." All those words meant the same to me. Love equals service to others. It was the same in my family. Loving my mother meant not being who I was—really who I still am. My mother was very young when I was born—nineteen—and her marriage was not happy. I, her oldest child, was supposed to make her feel good—to validate her life—to live out her dreams—to serve her by giving over myself. This would have meant merging myself with her. Same thing with God—merging myself with Him. Last year I had an experience that was overwhelming. I went to an Episcopal church with a friend. I was really excited because a woman priest would be officiating. I was to see a woman in this powerful role, reserved for men. I was expecting to be proud, to feel female solidarity—all that. Instead I became very upset, hysterical almost. There was a woman standing at the pulpit wearing vestments with high heels sticking out from beneath, and she was speaking those despicable words—"It is in giving that we receive; love others." Those words coming out of a woman priest's mouth were my mother's words, the nun's words, the Church's words—all at once. It was a totality and there was no escape. That's the way I experienced it as a child . . . there was no escape.

We talk about how she protected herself from this fused threat to self made by her mother and religion. She describes how she turned to literature, discovering truths for herself about life in books. The first significant one, she remembers, is *The Secret Garden.*

I tried a couple of ways to protect myself. When I was in elementary school, I kept everyone away by being mean—or so they said. I see now I was depressed and lonely, but everyone then called me mean and grouchy. Then when I got to high school, I escaped by becoming very social. I laughed and played a lot and drank wine and smoked cigarettes. Then when I got to college, I escaped into major cynicism. I became an intellectual. I belittled religion and spirituality. I wanted nothing to do with it. I would pick apart everything, every little detail—expose inconsistencies and impossibilities. I just stepped back from religion for many years and assumed I was not religious. I'm still uncomfortable with spirituality.

But what was really important—what I really believed saved me—what showed me that pain could be transformed—that life could be whole—was books. From the time I was seven or eight, fiction was my major source of—not just pleasure—but life. I lived in books. In books, I lived other people's struggles and saw them transformed. In that way, I guess I began to transform some of my own. My family was uncomfortable with hurt—especially the inner pain that comes from rejection or loneliness or even death. My grandfather died when I was five. He'd been very important to me—a person who seemed to love me just as I was. My uncle, who also loved me, left shortly before that for Europe in World War II and my sister was born. These are the tragedies of every child's life. But no one helped me deal with them. No one acknowledged how much my world had changed, how lonely I was. But books helped. They really did. They gave me wholeness. They were about whole lives . . . The most significant novel for me when I was little was *The Secret Garden*. It's about a little orphaned girl who lives with an embittered, cynical old uncle. She finds some relief from her unhappiness in a tangled garden which had been untended since the death of the uncle's wife. And then the little girl discovers in the middle of the night a small boy, more miserable and sallow than she . . . a cripple who can't even walk. And she and the maid and her rosy-cheeked young brother teach the boy to walk and she learns to live and love herself . . . and all of them together teach the uncle by their example to give up his misery and begin life again. Everyone is transformed by the struggle. Everyone is whole.

I ask if the story of *The Secret Garden* isn't actually about something Lilli disbelieves, i.e., the saving power of love. She responds:

> That is a different kind of love. That is not the love that our religion is talking about, which is about giving yourself over. It is the kind of love that allows you to find yourself. Maybe that is what is meant by God, and the love of God. But I sure never heard it that way. I never experienced it that way. I never felt it that way.

I observe that there seems to be some fundamental link between how she sees God, the institution of the Catholic church and her early experience with her own mother.

> Yes, it is not separate . . . the church as an institution and God are the same thing. I've never understood my high school friends who became mystical . . . I mean, it's like giving the self, just giving it right over. My experience with giving over is pain, and there isn't anything redeeming about giving over.
>
> I experienced saving myself, holding myself, protecting myself, rather than giving myself over. I don't fit into groups easily. Religion seems like such a lousy idea . . . and it is completely beyond me how anybody could have faith in something outside herself. Everything becomes externalized . . . there is no self to hold onto . . . and I feel eaten and swallowed up. When I have what I would call spiritual experiences, it is when I feel almost totally myself—not even a self-consciousness intrudes. And these times are usually highly emotional, and I feel totally me—there is nobody else.

Lilli goes on to talk about her ideas about God and how the idea of God affects human behavior.

> I think the whole notion of a transcending God completely destroys our basic freedom. The idea of something transcendent—outside of yourself—is repugnant to me. There seems to be a basic contradiction between that idea and the idea that we have freedom. I don't usually think about a God. When I do, I often get angry; it seems like such a thieving notion. I probably am influenced by Dostoyevsky—especially *The Grand Inquisitor*—the whole idea of God robbing us of our freedom.

God, in a way, is the death of freedom. It seems to me that the concept of God is an attempt to run away from, to escape from, the inescapable despair that comes just facing your own life and living with that despair, going on and being loved in spite of the despair, choosing to go on living as fully as you can.

I never had God. In some ways I never really had God.

For a very short time, ten or twelve years ago, I went back to the Catholic church, and at first it felt wonderful. I felt I finally understood what the mystical body was and I felt united with the universe—with the spirit of everything. Then, again, I began to notice the institution and the priests and the sexism and I couldn't take it. It was not for me—not for a woman with a desire to live her own self. Again, I couldn't fit. Now to fit meant to accept my role as a woman as inferior. To fit meant to lose myself. Basically, religion had nothing to do with my life as a woman. It didn't seem to speak to my real everyday life of mothering, working, being. What did Jesus, a man who never married, never attached, have to do with my life, a life of being myself and of attaching to others. He could live out his destiny, be autonomous. He didn't relate to people as I did. At about this time I had a religious discussion with my mother. I said that Jesus's life seemed antithetical to relational, human love. She threw me out of her house.

Existential Truths in the Everyday

Lilli and I begin to talk about what it means for her to have dismissed religion, and of how she has had to come up with her own formulation to explain existence. To do this, she relies on literature, art, and her own personal experience.

Everyone suffers so, we are so isolated, it seems that the only overcoming of that is in the smallness—but the significance—of your everyday life—being fully with it, fully there. I understand why people have to go outside of themselves—it's very hard. I think there is a very great burden to our freedom . . . but also the greatest joy. When you just absolutely are struggling to be, it is not even being, its struggling to be. There is no time that feels better. (I've gotten more truthful as this is going on.) It is a heroic struggle. I feel the meaning of my life is in overcoming despair. Sometimes that is a spiritual experience. Facing the essential nothingness, meaninglessness, and still choosing to find the truth in whatever I am doing, the meaning in whatever I am doing. So it's real tiny, becomes very tiny. It's all my responsibility to do it. I feel I am a living struggle. When I feel most alive, I'm conscious of the struggle. I'm not overwhelmed by it, yet part of the struggle also is being overwhelmed by it, sometimes in the middle of the maelstrom of our life.

Lilli goes on to talk about wholeness, transformation, evil, and love.

We all are alone—and yet we also connect with one another through our common experiences, visions . . . I mean, that is the wonder of art . . . it's the wonder of any idea. We connect up with the wholeness of the experience. You watch King Lear. You see the whole of his life, you can see its beauty and its wholeness, the fact that he constantly struggled for his own truth. That seems like that is my religious experience, the struggle for your own truth.

I ask Lilli a question about the relationship between her interest in Jungian psychology, with its concepts of a collective unconscious and archetypes, and the existential dilemmas we have been talking about.

There are connecting threads. It's human nature that's connecting and I think that the thing that is so appealing about that is the recognition that everybody is searching for that, everybody is struggling to understand, to make meaning. Everybody is struggling and it's fascinating that people come up with similar concepts. I guess I suspect that it is genetic. I like it, because it is interesting and it is a contradiction. The thing I like about a Jungian perspective is that, unlike a lot of the psychoanalytic discussion, it's not reductionistic. It has a basic integrity, a wholeness. In the worst of psychoanalysis they focus on some isolated incident . . . isolated from any meaning. Jung talks about the search for meaning . . . and I think that inherent in our human nature . . . our genetic inheritance . . . is this pull from within to search—to seek.

I think Jung's notion of transformation is really important. Well, I think you can . . . there are all sorts of things that occur that transform you and increase your wholeness. Even tragic things can transform. You can go down and use them, not because they are ultimately good and that evil does not exist— but somehow or another they get into you and they transform you. They help continue making you. You keep discovering and discovering and discovering pieces of yourself through all of them. That is what is interesting about Jung to me. It's not that you're not touched by evil . . . it's that you use it . . . you transform it so it's not so depleting. But you have to live with it, to face it, to know it. You can't be saved from it, and that's the lie of a lot of religious explanations.

And it's not the love of religion that saves . . . it seems to me that the only thing that saves is going deeply inside yourself . . . it's nothing outside of yourself.

I ask Lilli how this relates to her work as a therapist. She responds:

In therapy there is a love, but it's a different kind of love. It's not the love that I heard of when I was growing up, not the love of religion, not a love of self-sacrifice. The love I talk about in therapy is the love of totally accepting another person . . . and at the same time, there is a respectful distance between you . . . an integrity given to your individuality.

I have had an ordinary life and I guess that is what makes me believe in the kind of people I work with in therapy . . . I am just ordinary . . . and yet I feel lucky and alive.

Transformations

We next talk about how her ideas of facing and transforming despair, of struggling to find one's own truth, have occurred in her own life.

The writing of my poem "Medusa's Legacy," which was what I chose as my spiritual experience, . . . that was a transformative experience. I found some truth at that moment that transformed darkness, evil, anger into something greater. I integrated it into myself and then there was more.

Lilli gives the background for the writing of her poem.

> I was attending a workshop at a conference that was run by Quakers. The workshop was about the fierce Indian Mother Goddess, Kali, or what she represented. The idea was to get in touch with your own fierce, dark, rampaging anger, to think of Kali, this all-devouring mother witch, who is destruction, who denies the child. Anyway, I had this emotional experience of writing the poem, and then we came back in and reassembled to do a role play. I was to play the part of the wife—this was the actual life situation of someone at the workshop. Anyway, I was to play the part of the wife who had to get off to work each morning. And each morning there would be confusion, too little time, and she would yell and scream at her young child. The husband—who I had very little sympathy for—he was staying home to find himself, and he was very upset by his wife's fierce anger, and her destructive rage toward the child. Well, I really got into that role. I became the wife, the destructive mother, and within seconds I was ready to destroy that child, who was being played by another workshop participant. I was so angry I just lost myself. Everybody became terrified of me. I felt like a pariah. No one felt comfortable talking to me after the role play; they didn't understand what had happened, didn't feel comfortable.
>
> But what had happened . . . I had experienced the denial of self. That is what the mother witch is . . . and that is what religion does . . . and the irony is, that is what makes the mother witch. She is venomous because she is expected to deny self, to give up in the service of others. And the anger and fury and destructiveness the mother witch spewed out was evil, but the evil grew out of the self-denial.
>
> I think that evil originates in the denial of self, in being told to conform, to give over. It doesn't come from anything external, it comes from a basic threat to self, of not being able to be.

I note that Lilli's proposal that evil originates in the denial of self coincides with feminist theologian Valerie Saiving's thesis. She posits that the experiences of women are more likely to lead to the sin of self-abnegation, of failure to take responsibility for self. It is men, not women, who are vulnerable to commit sin explained as the "will to power," which Saiving contends is derived from the male experience. Lilli agrees, and continues to explain how the writing of the poem became a formative moment in her life.

> The experience of writing the poem, and doing the role play of the mother witch at the workshop, really brought together a lot of these issues I had been struggling with all my life. My daughter was fifteen at the time, and I was terrified I was going to give to her the legacy my mother had given me: "If you can be, then I can't." That's the notion she had in her head, I think. It's either you or me. And she chose me—and the other children—but she never let us forget it. She made the ultimate sacrifice; she sacrificed herself. And in many ways she did choose us. In many ways she was good. Anyway, I was able to write this poem that expressed what the struggle was about. It didn't offer any resolution . . . it was just a naming . . . making a whole. The struggle was within me, and I could name it, and somehow that was transforming. I was able to work with the experience in a different way, because I could see it, it was out there—it was outside . . . I no longer was lost in the circle.

Our conversation now shifts to how this transformative experience of Lilli's is related to the truth that mythology and literature try to express, and how transformation is found in the everyday.

> Mythology is meaningful because it expresses the truth of human experiences. It's not just someone's individual truth. It's everybody's . . . it touches on some natural truth. I believe there are some inherent truths . . . truths in the struggle . . . that you have to descend, to be reborn, to transform experiences. Not that there is a cycle of life . . . there is a cycle of experiences.
> In the experience I was speaking of with my mother, I had to go deep into the misery of what it means to be a witch myself, what it means to have been a witch. I have to go into that . . . I have to go into that, to descend into it, to die into it. I have to get despairing and then somehow pull out of it a crystal,

like a poem, a painting, a dissertation, or a conversation. Something comes out that is whole and from that I can then learn something else.

And this all comes out of an ordinary life . . . it is all in a little tininess. It's in my own life, and it is a little tiny bit of a thing. And it's at that level that mythology is truth, because it describes the truth of human experiences . . . the process of life.

It's the process that it describes that has significance, the process of struggling with the miserable despairing. I write a poem. Sometimes it's not anything other than a conversation or an insight. But something comes out that is nameable. It gets made in its naming. Then you can take it back in a new way.

And you can get it from literature, from novels . . . and it is what I couldn't get from religion . . . I could not relate to a man named Jesus who never married, never had children, who didn't lead an ordinary life . . . full of disconnections . . . and I couldn't relate to some transcendent, removed God who didn't participate in these processes of life. The cosmic truths and large belief systems didn't work for me. They killed me . . . they tried to kill me. Transformation—it's found in the everyday. And that's what I try to do as a therapist and a parent. I mean that is my goal, at least in the last few years . . . when my child was struggling, not to deny the struggle, not to tell her everything would be OK, but to just live it with her and help her name it, and use it. Not use it to grow, I mean, I think that the whole notion of growth is ridiculous.

Lilli and I talk about how much of her struggle in life has been to lead her own life, to be herself, and not her mother. As we are musing about this, Lilli speaks about her mother's struggles.

In some ways my mother is a mess, but she is proud, and she has never given over. She has maintained the struggle . . . she continues to evaluate, to look at life. She continues . . . she has not had things go her way. She had probably made some really crummy choices about her life. In the face of all that her life is meaningful.

We both realize that we are at the end of the interview, sensing a completion with our topic. Lilli concludes our discussion by observing, once again, what has been an organizing principle of her life.

Nothing is given up in transformation.

Medusa's Legacy

I swam among the lily blooms
My feet were free; my hair was wild
From dark below in sacred tombs
a mother's cry: Come deep my child.

I swam up close and entered there
She smiled wide and pampered me
She tied my feet; she bound my hair
You're mine You're mine You're mine, said she,

I pulled, I screamed, I sunk my teeth
into her soft and shackled arm
Upon my head she placed a wreath—
A gorgon's crown of slip'ry charm.

Medusa mine, it's me you'll be.
Your breath will stink; your heart will groan
Although your fearsome eyes won't see
Your tears will turn brave men to stone.

I squat now in my own cold cave
I echo mother's lonely plea
I moan, I screech, I cry, I rave
And call my daughters home to me.

The Naming of Laura-Athene

Not flesh of my flesh are you
But flesh of my heart.
Born from a child mother
Yours was a difficult birth.

Before me only was Zeus
Mighty King of the gods
Even he had a splitting headache
On the eve of Athena's birth.
But she—bright eyed and bold—
Sprung forth—full grown from
His head—A warrior girl.

My heart was heavy with you
I could not walk for your weight
Nor rest, nor sleep, nor dream
For pain, for fear, for awe.

An induced labor, they say
is hard and quick, but ours
It was arduous and long
I was not prepared for your force
for the strength of your bright grey eyes
For power you had, my girl,
my cat-eyed Athene.

And so we suffered, you and I
Through the long dark night of the
Soul until with a last o'erwhelming
You tore through my sparrow ribcage.
Blood covered me. I reached inside
My breast and found my heart and you
Stepped out—full grown—A warrior girl.

And now I sing of thee clear-eyed
Athene—dressed in golder armor
carrying Medusa's head on your
unblemished shield as you walk
in your long, proud stride.
    GODDESS OF WAR

And I sing to you, gentle Pallas
Athene, child of my heart
carrying your palette and brush
dressed in the dappled colors
of morning.
    GODDESS OF ART

Emma
Reference: Interpersonal Event pp. 58–60

Emma has had an abiding interest in her Jewish heritage and religion since she was a child, although her relationship with her tradition has changed through the years. When younger, she eagerly learned about Jewish history and beliefs and participated in ritual and community life. In early adulthood, however, she began seriously questioning many of the religious suppositions she had accepted without challenge as a child. She continues to search for her own voice, seeking to create her own meaning out of her tradition. An integral part of her search is to find her place within a larger community.

Emma was raised in a closely knit middle-class professional family in a mid-Atlantic city. She is the oldest of four children. Her parents live near Emma and her husband, and they have maintained close family ties. Emma is an educator.

A Fall from Grace

Emma and I begin by talking about the event she chose as her spiritual experience, an abortion she had at the age of twenty. We talk in general about the practical as well as emotional difficulties of having an abortion before they were legalized. Our conversation then turns to the personal significance Emma's abortion had for her life and for her relationship with her mother. Until the time of her abortion Emma was her mother's "shining star." The abortion, however, caused a disruption in her relationship with her mother and father and made Emma feel as though she "had fallen from grace." A major difficulty between Emma and her mother was the way her mother found out she was pregnant. Emma remembers that she was discussing her pregnancy with her steady boyfriend on the telephone. His mother, unaware that the phone was in use, picked up an extension to make a call and listened in on their conversation. The boyfriend's mother, acting precipitously, called Emma's mother and told her of the pregnancy before Emma had time to tell her herself. Emma describes this as a "horrendous experience." I remark that this must have been quite a shock to her mother and ask her if she was upset. Emma responds:

> Ohhh . . . to put it mildly. She screamed, she yelled . . . she was just very disappointed. The disappointment was that she had to find out that way. That was where the disappointment was, not that I was pregnant, but just that she found out that way . . . from my boyfriend's mother, not from me.
>
> I know she was dreadfully hurt . . . that I hadn't come to tell her. I don't remember how our initial conversation went. She asked me if I was pregnant, and I said I'm not sure or I might be . . . whatever . . . and then the conversation went from bad to worse . . . you know, because of her already knowing. It was just a horrendous experience, and it affected me for years. The separation from her was so severe, the pain around that disappointment was so severe I couldn't deal with it . . .

I ask Emma if she would elaborate on how she had disappointed her mother by not telling her about her pregnancy before someone else did. Emma comments:

> It's an issue of trust . . . It's much more an issue of trust, and betrayal. I could tell her the worst things. I could tell her that I murdered somebody! That would be OK, she would be there for me, but if she read it in the paper, if she didn't think that I could come to her, that would freak her out. In our relationship there wasn't anything we couldn't tell one another . . . and know . . . the other person would be there to support you through it . . . but not to have someone else know, especially someone outside of the family.

Without any discussion, Emma's father quietly arranged a trip to New York City so that she could have an abortion, which was illegal at the time.

> My father and I went on a "business trip." We planned it, it was in the summer . . . a short trip. I got to go to New York with my father. We went shopping . . . I still have the skirt and jersey he bought me . . . to this day. I'm about to give the jersey away. Anyway, we went shopping together, then he took me to the doctor's office. We waited till everybody left. My father was there, the doctor, and his nurse were there. I think the doctor gave me a shot—probably sodium pentothal. I'm trying to remember whether he did or not, as a matter of fact, I don't think he did. I think he did it pretty much locally. Because I was aware . . . He told me when there'd be discomfort around the cervix; I think he basically gave me a D & C. I think I was about eight weeks along, no more. We were out and we went back to the hotel on one of those city buses. Then we slept over and went home the next day. I was on tons of Vitamin B complex and C. You're supposed to eat like six lemons a day, for the Vitamin C. I was drinking gallons of tomato juice for about three weeks. It was amazing. And what I remember was that I never talked about it with my dad.

I ask Emma if, at the time, she was certain about her decision to have an abortion. She replies:

> At that time I didn't think about it. I had read so many *True Confession* magazines . . . about all that garbage that people go through . . . the melodrama, there was no way I was going to put my parents through the whole experience . . . my going off and being pregnant. I never thought of it. I have never thought of it along the ideas of struggle or agonized over it at that time. It was simply that there was no choice. That was the only choice. It had nothing to do with me. I didn't even think about me having the baby—about the fact that I was pregnant, I would be a mother. It was that I had let my parents down . . . they didn't find out through me. That in itself was so bad that there was no way I was going to go off for nine months, or have to put my parents through all that . . .
> The thing that happened to me . . . the abortion . . . it

was something that wore very hard on me, for a long time. I remember the day . . . I had the abortion on my brother's birthday, so I remember it every year. You know, I would have a child this July who's seventeen years old, and I look at some of the young people that I'm working with and think about having a child this old. Every now and then, I've thought about it. I look at it.

Redemption at the Wailing Wall

I tell Emma that I am impressed by the significance she placed on what she saw as her responsibility to her parents. I observe that her feelings of remorse did not come from having an abortion, but rather because she felt that she had failed her parents. Emma explains that the year after her abortion she was in a kind of daze, full of anguish because she thought she had disappointed her parents, and hurt by the estrangement between them. We talk about how painful that time was for her. I ask Emma how she was able to finally come to terms with what happened. The summer following her abortion, Emma explains, she took a trip to Israel and began a process of healing the breach with her parents.

> I went to Israel, and one of the first places that I went to was the Wailing Wall. That is where I had this long talk with God. It was the first time that I was able to talk to anyone about my experience. I told God about the whole experience, and basically asked to be forgiven. That was the first time I felt like I could live with myself . . . I was so aware of . . . being in touch with somebody else, and that there really was something that was out there . . . I felt so connected. It was as if I had finally given myself permission to take my own life back. That whole past year was lost. I was barely functioning . . . I was so out of touch. I felt so distanced from my parents. I was living at home, but I was totally out of connection with my mother, who was a major woman in my life, and I felt I had caused his major disappointment.
>
> Until the Wailing Wall, it was as though I didn't feel

that there was anybody that I could tell . . . that would still like me, except God. My visions of God at that time included the idea that it wouldn't matter what had happened in my life—God would still love me. Then there is the whole issue of repentance, recalling, and baring your soul, too. I really felt it then. I just stayed there, at the Wailing Wall, for a couple of hours. I sobbed and sobbed. I was just sitting there . . . I had no idea what any other people were doing. I was sobbing, but it didn't make any difference to anybody, because everybody else there assumed that you were there to talk to God.

And I knew as soon as I got to Israel, that the Wailing Wall was where I had to go. It wasn't a temple, it wasn't anyplace else. Because that's where I knew . . . that's where God was, in some important way. Not that you couldn't talk to God anywhere . . . but it was just that . . . well, it was like going home . . . like you knew somebody would be there.

When I left the Wailing Wall, it was as if I could breathe easily for the first time in a long time . . . the wind was back . . . the sun was there. I made it through the next three years. In going there I found some way of unburdening. I think that going there probably kept me out of a psychiatric ward.

We talk about how this experience gave her a renewed sense of connection when before she had felt apart. I ask Emma if this experience at the Wailing Wall closed the issue for her. She explains that the process of healing was not complete, that she continued to work through her experience and the isolation from others that she felt.

It was a major secret . . . I never told anybody. For years I didn't tell anyone . . . I just told one of my sisters last year. But I always felt that everybody knew . . . that there was some sign on me or something. I'd go to all these women's groups, and they would be discussing abortion, but me, never! It didn't go with my image. It wasn't until a personal growth workshop that I was able to tell someone else. There was a woman there . . . she had been to introductory counseling workshops and knew very little about counseling. I knew that I liked her, and somehow I wanted to tell her this terrible secret that I needed to get off my chest. She let me tell her, and cry, and cry, and cry, and cry . . . it was like this weight was lifted. And then, later, I remember that I was able to tell this man that I was driving with to Pittsburgh . . . but, God, it felt like I had nobody at home that I could ever tell. And, in reality, it took a few years before I could do so.

I ask Emma if she ever told her mother about what she had gone through. She tells me that eventually she and her mother were able to talk about the experience around the abortion.

> She forgave me . . . after a while we were able to joke about whether or not I was her shining star. She was amazed that I thought that I wasn't. We've had some heart-to-heart talks, wondering what would have happened if she hadn't been so freaked out. We wonder whether she would have wanted me to have the baby. She's anguished a whole lot about it, and felt badly about letting her feelings get in the way of being able to have said, "It is OK, it's happened, think about it, have the baby. You're going with this man, you're thinking about getting married anyway, so why don't you do it this summer instead of next summer?" I really didn't know for a number of years that she anguished over it, and she didn't want to discuss it with me because she thought it would be too painful for me. But we got a chance to talk. I reassured her that it was not her fault; it was not her unclear thinking. It worked out for the best. I don't know whether or not I would have been able to have handled it at that point, suddenly being married, suddenly being pregnant, everybody knowing that I was pregnant at the time. I mean, given where I was in terms of who I was as a woman, I don't think I would have been able to deal with that image of myself, and having to live with that, at that time.

I ask if she has ever talked to her father about the abortion, and her feelings that she had disappointed them.

> I've thought about it, but, I can't quite think about why I would do it. Obviously it would be for my benefit; I'm sure my dad never thinks about it. Why drag it up? And I'm making an assumption. Maybe he does. With all the information on abortion and everything else, women's rights and all kinds of things—both my parents were for the women's movement . . .

> What my father did for me then—it was a hell of a thing for him to do as a man . . . to come through for me that way. Sometimes I've cried a lot over that; it was just his love for me, which is expressed so differently than my mother's. My dad had to make the arrangements, talk to his friends, let them know his daughter was pregnant, find an abortionist, when abortion was illegal.
>
> He had never mentioned it, never said anything, never alluded to it . . . even when we talk about children, abortion, . . . my dad isn't one to dwell on the past. You can't spend your life in the past.

I ask Emma if she knows whether or not her mother and father have ever talked to one another about their experience with her abortion.

> I never asked her directly if she talked to Dad. My mother and father talk about everything, so I'm sure when my mother was anguishing about her decision—whether or not that had been a good decision—obviously she's talked about that with my dad. I'm sure over the years they have talked about it together. But I think for my dad his way of taking care of me was to let it lie. Let's get over it. Let's put it behind us. Let's move on.

A Mother's Love and Influence

I observe that Emma's relationship with her mother comes up repeatedly in our conversation. She agrees, commenting, "Well, she's had a great impact on my life; she's a major figure." She then recalls an example of her mother's influence.

> I remember being in the sixth grade . . . practicing the piano and all of a sudden I just started sobbing . . . my mother heard me stop playing and came down the stairs, put her arms around me, and said, "What's wrong?" I felt like none of my friends liked me because I was being friends with one of the little girls that the other girls on the block didn't like. She just told me that I should never hurt Robin—that was the little girl's

name—because of this other "cliquey" group. She said if they would do that, then they're not worth that.

She also recalls a time in high school when she was horrified to find out that her younger sister had betrayed her mother by disclosing a family matter to someone outside the family.

> My sister was in tenth grade—I was in the twelfth grade. She was writing an English journal as an assignment from her teacher and said I could read it. She had written about some incident with my mother, when she was very angry with my mother. I couldn't believe she wrote about it and let someone else read it . . . I ripped it out of her journal . . . you don't just tell someone . . . do you know I still have it?

I ask Emma if this incident with her sister caused any lasting friction between them. Emma recalls that throughout the 1960s, she and her sister had a troublesome relationship. Around ten years ago, however, Emma explains that she began to pursue her sister.

> I decided to have it out—and I tried to talk to my sister about what I had done. She just felt so betrayed. It took a long time. I called her once a week, no matter where she was living . . . We finally began to deal with it . . . I did that to her out of my relationship with my mother . . . I just felt that no matter how disgusted you get, you didn't tell your English teacher about your mother . . . It felt like such a betrayal of family trust.

I note, with humor, that her attitude would rule out psychotherapy. She replies, laughing, "At that time, it would, it certainly would!" I ask Emma if she still feels that she should not hold back anything from her mother.

> Well, there are some things that I haven't shared with her . . . difficulties that [my husband] and I have had, or struggles around certain kinds of things because it felt like too much of a soap opera. Also, she understands that we can handle a lot of things ourselves, and we can deal with it rather than running to mother. She takes up everybody's family problems. My mother is a real good listener, she has a good perspective and talks to people about issues . . . so many people come to my mother. My

mother has this capacity for unquestioning, unrelenting love. They want to talk with her and use her as a confidant . . . My mother takes all this to heart. Sometimes she doesn't get enough sleep, her mind doesn't rest. So I feel that if there is a short–term problem, then it doesn't make any sense to worry her. And there also are times when I'll say, "OK, I'm not going to protect my mother." It makes much more sense to tell her and share this with her—it makes sense then for her to know what's going on, and she'll figure out how she's going to deal with it. At those times I don't try to take care of her, protect her . . . I mean, if there are really important things going on, you really don't have a relationship unless you can tell the other person . . . to know that they'll be strong enough . . .

I note that unlike some other women, who feel as though their mothers are trying to intrude in their life, Emma genuinely appreciates her mother's interest in her life.

Yes. There are definitely things that I have to share with her. And that's OK. And there are many things that I do share with her. The thing that's important is that I know how she'll take it. I know I will be accepted, and, of course, it wouldn't matter what it was. It's bonding; she knows that I could come to her and that together we would try and figure out some way of dealing with the issue. I wouldn't be ostracized, thrown out, or ridiculed, or humiliated, or disapproved of. And it's interesting, I could probably even imagine a situation where I could think of something to tell my mother that she might disapprove of, but she would not abandon me in the solution to the problem. What she is saying is that the two of us will always be together—whatever the problem is. We're going to stick together through this.

Religious Training and Appreciation

We begin to discuss Emma's religious training and the development of her ideas about God, and religion, and the meaning of life. Here, too, her mother has a significant influence on her.

My mother is a very religious person, though not around ritual. She was brought up in an Orthodox home and my father was not. She gave up a lot of things when they went to live with his family. There were a lot of rituals that went by the wayside. My mother is a very religious person in her spirit—in her faith, in her relationship to God and how the world works. She communicated a lot of that. So growing up, interestingly enough, there was this very powerful sense of God being present. And much more as a concept, rather than as this little old man with a long white beard, flowing, and whatever.

I've struggled with God for a long time. God seems to be this particular spirit that was always powerful, that was loving, that pretty much was in charge of what was happening . . . someone to whom you could talk. I know my mother sometimes views God as having powers of intervention, being able to act; but I don't. God was just out there.

I ask Emma what kind of religious involvement she had as a child. She recalls how she loved going to temple and participating in Jewish community life. She began Hebrew school in the third grade, attending after her public school classes ended. This association became a vital part of her life.

I loved going to temple, you know. I loved doing cantorial things in the junior congregation, just being there. I had been in Hebrew school, and one year I decided I wanted to get the pin—the congregation's pin. You would get that pin for going to services regularly every week for a year. Anyway, that was in the third grade, so I was about seven years old. They start you out in Hebrew school in the third grade, because you have to be able to read and write, unlike public school. I'd go from 2 or 2:30 to about 4:30 in the afternoon, about two days a week. Then I'd also go on Sundays. I learned well. I was fast. I was real smart. I got lots of admiration and appreciation about how bright I was, so I loved Hebrew school. When I decided to go to the junior congregation, I decided to be a cantor and I sang all of the prayers. I loved to go, because I loved the Hebrew and all that . . . I loved to go there—you know, all those kinds of things, and friends you met. I loved all the information. I loved the holidays . . . I remember Sukkoth, which is in the fall. It is a celebration of the fall harvest—celebrating plenty. And there are all kinds of fruits and sweets. So it was a lot of fun. And when I finished . . . you finish after six years, so you are in eighth grade of public school. When I graduated, the principal gave a speech. He held out his hands, palms down, waist high, to indicate the point where you start school. He began to raise his right hand a few inches, indicating that's how high you get when you graduated from elementary school, then he raised it a little higher, indicating that's how high you get when you graduated from high school, and on up until his hand was very high, showing graduation from graduate school. Then he raised his other hand, saying, "And, when you graduate from Hebrew school, you stop here (which was well below the other hand). Now what does that say about your Jewish education?"

The visual effect of his hands, showing a lack of equality between Jewish and public education was significant. I always enjoyed the beauty of symmetry. And I knew then that I wanted to go all the way through (so both hands would be on the same finished plane). And I did. I attended four years of Hebrew high school and then four years of Hebrew college. I wanted to know about being Jewish, and to integrate what it meant to be a Jew with all the other information I was getting. (At the time, that's what I thought of my public school education, as that "other information.") So, for the rest of my school career, I went to public school, then I attended Hebrew school, and I did that through college.

And throughout, I always felt very connected to God. That was a very important part of my life—attending Hebrew school. Those were the people I hung out with. You ate dinner there. You came home late at night from there. You had a whole other life.

The Emergence of Doubt

Because I knew that Emma's current conception of God and religion is different now than it was when she was younger, I ask her when she began to doubt.

Nobody in the community that I belonged to challenged the idea . . . then I attended a humanistic Jewish seminar and the people sitting around the room began to admit they were practically atheists.

I ask her if this is when her doubts began. Emma answers:

Oh, I think it had to do with the people I began spending time with. I began spending time with people who were in the women's movement, I began learning. . . . How old was I? I was about twenty-two. And then I began to have my eyes opened. I was with some of the women who were in the forefront of the movement—the women's collective. I started to question a lot of things . . . and God certainly came in for his share of questioning.

A number of these women were often Jewish women. It was hard for me to deal with their socialist politics, things that I had never thought about before. And then, a couple of women and I took a course in economics from [a local university]. And, part of my questioning—the doubt—had to do with my experience in the personal growth workshop, when I had a chance to talk with a woman about my abortion for the first time. That got me involved with a counseling group and it was the counseling class where I began to get hooked up with these people who were involved with the women's movement. These were people from [a local university] and a few other places. Very quickly, I became very good at counseling. I began to be a leader of the counseling community very early. I was very good at helping other people talk about the most intimate details of their life. I, on the other hand, was harboring this major secret about my life—which still impacted on my life. There were other things that I'd share and deal with about self-doubt and other things.

I knew that Emma had met her husband through this counseling community. I ask her about meeting her husband. She explains that whereas others in the counseling community assumed that all of Emma's self-confidence was real, he saw through her "self-assured image." He recognized, Emma says, "where I was really hurting and suffering."

[My husband] just began to go after that . . . and I gravitated toward him. I was able to share who I really was . . .

the idea of feeling adequate in this area, but scared in another. I could never tell anybody I was scared. When I got scared, instead of getting panicky or anxious, I go to the other extreme. I look very relaxed, very calm. Nobody recognized what was really happening to me, that I was dying inside. It was not part of my image to reveal that I was afraid of things.

We talk about how hard it is to live that way, presenting a false self to the world, especially when one's real self is in need. I ask Emma if she understood how this happened, and she then describes how she discovered the origins of her fears.

I was always afraid as a child and later that I was not good enough, and I think that had to do with being the oldest of the children. I think, as a child, I concluded that my parents must have kept on having more children because I wasn't good enough. So they had to have another child, because I wasn't providing enough . . . No matter how I tried, I was never good enough. Through counseling sessions and workshops, I was able to figure out . . . to realize there was another explanation. I realized that it also was possible that they continued to have children because I was satisfying—quite the reverse of my first reaction. Because I felt secure enough to understand this possibility—that the other children indicated my parent's satisfaction with me—I was able to ask my mother about this. I told her my fantasies as a child, and what I thought might be the case now. She confirmed what I had just realized. She said, they thought "she's so wonderful, let's have another one."

We return to our discussion of how serious religious doubts emerge as she is exposed to a number of new and challenging systems of political thinking.

I began meeting a number of people who were looking at important issues—racism, homophobia, women's issues, anti-Semitism. We couldn't begin to look at those without taking a look at the politics.

Patriarchy was an issue . . . the feminist women began to talk about whether God could be female . . . challenging the whole issue. It made you realize that when you thought of a God "up there," then you have the easiest excuse to abdicate any self-responsibility if you assumed God took care of everything.

I had this whole community of women who were talking about God. "Did He exist?" "Didn't He exist?" "Need He be a He?" I'm listening to all these things and wondering about my beliefs. While I was involved with these women, I also was getting my scientific training . . . I was a pre-med major in school. I never had any conflict with my religious beliefs and my scientific training. God created the world in six days—well, scientifically, six days is a whole different time length. In fact, I had an explanation for how miracles happen—it never dented the love I had for the miracle in my own mind. I could separate those two—the religious and the scientific—and just love each of them. It's still something near and dear. It's a childhood image that I had about the burning bush, or that I had about the Red Sea . . . or I had about Elijah and his vision, or Isaiah's. Almost like art . . . just another way of taking scientific fact.

So I went through this phase where God and I were at odds and I sometimes didn't know whether or not I really didn't believe or whether or not it was a phase—a God-is-dead phase. It was an intellectual challenge; it streched me in an area that, as a child, I had accepted and never challenged. It didn't mean I couldn't come back to God. But it would be by choice and by thought, and I could then change my views as to who God was. I'm at that point, again; thinking about God . . . what is God, who is God, or does it have to be. I still like the idea of there just being these attributes that all humans strive for . . . women and men. And I think of God being red, black, gay . . . of God as just holding out acceptance of all humans. So I see God as having all of the human attributes, outside of all the pettiness, outside of all the patterns we get trapped in, outside of all those things that distance us from each other . . . racism, sexism, homophobia, anti-Semitism.

Emma recalls that as a child, "I was really into the notion of the chosen people. I was so into the chosen people. And I was even chosen amongst the chosen." Emma recalls that she derived a great deal of security from the thought that she was someone special. Then she returns to her present ideas about God.

Obviously, I look back and I see things very differently. Today, if I want to sit down and "talk to God," it is basically myself getting a chance to think out loud. It all has to do with focusing your attention on being able to deal with whatever you have to deal with . . . and really developing self-reliance, but not self-reliance to the point of isolation.

Finding Her Own Voice and Locating Community

Thinking of a conversation I had with Ellen, one of the other women I interviewed, I remark how it requires more effort when one's beliefs don't fit into some neat and conventional system, because there seems to be a constant demand to construct one's own explanations rather than to rely on preexisting ones. Emma then begins to talk about her continuing search to find her own meaning in the context of her Jewish heritage, but how this process is made more difficult because her husband isn't Jewish. When she and her husband discuss children, religious issues come to the forefront of their marriage. Her husband, who is willing to raise any of their children as cultural Jews, has rejected all religious traditions. Emma, however, still sees possibilities for herself, and any possible children, within her Jewish tradition.

> At first, when we were married, I focused on female-male relationship issues. That took precedence at first. I put being Jewish, and what that meant, aside. First, I had to continue to figure out what it was to be a woman. Then when I had the female-male issues pretty well resolved, I became frightened about questioning my Jewishness. I knew that by taking it up—what it meant to be a Jew—might challenge my relationship with [my husband] . . . because he isn't Jewish. When I understood this, it was very frightening to have to deal with my having given up something of my own Jewishness . . . my functioning as a Jew in the world . . . and this continues to challenge me.
>
> I'm still looking. That's why visiting all of these different Jewish congregations has been so important. It's part of a search to reclaim a lost piece of myself.

Emma now has no association with a Jewish temple or community, and she has left the counseling community. The desire for community in her life still persists, however, and she talks about it.

> I miss a sense of community. It didn't matter what color you were, etc., there were certain ideas that were held in common . . . part of the difficulty is, how do [my husband and I] develop community together? We don't have a religious community together; we don't have an idea of community; we don't have a PTA.
>
> Lack of communities has always been difficult for me. But the other thing is to take another look at the concept of community, to get outside of my own stereotypes of what I thought community was. I was thinking, I know so many people, but we don't spend time together—most of my friends don't know one another. So I used to try to figure out how to have activities that could get people together, and be able to know one another.
>
> Now, community seems to be just developing strong friendships. . . . It doesn't necessarily mean they all have to know one another, but that I have a solid connection to each of them.

We conclude our conversation with Emma's assessment of her current relationship to God and religion.

> At this point, I don't feel isolated from God. I feel much more freedom . . . to interact . . . to think about the concept. Everything at this point feels very fluid. I feel at a very different place in my life. I can now experience all kinds of things that before I put off limits, and all kinds of things that before did not seem to fit part of my image. I've freed myself from much of the rigidities of my old self-image. I give myself permission now to investigate and participate more fully in life. I can choose.

Postscript: Finding Meaning
in Relationship to the Ordinary

We have, as aware beings, a "burden of under-standing,"[1] to imagine, to seek meaning. It is this human capacity to envisage, to reach for some truth, that defines us as human. "The activity of being a person is the activity of meaning making,"[2] we have heard. And the activity, or process, of being a person can occur only in relationships. Our relationships may be with an actual other person, or they may be an intrapsychic or intrasubjective relationship, as we internalize our experiences with significant others in our lives and they become part of who we are. The mythic relationships we enter are just as real as our actual and intrapsychic relationships in our formation and reformation. As I have reported on the spiritual experiences of the ninety-four women of this study, I have argued that the significance of relation-ships for these women's lives implies a fundamental reality of relatedness,[3] and that the relationship of psyche and spirit meta-phorically depicts the relationship between being-in-relationship and being-in-relatedness. Both depend on one another for their vitality and for their very existence.

Now we have had a chance to meet and to know better six of these ninety-four women. The portrait of each of these six women offers more than an account of one or two significant moments in a woman's life. The in-depth interviews given by each woman allow us to see the process each goes through to find meaning for her life and the influences on that process. Each woman's story depicts the process of human living, which is the process of meaning making, of coming to some understanding of her relationship to the world, to others, and to herself.

A traditional-charismatic religious explanation satis-fies Beth's questions about meaning. Her life is given a structure by her belief in, and her adherence to, the tenets of her faith. Other women, like Barbara, Emma, and Ellen, while acknowledging some historical debt to the religions in which they were raised, continue to reformulate and integrate what they have been taught in the past with their personal experiences and broadened perspectives. Emily, although active in her religious group, always has relied more on her own sense of purpose than on the teachings of any organized religion. And, Lilli, more than the other women, has renounced all organized religion. A self-described apostate, she has created meaning for herself without an organized religious community. Instead, she relies on symbolic communities that she locates in literature and art, and on an actual community of family and friends.

Although each of these women has her own story to tell, and each arrives at different interpretations of her relationship to the world, all describe the same processes. Whatever conclusions they have reached, all are seekers of meaning. Every one of these six women imagines "not only . . . a place, but . . . Space; not only . . . time, but . . . History."[4]

These six women's lives not only reveal the human drama of meaning making, but they also offer another lesson about the nature of human existence, I believe. They are able to teach us, not because they are in any way a "special" group of women, but precisely because they are not. These women's lives are probably much like many other women's lives, and yet if we reflect on the process, and not the content, of the lives of these six ordinary women, we learn more than the facts of their particular personal stories. We gain a deeper insight into the human condition. It will not be prophets, gurus, saints, or experts in psychology who will make our meaning, offer us wisdom about how to live our lives, or explain the world. Scientific theories and theological explanations may point us in a particular direction, but ultimately we learn about life through the living of our own lives and the lives of others.

We may not make the same choices for ourselves as any of one of these women made for herself. We do not have to adopt, or even admire, the particular way a person arrives at her interpretation of the world or the conclusions she reaches. What endures is not a particular woman's belief or the current resolution of her relationship to that which is important, because these very likely will change. This was illustrated by one woman who, when listening to herself in the dialogue of the interview, came to realize that she had not adequately worked through her childhood experience with religion, and with this awareness began the process of reexamination and, perhaps, reformulation. It is the human striving to understand, to believe, to find coherence, that remains the same. It is not necessarily the facts about a person's striving that are important, but the fact that they strive.

I agree with Lilli that truth, beauty, and wholeness are found within the living of our ordinary lives. At the same time, and I think Lilli would agree, I have come to realize in my work as a clinician something of a paradox: although truth and beauty arise out of the ordinary, there is nothing "ordinary" about any one person's life. Each of us repeatedly face challenges that call into question a sense of order or coherence we once felt, but no longer do. There are "dark nights of the soul" for all of us, times when we don't know where we belong or why we are here. And, as a condition of being human, we must somehow tolerate the conflict created by our longing to separate and go out into the world, to make our own statement, with the equally poignant pull to be included, attached, connected to another. Somehow, over and over again throughout our lifetimes, each of us must arrive at some resolution to these challenges and opportunities that life inevitably presents to us.

At times any one person's resolution may cause pain and injury to herself, to others, and to the world. Not all resolutions work, or are wise, or just. Human pathology cannot be separated from this desire for wholeness or truth, however. Instead, it reveals how the human need to find a Space and a History can become distorted by circumstances, personal choice, and, perhaps, by chance. It is in this ordinary and very human struggle to live with the responsibility for our freedom, the knowledge of our death, and the uncertainty about our future, that some of us find some of the time the possibilities for our extraordinary courage to strive for a coherence or wholeness in life.

All of us have a story to tell. It is the story of being human, of reaching for new understandings, of appreciating mystery, and of seeking wholeness, beauty, and truth. All we need to do is to ask, and to listen.

Notes

Prologue

1. John McDargh, *Psychoanalytic Object Relations Theory and the Study of Religion: On Faith and the Imaging of God* (Lanham, Md: University Press of America, 1983).
2. Susanne K. Langer. *Philosophy in a New Key: A Study in the Symbolism of Reason, Rite, and Art* (Cambridge, Mass.: Harvard University Press, 1942) p. 241.
3. Heinz Kuhut, *How Does Analysis Cure?* (Chicago: University of Chicago Press, 1984).
4. Harry Stack Sullivan, *The Interpersonal Theory of Psychiatry* (New York: Norton, 1953); Karen Horney, *Feminine Psychology* (New York: Norton, 1967); W.R.D. Fairbairn, *An Object Relations Theory of the Personality* (New York: Basic Books, 1954); Harry Guntrip, *Personality Structure and Human Interaction* (London: Hogarth Press, 1961); Guntrip, *Psychoanalytic Theory, Therapy, and the Self* (New York: Basic Books, 1971); D.W. Winnicott, *The Maturational Processes and the Facilitating Environment* (New York: International Universities Press, 1965).
5. Robert Kegan, *The Evolving Self* (Cambridge, Mass.: Harvard University Press, 1982); Robert Kegan, Gil G. Noam, Laura Rogers, "The Psychologic of Emotion: A Neo-Piagetian View," in *New Directions in Child Development, Emotional Development*, D. Cicchitti and P. Hesse, eds. (San Francisco: Jossey Bass (1982); Gil G. Noam, Lawrence Kohlberg, John Snarey, "Steps Toward a Model of the Self," B. Lee and G. Noam, eds. (*Developmental Approaches to Self*) (New York: Plenum Press, 1984); Gil G. Noam, "Stage, Phase, and Style: The Developmental Dynamics of the Self," M. Berkowitz and F. Oser, eds., *Moral Education* (Hillsdale, N.J.: Lawrence Earlbaum, 1985).
6. Jean Baker Miller, *Toward a New Psychology of Women* (Boston: Beacon Press, 1976); Miller, "The Development of Women's Sense of Self," *Work in Progress*, No. 84–01, Wellesley College, Stone Center for Developmental Services and Studies, 1984; Nancy Chodorow, *The Reproduction of Mothering* (Berkeley: University of California Press, 1978); Dorothy Dinnerstein, *The Mermaid and the Minotaur: Sexual Arrangements and Human Malaise* (New York: Harper Colophon Books, 1977); Carol Gilligan, *In a Different Voice: Psychological Theory and Women's Development* (Cambridge, Mass.: Harvard University Press, 1982); Helen Block Lewis, *Shame and Guilt in Neurosis* (New York: International Universities Press, 1971); Lewis, *Psychic War in Men and Women* (New York: International Universities Press, 1976).
7. Otto F. Kernberg, *Object Relations Theory and Clinical Psychoanalysis* (New York: Jason Aaronson, 1979).
8. Carol Ochs, *Women and Spirituality* (Totowa, N.J.: Rowman and Allanheld, 1983), p. 111.
9. Kegan, *The Evolving Self*, p. 11.

1. Women's Lives and Reality

1. I. Broverman, D. Broverman, F. Clarkson, P. Rosenkrantz, and S. Vogel, "Sex-Role Stereotypes and Clinical Judgments of Mental Health," *Journal of Social Issues* (1972), 28:59–78.

2. Although Kohut has very insightfully discussed the probability that minimal shortcomings in early childhood allow one to develop "the transmuting internalization and creative change," he does not refer to women, or to the effects differential power relationships in society have on children's development of self.

3. Jean Baker Miller, *Toward a New Psychology of Women* (Boston: Beacon Press, 1976), p. 27.

4. Susanne Langer, *Philosophy in a New Key* (New York: Harcourt Brace & World, 1963.)

5. Valerie Saiving Goldstein (now Saiving), "The Human Situation: A Feminine View," *Journal of Religion* (April 1960), 40:101.

6. Jessie Bernard, *The Female World* (New York: Free Press, 1981).

7. Carol Gilligan, *In a Different Voice: Psychological Theory and Women's Development* (Cambridge, Mass.: Harvard University Press, 1982).

8. Elizabeth Schussler Fiorenza, *In Memory of Her: A Feminist Theological Reconstruction of Christian Origins* (New York: Crossroad, 1983), p. xx.

9. Rosemary Radford Ruether, *New Women, New Earth: Sexist Ideologies and Human Liberation* (New York: Seabury Press, 1975), p. xiv.

10. *Ibid.*, p. xii.

11. Noami Goldenberg, *Changing of the Gods.* (Boston: Beacon Press, 1979).

12. Goldstein (now Saiving), "The Human Situation: A Feminine View."

13. Judith Plaskow, *Sex, Sin, and Grace.* (Washington, D.C.: University Press of America, 1980), p. 151.

14. Helen Block Lewis, *Shame and Guilt in Neurosis.* (New York: International Universities Press, 1971).

15. *Ibid.*, p. 248.

16. Eleanor E. Maccoby and Carol N. Jacklin, *The Psychology of Sex Differences.* (Stanford, Calif.: Stanford University Press, 1974); Helen Block Lewis, *Psychic War in Men and Women.* (New York: New York University Press, 1976).

17. Carol P. Christ and Judith Plaskow, eds., *Womanspirit Rising: A Feminist Reader in Religion.* (San Francisco: Harper and Row, 1979); Mary Daly, *Beyond God the Father: Toward a Philosophy of Women's Liberation* (Boston: Beacon Press, 1973); Daly, *Gyn/Ecology: The Meta-Ethics of Radical Feminism* (Boston: Beacon Press, 1978); Carol Ochs, *Behind the Sex of God* (Boston: Beacon Press, 1977); Rosemary Radford Ruether, *New Woman, New Earth*; Ruether, *Sexism and God-Talk: Toward a Feminist Theology* (Boston: Beacon Press, 1983).

18. Vicki Nobel, *Motherpeace: A Way to the Goddess Through Myth, Art, and Tarot* (San Francisco: Harper and Row, 1983); Hallie Inglehart, *Woman Spirit* (Wolf Creek, Ore., 1983) a magazine published quarterly containing articles, poems, and art in which women express their spirituality. In addition to these writings from the women's spirituality movement, this new conception of God also can be seen in the liturgical events created by the Women's Alliance for Theology, Ethics, and Ritual.

19. Jean Baker Miller, "The Development of Women's Sense of Self," Work in

Progress, No. 84–01, Stone Center for Developmental Services and Studies, Wellesley College, 1984.

20. W. R. D. Fairbairn, *An Object Relations Theory of the Personality* (New York: Basic Books, 1954); H. Guntrip, *Personality Structure and Human Interaction* (London, Hogarth, 1961); Heinz Kohut, *The Analysis of the Self* (New York: International Universities Press, 1971); Kohut, *The Restoration of Self* (New York: International Universities Press, 1977); D. W. Winnicott, *The Maturational Processes and the Facilitating Environment* (New York: International Universities Press, 1965).

21. Carol Ochs, *Women and Spirituality* (Totowa, N.J.: Rowman and Allanheld, 1983), p. 13.

22. Martin Buber, *I and Thou*, Walter Kaufman, trans. and intro. (New York: Scribner, 1970), p. 62.

23. *Ibid.*, p. 80.

24. Mary Hunt, "Lovingly Lesbian: Toward a Feminist Theology of Friendship," in Robert Nugent, ed. *A Challenge to Love* (New York: Crossroad, 1983), pp. 139 and 137.

3. Views of Self

1. Carl Rogers, "A Theory of Therapy, Personality, and Interpersonal Relationships, as Developed in the Client-Centered Framework," in *Psychology: A Study of Science*, S. Koch, ed. (New York: McGraw-Hill, 1959), 3:201.

2. Gil G. Noam, Lawrence Kohlberg, and John Snarey, "Steps Toward a Model of the Self," B. Lee and G. Noam, eds., in *Developmental Approaches to Self* (New York: Plenum Press, 1984), p. 62. John Snarey, Lawrence Kohlberg, and Gil G. Noam, "Ego Development in Perspective: Structural Stage, Functional Phase, and Cultural-Age Period Models," *Developmental Review* (1983), 3:303–338.

3. Robert Kegan, Gil G. Noam, and Laura Rogers, "The Psychologic of Emotion: A Neo-Piagetian View," in D. Cicchitti and P. Hesse, eds. *New Directions in Child Development, Emotional Development* (San Francisco: Jossey Bass, 1982), p. 105; Robert Kegan, *The Evolving Self* (Cambridge, Mass.: Harvard University Press, 1982).

4. Lawrence Kohlberg, "Stage and Sequence: The Cognitive-Development Approach to Socialization," in D. A. Goslin, ed., *Handbook of Socialization Theory and Research*, (Chicago: Rand McNally, 1969); Carol Gilligan, *In A Different Voice: Psychological Theory and Women's Development* (Cambridge, Mass.: Harvard University Press, 1982); James W. Fowler, *Stages of Faith: The Psychology of Human Development and the Quest for Meaning* (San Francisco: Harper and Row, 1981); Robert L. Selman, *The Growth of Interpersonal Understanding: Developmental and Clinical Analyses* (New York: Academic Press, 1980).

5. Kegan, *The Evolving Self;* Kegan, Noam, and Rogers, "The Psychologic of Emotion."

6. Noam, Kohlberg, and Snarey, "Steps Toward a Model of the Self," p. 129.

7. Teilhard de Chardin, *The Divine Milieu* (New York: Harper and Row, 1965).

4. The Interpersonal Event

1. Janice R. Mokros, Sumru Erkut, Lynne Spichiger, "Mentoring and Being Mentored: Sex Related Patterns Among College Professors," 1981, Working Paper No. 68, Center for Research on Women, Wellesley College, Wellesley, Mass.

2. Grace Baruch, Rosalind Barnett, and Caryl Rivers, *Lifeprints: New Patterns of Love and Work for Today's Woman* (New York: McGraw-Hill, 1983).

3. Sally I. Powers, Stuart T. Hauser, Alan Jacobson, and Gil Noam, "Ego Development of Parents and Their Children," Laboratory of Social Psychiatry, Harvard Medical School; John Snarey, Karen Friedman, and Joseph Blasi, "Sex Role Strain Among Kibbutz Women: A Developmental Perspective," 1985, Working Paper No. 151, Center for Research on Women, Wellesley College, Wellesley, Mass.

4. John Snarey, Lawrence Kohlberg, and Gil Noam, "Ego Development in Perspective: Structural Stage, Functional Phase, and Cultural Age-Period Models," *Developmental Review* (1983), 3:303–338.

5. Robert Kegan, *The Evolving Self: Problems and Process in Human Development* (Cambridge, Mass.: Harvard University Press, 1982); Robert L. Selman, *The Growth of Interpersonal Understanding: Developmental and Clinical Analyses* (New York: Academic Press, 1980).

6. Carol Gilligan, *In a Different Voice: Psychological Theory and Women's Development* (Cambridge, Mass.: Harvard University Press, 1982).

7. Carol Ochs, *Women and Spirituality*. (Totowa, N.J.: Rowman and Allanheld, 1983).

8. Martin Buber, *I and Thou*, Walter Kaufman, trans. and intro. (New York: Scribner, 1970).

9. *Ibid.*, p. 67.

5. On Death and Dying

1. Robert Jay Lifton, *The Broken Connection: On Death and the Continuity of Life* (New York: Basic Books, 1983), p. 179.

2. Harold F. Searles, *Collected Papers on Schizophrenia and Related Subjects* (New York: International Universities Press, 1965).

3. Otto Rank, *Will Therapy* (New York: Norton, 1936).

4. Sigmund Freud, *Civilization and Its Discontents*, vol. 21 of *Standard Edition of the Complete Psychological Works of Sigmund Freud*, 24 vols., James Strachey, tr. and ed. (London: Hogarth Press, 1953–1974).

5. C.G. Jung, *The Collected Works*, Bollinger Series XX, G. Adler et al., eds. R.F. Hull, trans., 2d ed. (Princeton: Princeton University Press, 1968).

6. Herman Feifel, "Death-Relevant Variable in Psychology," in Rollo May, ed., *Existential Psychology* (New York: Random House, 1960); Rollo May, "Contributions of Existential Psychology," in Rollo May, Ernest Angel, Henri F. Ellenbergh, eds., *Existence* (New York: Simon and Schuster, 1958); May, *Love and Will* (Norton, 1969); Irvin O. Yalom, *Existential Psychotherapy* (New York: Basic Books, 1980).

7. Lifton, *The Broken Connection,* pp. 17 and 3.

8. *Ibid.,* pp. 20, 25, and 31.

9. *Ibid.,* p. 392.

10. *Ibid.,* p. 7.

11. *Ibid.,* p. 17.

12. Carol Ochs, *Women and Spirituality* (Totowa, N.J.: Rowman and Allenheld, 1983).

6. Views of God

1. John McDargh, *Psychoanalytic Object Relations Theory and the Study of Religion* (Lanham, Md.: University Press of America, 1983), p. 113.

2. *Ibid.*

3. Ana-Maria Rizzuto, *The Birth of the Living God: A Psychoanalytic Study* (Chicago: University of Chicago Press, 1979), p. 209.

4. *Ibid.*

5. Rizzuto, pp. 57 and 73; D. W. Winnicott, *Playing and Reality* (New York: Tavistock Publications, 1971).

6. Rizzuto, p. 185; D. W. Winnicott, *Playing and Reality,* p. 55.

7. Rizzuto, pp. 190 and 193–194.

8. Winnicott, *Playing and Reality,* p. 14.

9. Carol P. Christ and Judith Plaskow, eds., *Womanspirit Rising: A Feminist Reader in Religion* (San Francisco: Harper and Row, 1979); Mary Daly, *Beyond God the Father: Toward A Philosophy of Women's Liberation* (Boston: Beacon Press, 1973); Daly, *Gyn/Ecology: The Meta-ethics of Radical Feminism* (Boston: Beacon Press, 1978); Carol Ochs, *Behind the Sex of God* (Boston: Beacon Press, 1977); Rosemary Radford Ruether, *New Woman, New Earth: Sexist Ideologies and Human Liberation* (New York: Seabury Press, 1975); Ruether, *Sexism and God-Talk: Toward A Feminist Theology* (Boston: Beacon Press, 1983).

10. Rizzuto, p. 204.

11. McDargh, *Psychoanalytic Object Relations Theory and the Study of Religion.*

7. Stepping Back

1. I was introduced to the concept of being-in-relationship and of a reality of relatedness by the work of Carol Ochs, Harold Oliver, and Alfred North Whitehead; I am indebted to all of them. The responsibility for applying their thinking to psychology, which I have done here, rests solely with me, however.

2. Alfred North Whitehead, *Process and Reality,* ed. David Ray Griffin and Donald W. Sherburne, eds. (New York: Free Press, 1978), p. 67.

3. Alfred North Whitehead, *Adventures of Ideas* (New York: Free Press, 1967).

4. Rosemary Radford Ruether, *New Women, New Earth: Sexist Ideologies and Human Liberation* (New York: Seabury Press, 1975); Elisabeth Schussler Fiorenza, *In Memory of Her: A Feminist Theological Reconstruction of Christian Origins* (New York: Crossroad, 1983); Carol P. Christ and Judith Plaskow, eds., *Woman Spirit Rising: A Feminist Reader in Religion* (San Francisco: Harper and Row, 1979), Carol Ochs, *Behind the Sex of God* (Boston: Beacon Press, 1977).

5. Robert Kegan, *The Evolving Self: Problem and Process in Human Development* (Cambridge, Mass.: Harvard University Press, 1982); Gil G. Noam, Lawrence Kohlberg, and John Snarey, "Steps Toward a Model of the Self," in B. Lee and G. Noam, eds., *Developmental Approaches to Self* (New York: Plenum Press, 1984); Robert Jay Lifton, *The Broken Connection: On Death and the Continuity of Life* (New York: Basic Books, 1983); Ana-Maria Rizzuto, *The Birth of the Living God* (Chicago: University of Chicago Press, 1979).

6. *The American Heritage Dictionary of the English Language*, New College Edition, s.v., "psyche," "spirit."

7. American Psychological Association, "Background: The Practice of Psychology," February 1983.

8. Alfred North Whitehead, "Immortality," *Essays in Science and Philosophy* (New York: Philosophical Library, 1948).

9. *Ibid.*, p. 69.

10. T.S. Eliot, *Collected Poems, 1909–1962* (New York: Harcourt, Brace and World, 1970), p. 79.

11. Harold Oliver, *Relatedness: Essays in Metaphysics and Theology* (Macon, Ga.: Mercer University Press, 1984).

12. D.W. Winnicott, *The Maturational Processes and the Facilitating Environment* (New York: International Universities Press, 1965); W.R.D. Fairbairn, *An Object Relations Theory of the Personality* (New York: Basic Books, 1954); Harry Guntrip, *Psychoanalytic Theory, Therapy, and the Self* (New York: Basic Books, 1971).

13. Heinz Kohut, *The Analysis of the Self* (New York: International Universities Press, 1971); *The Restoration of the Self* (New York: International Universities Press, 1977).

14. Erik H. Erikson, *Childhood and Society* (New York: Norton, 1963); Erikson, *Identity: Youth and Crisis* (New York: Norton, 1968).

15. Robert Kegan, *The Evolving Self*; Robert Kegan, Gil Noam, Laura Rogers, "The Psychologic of Emotion: A Neo-Piagetian View," in D. Cicchitti and P. Hesse, eds., *New Directions in Child Development: Emotional Development* (San Francisco: Jossey Bass, 1983); Gil G. Noam, Lawrence Kohlberg, John Snarey, "Steps Toward a Model of the Self."

16. Alexandra G. Kaplan, "The Self-in-Relation: Implications for Depression in Women," Work in Progress, No. 84–03, Wellesley College, 1984; Jean Baker Miller, *Toward a New Psychology of Women* (Boston: Beacon Press, 1976); Miller, "The Development of Women's Sense of Self," Work in Progress, No. 84–01, Wellesley College, 1984; Irene P. Stiver, "The Meaning of 'Dependency' in Female-Male Relationships," Work in Progress, No. 83–07, Wellesley College, 1984; Janet Surrey, "The Relational Self in Women: Clinical Implications," Work in Progress, No. 82–02, Wellesley College, 1983.

17. Carol Gilligan, *In a Different Voice: Psychological Theory and Women's Development* (Cambridge, Mass.: Harvard University Press, 1982).

18. Jessie Bernard, *Women and the Public Interest: An Essay on Policy and Protest* (Chicago: Aldine Atherton, 1971).

19. Gil G. Noam, "Stage, Phase, and Style: The Developmental Dynamics of

the Self," in M. Berkowitz and F. Oser, eds. *Moral Education,* (Hillsdale, N.J.: Lawrence Earlbaum Assoc., 1985). He integrates a presentation of relational style with stage of development and phase of life, but that will not be discussed here.

20. See chapter 1, "Women's Lives and Reality," for a discussion of Saiving's argument.

21. Noam, "Stage, Phase, and Style," p. 339.

Postscript

1. Susanne K. Langer, *Philosophy in a New Key: A Study in the Symbolism of Reason, Rite, and Art* (Cambridge, Mass.: Harvard University Press, 1942), p. 241.

2. Robert Kegan, *The Evolving Self* (Cambridge, Mass.: Harvard University Press, 1982) p. 11.

3. Harold Oliver, *Relatedness: Essays in Metaphysics and Theology* (Macon, Ga.: Mercer University Press, 1984).

4. Langer, *Philosophy in a New Key,* p. 241.

Index